A Nation Reconstructed

Also available from ASQC Quality Press

Quality Handbook for the Architectural, Engineering, and Construction Community
Roger D. Hart

Recovering Prosperity Through Quality: The Midland City Story
Robert A. Schwarz

Quality Management for Government: A Guide to Federal, State, and Local Implementation
V. Daniel Hunt

The Process Analysis Workbook for Government: How to Achieve More with Less
Gerard Bruno

Business Process Benchmarking: Finding and Implementing Best Practices
Robert C. Camp

Benchmarking: The Search for Industry Best Practices That Lead to Superior Performance
Robert C. Camp

The Change Agents' Handbook: A Survival Guide for Quality Improvement Champions
David W. Hutton

Mapping Work Processes
Dianne Galloway

To request a complimentary catalog of publications, call 800-248-1946.

A Nation Reconstructed
A Quest for the Cities That Can Be

Roger D. Hart, editor-in-chief
Sheryl L. Cooley, editor

ASQC Quality Press
Milwaukee, Wisconsin

A Nation Reconstructed: A Quest for the Cities That Can Be
Roger D. Hart, editor-in-chief
Sheryl L. Cooley, editor

Library of Congress Cataloging-in-Publication Data

   A nation reconstructed: a quest for the cities that can be / Roger D. Hart, editor-in-chief; Sheryl L. Cooley, editor.
      p. cm.
   Includes bibliographical references and index.
   ISBN 0-87389-409-X (alk. paper)
   1. Urban renewal—United States.   2. Urban policy—United States.
3. Total quality management in government—United States.   I. Hart, Roger D., 1946– . II. Cooley, Sheryl L., 1953– .
HT175.N34   1997
307.76'0973—dc20   96-9852
                                                                                      CIP

© 1997 by ASQC

All rights reserved. No part of this book may be reproduced in any form or by any means, electronic, mechanical, photocopying, recording, or otherwise, without the prior written permission of the publisher.

10 9 8 7 6 5 4 3 2 1

ISBN 0-87389-409-X

Acquisitions Editor: Roger Holloway
Project Editor: Jeanne W. Bohn

ASQC Mission: To facilitate continuous improvement and increase customer satisfaction by identifying, communicating, and promoting the use of quality principles, concepts, and technologies; and thereby be recognized throughout the world as the leading authority on, and champion for, quality.

Attention: Schools and Corporations
ASQC Quality Press books, audio, video, and software are available at quantity discounts with bulk purchases for business, educational, or instructional use. For information, please contact ASQC Quality Press at 800-248-1946, or write to ASQC Quality Press, P.O. Box 3005, Milwaukee, WI 53201-3005.

For a free copy of the ASQC Quality Press Publications Catalog, including ASQC membership information, call 800-248-1946.

Printed in the United States of America

∞ Printed on acid-free paper

Quality Press
611 East Wisconsin Avenue
Milwaukee, Wisconsin 53202

To my grandfather, born of Irish
immigrants in East St. Louis in 1876,
and to my family and parents.

Roger D. Hart

Contents

Preface xi

Introduction xvii

Part I: The Challenges

Chapter 1   A Total Quality Approach to Urban
Revitalization 3
Roger D. Hart

Chapter 2   Next Generation Policy Making: The Challenge
of Federal/Local Partnerships 11
Dick Swett

Chapter 3   The Crisis in Human Capital Development
in Distressed Urban Communities 27
William H. Brown

Chapter 4   The Lack of a Quality Focus in Urban Education
Sanctioned by Government 39
Wilbur L. Campbell

| Chapter 5 | The Family in Crisis........................ | 55 |

Sheryl L. Cooley

Part II: The Vision

| Chapter 6 | The Vision of Urban Revitalization............ | 71 |

Roger D. Hart and Sheryl L. Cooley

| Chapter 7 | Democracy and Total Quality................. | 93 |

Roger D. Hart

| Chapter 8 | Financing and Restructuring Debt in the Inner City .... | 113 |

Ishaq Shafiq

| Chapter 9 | Fighting Drug Crime in the Distressed City ... | 135 |

Gordon D. Bush

| Chapter 10 | Solving Urban Education Problems Through a Quality Focus............................ | 151 |

Wilbur L. Campbell

| Chapter 11 | The Economic Well-Being of the Inner City.... | 171 |

Sheryl L. Cooley

Part III: Quality Techniques

| Chapter 12 | Planning the Quality Program for Customer Focus and Effective Implementation........... | 199 |

John P. Jackson

| Chapter 13 | Deming and Juran and a Quality Strategy That Incorporates Their Philosophies............... | 221 |

Eugene Danylyshyn

| Chapter 14 | Getting Started and Getting Results........... | 237 |

Roger D. Hart

Part IV: Epilogue

Chapter 15	A Vision of the Cities That Can Be in 2010 ... *Roger D. Hart*	259
Appendix	An Example of a Holistic Total Quality Approach....................................	275

Author Biographies 285

Bibliography... 291

Index.. 297

Preface

I spent much of the summer of 1995 working with Roger Hart to help a community in the Midwest develop a test bed approach to implementation of an urban revitalization program. The city, which has been undertaking the arduous task of rebuilding its physical, economic, political, and social infrastructure since the early 1990s, had latched onto the idea of governing its entire program from a total quality standpoint. By 1995, city officials were working with Roger—a well-known quality professional, ASQC vice president, and past member of the board of examiners for the Malcolm Baldrige National Quality Award—to develop a more formal urban quality plan. In turn, they hoped to draw more attention from the federal government by recommending that the community be used as a test bed to try this unique approach to urban revitalization.

In support of this effort, I spent considerable time reviewing the published literature on community development. Newspaper and magazine articles tended to focus on current legislation, failed programs, or extensive discussion of the components of any or all urban problems. Books, on the other hand, appeared to be published versions of theses or research papers. They were thorough, but dry, and prone to minutiae. The were statistically precise. They offered ample evidence of the urban hydra, but little in the way of solutions. Crime in the inner city, for example, was explored in terms of other studies and findings regarding relationships between crime and income levels or crime and numbers of police officers or crime and the number of single-family households. While the data were conclusive, they offered little in the way of practical advice for implementing crime prevention programs.

Even the book *Interwoven Destinies: Cities and the Nation*, edited by Secretary of Housing and Urban Development Henry G. Cisneros (1993), was designed to be a compilation of "talking papers" for use by the American Assembly—a group that meets to discuss public policy at Arden House in Harriman, New York, under the auspices of Columbia University. Again, the challenges of urban revitalization were documented by the many contributing authors. But few solutions were offered, and the Assembly could not find enough consensus among its many participants to develop its own.

Our book, however, has the luxury of bias. Authors here who have given of their time, talents, and experience firmly believe in a quality approach to finding solutions.

Part I of the book describes the most basic challenges that face a community in crisis: unrecognized human resources, the decline in educational effectiveness, the dissolution of the family, and the effects of our political system on these problems. For example, Former Congressman Dick Swett offers an insider's view of some of the difficulties of establishing federal/local partnerships in urban revival programs.

Part II gives a glimpse into inner-city projects that have worked and promotes new ideas for meeting a diverse range of problems. The section covers everything from Roger's vision of revitalization by improving the democratic process using quality techniques, to Gordon Bush's down-to-earth description of how drug-related crime is being fought in one of the nation's toughest cities, East St. Louis, Illinois. Bush is the mayor there, and he tells a story of courage and faith and practical solutions. The other chapters are of equal interest and delight.

Part III is devoted to an overview of the application of quality techniques. John Jackson, a noted management consultant, insists that city governments cannot divest themselves of direct management responsibility for their urban projects. He describes in detail what quality techniques they must use to ensure the success of their programs. Also within this section is a chapter that espouses the practical techniques of getting and measuring real results through focusing on the "significant few" quality elements of urban revitalization. It also includes a general discussion of J. M. Juran and W. Edwards Deming's principles of quality as applied to the revitalization process.

Part IV, Epilogue, expands on the title of the book. It is a vision of the cities that can be in the not-too-distant future. It is a discussion of trends and presents an image of hope and prosperity brought on by a renewal of spirit in ourselves and our nation.

The purpose of this book is to make the reader aware of the value of adopting formal quality strategies in concert with urban reform and the worth of making quality the backbone on which related programs can be built. It shows just how important integrating quality is to the success of many inner-city projects. *A Nation Reconstructed* is written for those who are looking for practical quality ideas to incorporate with the design of an urban revitalization program. It is written for the person who is not a quality expert, but believes in the absolute necessity of real results in the revitalization process. It is written for those who seek to make a difference in our nation's fortunes—who recognize the drag of urban blight on our citizens, our economy, our reputation as Americans, and the promise that this country holds for future generations.

It is not designed, however, to work only in the United States. The quality solutions described here are global in concept. They will work anyplace where leaders want the best for their people and understand the satisfaction that innovative ideas and empowerment can bring to them. Quality is, in the end, an attitude—a vision distilled into principles and practices and a formal means to improve the quality of life everywhere.

The reader will note that East St. Louis plays center stage in much of the book. This is intentional. We felt that by providing some real-life scenarios, we would take the literature in a new direction. We also believed that, by highlighting one city, we could better show how a systemic approach worked: The chapters on East St. Louis highlight financial debt restructuring, efforts to reduce crime, and endeavors to provide a paradigm shift in the approach to education. Each is related; in fact, at times we had to summarize some material from one author's chapter because it was repeated in detail in another. The context was different, but the stories were the same.

As different as they are, all of the chapters echo the central theme of total quality as embodied in a long-term, systemic approach. These authors believe that the introduction of a quality strategic plan as part of the an urban revitalization program will produce better results that, in the long run, will cost local citizens and the nation's taxpayers less than results achieved with cost, schedule, or political might as the primary goal. Those in the architecture/engineering and construction (A/E&C) community are familiar with such concepts as life cycle costing, design review, milestone scheduling, and facilities maintenance management—a few of the many processes that optimize all factors related to building or maintaining a facility. Successful social programs employ quality techniques, too. Leadership development, objective benchmarking, strategic planning, empowerment, training, managing the quality process, measuring results, and, most importantly, focusing on the customer—these are all quality tenets. The authors agree that when such quality techniques are added to public/private partnership factors and incorporated with a community development structure, a quality approach to urban revitalization is born.

Unfortunately, because of page limitations, not all problems and certainly not all solutions to the issues of urban blight have been covered. But just as *Interwoven Destinies* attempted to show the link between the health of cities and that of the nation, so did we endeavor to cover many of the interdependent factors that affect the distressed neighborhood—poverty, education, crime—and sought to provide glimpses into solutions that are working in cities across the nation. We covered quality at a conceptual level in most chapters, total quality in general in some, and particular techniques of quality management in yet others. It is eclectic, as a book by many authors will be, but we believe that together the chapters tell a convincing story, with quality at the core.

Roger and I are indebted to all of the contributing authors, each of whom brings a great deal of expertise to the book. Our time frame was short, and these are busy people. We are grateful that they could find time to make this a book of which we can all be proud. We would also like to thank the staff of ASQC Quality Press, who provided us with support when asked, direction when needed, and added their own expertise in editing and publishing to provide the final polish for this book. To everyone who had a part in making *A Nation Reconstructed: A Quest for the Cities That Can Be,* we thank you. To the reader, we hope that you will find a few nuggets among the alluvia of our words.

Sheryl L. Cooley

Introduction

As Martin Luther King said, "I have a dream." I was recently in Washington, D.C., for meetings. I had a couple of hours to kill, and stopped in at the National Archives where I had an opportunity to personally see the U.S. Constitution. We all have seen copies of it, but I felt a sense of awe in looking at the actual document—the original ink and paper.

When looking at the Constitution, the thought came to me like a shot: This is an *awesome strategic plan*. I started analyzing its structure, format, outline, and form—excellent! Sometimes this is all that's needed: a good plan.

I offer to you in this book a plan or vision that is logical; pieces of it have worked for many smaller-scale ventures. Those pieces can be used to help create a program for urban revival on such a massive scale that it could literally stagger the mind. This is a vision of the future that can be: jobs, education, and new cities.

What the Book Covers

In this book, you will read about many things that need to be done in order to reconstruct our cities as outlined by several knowledgeable individuals. The issues and concerns of urban revitalization have been addressed in Part I, The Challenges. The section highlights the need to develop partnerships in the urban revitalization arena, the crisis in human capital development, the lack of focus in urban education, and the difficulties faced by the inner-city family. These are the root problems that rock the foundation of community stability and lead to a community beset with blight.

Part II, The Vision, describes the means by which these challenges can be met. The section covers the issues of financial debt restructuring, education, crime, economic redevelopment, and political gridbook. Specific instances of revitalization success are described, and quality principles and practices are outlined to show how quality techniques have been put into practice.

Part III, Quality Techniques, describes specific quality solutions. The first chapter in the section is devoted to a discussion of quality in terms of its application to capital projects. The second provides an overview of quality as espoused by J. M. Juran and W. Edwards Deming. It includes an organizational chart that describes the roles and responsibilities of key players during the first 100 days of urban program implementation. The last chapter outlines in detail a means for managing overall quality of the entire revitalization program through Pareto analysis and a quality focus on the "significant few." It briefly outlines quality-effecting techniques that can be employed on physical rebuild projects and social programs with real, measurable results.

Part IV, Epilogue, provides the reader with the quest for the cities that can be. It describes worldwide trends and global quality scenarios and offers a futuristic walk through a typical community built on quality.

What This Book Does and Does Not Do

Because there can be no single model for the process of urban revitalization, there can be no single quality program. Quality programs are based on work processes, and those processes vary greatly from community to community. Southern California city officials do not have to worry that their residents will freeze to death in the winter. Cities in much of the Midwest have significantly less need to provide services for non–English speaking people. The eastern seaboard has less trouble with the issue of availability of public transport. And the South, in general, is little troubled by working hand-in-glove with professed religious organizations. The issues that plague one urban community simply do not plague another. East Los Angeles is desperate for large plots of land on which to build; East St. Louis, Illinois, grapples with the problems of vacant lots. Vancouver, British Columbia struggles with the tremendous increase in real estate prices as wealthy Chinese flee Hong Kong and find refuge in that city. Wausau, Wisconsin copes with an eroding tax base caused largely by the influx of Vietnamese who first arrived at the invitation of the city but who have since sponsored hundreds of extended family members content to live on welfare.

All of these cities now harbor distressed neighborhoods. A single urban revitalization model for the kinds of diverse challenges they face defies common sense. Likewise, a single, practical quality model is of little value in the real world.

Quality is easy to recognize. We know it when we see it. In theory, it is easily defined; it is described in terms of degrees of excellence. But between definition and recognition traditionally has lain opinion. In cultures where opinion is sacrosanct, where a person has an inalienable right to his or her own point of view, developing quality standards has been considered tremendously difficult at best. Consensus has seemed impossible. Today quality, as practiced by experts, is still considered largely metaphysical by too many in America and, consequently, scorned as an unnecessary cost. Seldom are quality-effecting methods put into practice without a specific mandate to do so. Some industries remain skeptical of the entire practice.

Additionally, the history of quality control has limited peoples' response, as quality itself has been viewed as a result and not an activity incorporated into all aspects of a building or social program master plan. It was what you got if you did everything right, if everything went according to plan. And, in the long run, quality was considered to have been achieved if the client was happy with the project or if a social program appeared to be successful. The idea that quality could be more than just fostered on some informal basis is a relatively new concept. And even today, it may seem hard to believe that it can be effective on the large-scale programs of community revival.

Because of these factors, and others, there are few examples I know of where a formal quality program has been the cornerstone of an overall urban revitalization effort. No doubt quality has been employed on a project level as commercial and infrastructure projects within a redevelopment program have been executed, but in many instances quality has simply been the fortunate result of good workmanship and a lack of unexpected delays. And in the arena of social programming, *formal* quality has played an even smaller role. As a result, most people, even those intimately involved in a program, have been little able to objectively judge its success, leaving it open to often undue criticism.

This book, therefore, is not a compendium of urban plans that have successfully developed and incorporated the perfect quality "formula" into their programs. Rather, it is a frank discussion of some of the major issues facing many distressed communities, a fresh look at these issues from a quality perspective, and a brief forum on formally recognized quality principles and techniques as they relate to urban revitalization in general. Interspersed are concrete stories of success and failure, innovative ideas, and a vision of the cities that can be.

How Can We Pay for Quality?

There are diverse social issues at stake in the inner city. With all of the multitude of concerns, we might ask the question: How can we possibility pay for this? That's a good question.

In 1994, the U.S. gross domestic product exceeded $650 trillion. This is a whole lot of money in anybody's book. Almost 10 percent of this was spent in construction—$650 billion. This industry, construction, is sometimes referred to as the A/E&C community because of its size and multiple industries. The application of quality improvement techniques and systems can help us achieve significant cost and schedule savings on design and construction projects, thus reducing that $650 billion figure. Within the A/E&C community, organizations can spend money on quality in two ways: by investing in good quality, or by paying for poor quality.

Now think of the words *quality* or *excellence*. Can you relate these words to the product of the A/E&C community? Is there a quest for excellence in this industry? The answer appears to be no! But why not? The 11 million employees in this industry *care;* they want to do a good job. But many feel that they have no choice but to build cheaply, to operate in a down-and-dirty fashion. The not-so-subtle truth is that this is all they know. They are trapped in a massive industry that does not give individuals the opportunity for excellence. Many quality experts agree that, in the A/E&C industry, more than 25 percent of the work is mismanaged or executed inefficiently, resulting in waste, scrap, and rework. The first time I really thought about this, I nearly fell out of my chair. This says that more than $160 billion was wasted in 1994 in the United States alone. Could we do something about our cities with $160 billion? *Absolutely!*

Let's Do It!

Then why don't we do it? There are a million and one reasons why we can't do it, but only one good reason why we should.

This is a quest for the cities that can be.

You see, I too have a dream.

Roger D. Hart

Part I
The Challenges

Chapter 1

A Total Quality Approach to Urban Revitalization

Roger D. Hart

> *The city of truth cannot be built on the swampy ground of skepticism.*
>
> —Albert Schweitzer

Historically, most government agencies were organized expressly to provide for the common good. The common good was perceived to perform for the collective. Schools, hospitals, fire departments, libraries, public works, and transportation systems were developed, expanded, and maintained using community funds. These structures and systems were selected in support of then-present needs and with a vision of the future. The model was based on expansion and growth. However, the "common good" precipitated a geometric increase in public "needs," which severely constrained already limited capital resources. Today, the key question is how to fund the array of services communities have come to expect.

Additionally, as America continues to support the immigration of new and diverse peoples, and as the gap between the "haves" and the "have nots" grows, expectations regarding the kinds of services that should be made available have changed. Consider the following:

- Today it costs more money to put people in prison that it costs to send them to college. At the same time, many public schools are in terrible condition. It is common knowledge that billions of dollars are needed just to bring existing school buildings into compliance with existing life and safety codes.

- The definition of *public infrastructure* is changing. Twenty years ago, few people would have claimed that correctional facilities were key components of the required infrastructure. Today prisons and criminal justice facilities are considered essential. It is forecasted that in 20 years drug treatment centers, halfway houses, and public facilities for long-term child care will become part of the required institutional infrastructure.

The current approach to managing difficult human resources often lies in remedial measures, as evidenced by our burgeoning prison system. The Los Angeles County Central Jail spent $173 million to expand its facility in the mid-1990s. Today it stands empty because of lack of funds to staff it.

A quality approach to long-term, systemic resource development lies with our schools, our families, and our national integrity.

Efforts Toward Urban Redevelopment

Every new revitalization effort creates its own set of advocates and antagonists. In some instances, these efforts have also created their own sets of demographics, economic opportunities, and social conditions. The Dan Ryan Expressway dividing east and west Chicago was built using the best available engineering practices, the most comprehensive data, and the latest urban planning techniques. To the west, single-family homes predominate. To the east are Chicago's largest public housing projects. These structures are isolated between the chain-link fences and concrete causeways of Interstate Highway I-94 and Lake Michigan. The terrible consequences of such developments are still being revealed.

Today's socioeconomic conditions require a new total quality (TQ) approach. It is no longer possible to reduce community revitalization to a set of engineering statements. The old model of urban renewal is no longer financially, sociologically, or politically feasible. Today's community revitalization challenges involve major systemic issues.

The result of urban decay.

TQ is not a process; it is a fundamental approach. It is the means by which physical challenges (such as building renovation, efficiency improvement) and intangible issues (such as attitude, family values, poverty) are met. It is the means by which holistic solutions are found to medusa-like problems where the patient's root illness is treated, not the symptoms.

In this case, the patient is the decaying city. As the United States has shifted from a nation of manufacturers to one geared to service industries, many of those cities built on old manufacturing bases have fallen into disrepair. Once started along this path, they experience a downward spiral. Manufacturing leaves or dies. Jobs disappear. People leave to find work elsewhere. And the financial back of the tax base is broken in the exodus. Those who stay are left with crumbling buildings, underperforming city services, and poorly funded schools. Eventually, they are left with nothing.

Quality of old addressed the symptoms. FDR created the welfare state and LBJ expanded it. Hundreds of alleged quality programs were put in place, implemented, and overseen by a sea of bureaucrats. Public housing was developed. School lunch programs

A Total Quality Approach to Urban Revitalization

New canvases for the children of our inner cities. The popularity of "tagging," and the reasons youngsters do it, is indicative of the anger and disillusionment of the urban poor.

were initiated. Food stamps were introduced. Aid was given to dependent children so that they wouldn't starve. Survival was legislated, if not ensured.

But the educational problems remained endemic to the community. Poor communities provided poor schools and, often, poor schooling. A generation of minorities and women fought for equal rights, but the next grew up knowing that it was not enough—that none of it was enough. Quality education did not proliferate, but teenage pregnancies and drug deals and gang-related deaths exploded as the possibility of a quality future became more dim. These realities added to the already heavy burden of fixing the problem. Not only were the systems dysfunctional, but so were the people.

A New Approach

Most experts agree that the country currently has neither the resources to fully address the size of the infrastructure, commercial, and institutional renovation of the urban community nor the latitude to ignore it. It is widely felt that innovation is needed, and a TQ approach can fulfill this need. Improvements to old systems, innovative new ideas, and paradigm shifts are required to adequately anticipate future needs and to offer an escape from the capital expenditure dilemma. New political and economic forces are making such programs more important than ever.

Revitalizing the urban community requires a three-pronged approach. The physical decay of the city must be minimized. Life safety issues must be addressed. Old buildings must be upgraded, renovated, or demolished. Areas containing environmental hazards must be remediated. City services such as trash collection and street repair, and community services such as education, public health care, and local transportation, must be rejuvenated. This is the first prong. Second, new businesses must be enticed into the area and old businesses improved. Crime must be curbed. The tax base must

A quality approach to self-sufficiency is needed to replace the lethargy that welfare breeds.

expand to ensure that the city will continue to thrive after initial financial support ends. Third, people must have a reason to take pride in themselves before they can take pride in their communities. Sound and appropriate educational opportunities must not only be made available, but taken advantage of. People must have work to go to and must want to go to work. The welfare state must become the safety net it was originally meant to be, not the warm, embracing, smothering blanket it has become. People must become self-sufficient.

This three-pronged approach must be implemented on an overlapping, phased basis. Life safety issues need to be dealt with immediately. Other capital-intensive programs have to be identified and decisions made as to need. Those projects that can wait until apprentices in local community education programs become available, should be so addressed in the overall master plan of the city.

Others will require more immediate attention or will not lend themselves well to apprenticeship programs. For example, schools nearly always need immediate repair, but even more important, usually need more and better-trained teachers. The community cannot afford to "grow" its own on a short-term basis; the task would be self-defeating.

TQ is managing the development, implementation, and oversight of this scope of work—finding ways to ensure quality programs that remain on schedule and within budget, and, by "doing it right the first time," save 30 percent to 40 percent (per current estimates). TQ is the key: an all-encompassing, interactive approach to the revitalization of our urban communities, and a systemic approach to the problem of attitude and the solution to decay. No one has yet found all of the answers, but efforts are underway. TQ is the challenge—and the path for the distressed community to reach this goal.

Chapter 2

Next Generation Policy Making: The Challenge of Federal/Local Partnerships

Dick Swett

> *Because I have confidence in the power of truth and of the spirit, I believe in the future of mankind.*
>
> —Albert Schweitzer

"It was the best of times. It was the worst of times." Charles Dickens' opening to his classic *A Tale of Two Cities* is not a wholly inappropriate description of our own era. As we move toward the close of what historians have long since dubbed "the American century," we Americans, by many rational measures, should be feeling good about ourselves and our country.

Victorious in the Cold War, with an economy on the rebound from the downsizing and corporate anarchy of the 1980s, there is more than sufficient reason for Americans to be satisfied with their position in the world. Our economic productivity is rising for the first time in years. Our competitive profile is more positive than at any time since the early 1970s. Our once-intimidating economic competitors, Japan and a united Europe, are beset by economic miseries of their own. All of these signs and more are cause for some optimism or, at the very least, substantial relief.

But we Americans are not sanguine about the future; instead, we remain maddeningly dubious. As a nation increasingly obsessed with polls and addicted to frequent, seemingly daily readings of our collective national pulse, we know ourselves to be collectively uneasy—anxious about the future and uncertain as to what it may hold. Confidence in our ability to get and stay on top of events is at what may be an all-time low. Sometimes it seems as if we are even more than cynical—we are out-and-out depressed about our society's and our government's capacity to solve our problems and steer us safely toward a better future.

This pessimism strikes some observers as unique in our comparatively short national history. While it may be more myth than fact, Americans have long had a reputation as being, for the most part, an optimistic people. Until recently, that is how we've tended to view ourselves and, certainly, that is how others have viewed us. Yet this description would hardly seem to fit the American public's mood today.

What has happened in recent years to cast doubt on earlier but still recent readings of our national character? Why are we presently fixated on our fears, rather than our hopes for the future? What has become of the American brand of optimism that saw challenges as opportunities, progress as inevitable, and change as exciting?

There seems to be something especially pervasive and enervating about our current national "funk." We fear that the arc of this latest national mood pendulum swing is so wide that there is some chance it will never come back—that this latest cycle of alienation is so profound that it is somehow sapping the regenerative capacity of our system, damaging it beyond repair.

The present pessimism is, in part, a predictable manifestation of the uncertainty and economic insecurity generated by rapid economic change. This societal angst is aggravated by the information and technological revolutions of our time that, along with their many benefits, have made the world so much closer and more connected with our own lives that we feel overwhelmed. Our horizons, while broadened, are also crowded with events and problems seemingly beyond our control.

Capping off this tale of woe is the pervasive sense that government is not only incapable of dealing effectively with the challenges we face, but is, in fact, a major part of the problem. This skepticism seems widely and deeply held and, to that extent, is historically new in America. While it is true that Americans have always been inclined to view government as Alexis de Tocqueville's phrase of a century and a half ago, "not a blessing but a necessary evil," the present disillusionment of so many Americans is sufficiently strong to border on genuine despair.

Wariness at the Local Level

That despair translates into wariness at the local level. Local constituents believe that they cannot trust their national government. Federal support often is not timely, not appropriate, or not user-friendly. In seeking to ensure that federal funds are spent properly and federal programs implemented appropriately, the government tends to create volumes of rules and mountains of paperwork that often are at odds with intended program goals. People get so caught up in the process of meeting government-imposed regulations that they lose sight of the goals themselves. And because the bureaucratic wheels turn so slowly, projects and programs are phased in and, a few years later, out again before they have time to take root and flower. The political winds change regularly and sweep out with them the path down which the country has been headed, leaving the recipients of these program benefits to cope as best they can. Once again the taxpayer feels that his or her money has been wasted. And the wariness sharpens.

This is particularly true in the arena of urban blight. Here it is the story of the scorpion and the donkey, where the donkey allows the scorpion to ride on its head as it fords a deep stream, only to be stung just before they reach the shore. The donkey keels over and the scorpion is thrown into the water—both drown. Similarly, cities facing serious urban blight (almost always the result of a shrunken tax base) need federal support to survive, but that support is despised, too. Federal programs are seldom "made to fit," and having to take the bad with the good (using rules and procedures that make no sense for a particular community in order to gain access to those parts of the program that do) uses up tremendous capital resources—resources that are often in short supply in distressed neighborhoods.

This leads to a feeling of rebellion, a concern that the nation's lawmakers are not listening to their constituents; that there is no consensus, only people on Capitol Hill with little knowledge of the common folk and less inclination to help them. It fosters the belief that people are in politics for power and fame, creating policy at the national level of only limited value or that promotes the rise of yet another set of problems.

Take, for example, Aid to Families with Dependent Children (AFDC). By giving aid only to single-parent families, it seems the federal government encourages the poor not to marry. This may be a significant contributing factor in the dramatic rise in the number of undereducated, female-headed households. This is devastating in a society that tends to give the best-paying jobs to well-educated men. Marian Wright Edelman, head of the Children's Defense Fund, believes that there is a vast underground of men, particularly African-Americans, secretly living with their families but not married to the mothers of their children, in part because the family unit cannot survive without the help of AFDC (Edelman 1987). And if that seems to be merely a matter of morals, consider the surprising number of elderly couples in the United States who live together but do not marry because they cannot afford to live on a single Social Security check.

Many federal programs, while seeking to improve the state of the nation as a whole, seem to get shoved down the throats of local entities. It is not the intent of Congress, but sometimes it may look that way. For example, in 1991, while in Congress, I championed what seemed a simple, straightforward program to build three playgrounds in tough neighborhoods in Washington, D.C.

The Playgrounds Project

The object of the playgrounds project was to engage my colleagues and the local community in a joint effort where both financial and sweat equity were common contributions. It was to be a symbolic effort that would accomplish several goals. By employing the traditional community approach to barn raising, the local neighborhood and members of the U.S. Congress would have the opportunity to work side by side. At its inception, the need for such an effort was clearly present. Underprivileged neighborhoods with a paucity of recreational resources were (and still are) the norm in Washington, D.C. In terms of traditional language, the barn had surely burned down. But few people were moving to reconstruct something out of the ashes.

The first action taken was to build support among Congressional leaders. This was done by getting the need recognized by those in a position to initiate action and mobilize resources. The key person to

Decent playgrounds are often at a premium in inner-city neighborhoods.

fill this role was Representative Eleanor Holmes Norton. Not only did she have the political clout to carry out such a task, she had the desire as well. Another important organization that participated in the project was the American Institute of Architects (AIA), both the national organization and the local Washington, D.C. chapter.

The playground design involved the neighborhood kids and their parents; they were the most important elements of the project. It gave them a stake in the outcome, and we hoped their involvement would prevent the playground from getting trashed after we were gone. Material donations were collected from local businesses. Labor was provided by the neighborhoods, local architects, and members of Congress.

The synergistic relationship among the leadership/resource centers of my congressional office and Norton's office, and the grassroots leaders in the neighborhood where the playgrounds were to be built created an alliance of four distinct can-do players, mediated by me, each with a history of success and achievement. Where no member of the alliance was individually willing to take on the task of building playground projects in the District of Columbia, collectively our alliance lowered the threshold. We were able to share the risks among disparate parties and thus raise our confidence in the prospect for success. This, I thought, was a complete partnership that was more than a sum of its separate parts. It was a synergistic dynamic that, once established, empowered the individual components.

Another conscious requirement for success was to conceive specific, concrete tasks without being overwhelmed by the depth and breadth of Washington, D.C.'s woes. This discipline enabled the participants to look into the not-too-distant future and actually visualize the results of their labors. Albert Camus once said,

> *Perhaps we cannot prevent this world from being a world where children are tortured. But we can reduce the number of tortured children. And if you believers don't help us, who else in the world can help us do this?*

It was clear that we were not going to change the world, but everyone was excited about making a small difference.

The implementation took a tremendous amount of coordination and planning. Much of the flesh was put on the project bones through the expertise of the local Washington, D.C. AIA chapter, backed by its national organization. Nevertheless, the political component of the partnership (Norton/Swett) found itself having to do a tremendous amount of brainstorming in order to overcome the hurdles put up by the local government.

Although this was to be a project donated at no cost to the city except to locate three sites at existing housing projects, there was an unbelievable number of problems with the D.C. government. We encountered indifference, even veiled hostility, toward the project. There was a tremendous amount of skepticism on the part of the local government as to the motives and staying power of the project initiators. There was the usual slothfulness and imbecility found in large bureaucracies. Constant delays were caused by battles over turf issues. Constant arguments erupted over who was to make what key decisions. Local officials appeared jealous and defensive when faced with an outside or nontraditional initiative. There was also considerable concern among the petty bureaucratic kingdoms regarding who would take credit if the initiative were successful as well as who would take the blame if it wasn't.

To the credit of the alliance, the response to the obstacles was, for the most part, constructive and positive. We realized that the local D.C. government had not bought into the picture; that in developing a partnership with the local neighborhood associations we had bypassed a vital link in the city's urban development efforts. We had assumed that, if the neighborhoods were in favor of the effort, their political representatives would be delighted to get the help. We had seen those representatives as support members, not part of the mainframe of the project. They felt that we were pushing a program down their throats without their having much say in the matter. In retrospect, we could have eased the project's progress and improved the quality of our project management efforts had we been more mindful of the inherent suspicion with which even the most benign federal efforts are viewed by local officials.

A lot of patience and perseverance was necessary to carry this project forward. Much time was spent giving reassurance to local officials, salving sensitive egos, and making a demonstration of commitment over an extended period. Meanwhile, the fate of the sites hung in the balance. A key quality factor in this small urban revitalization project was to keep our eyes on the prize and not let obstructive bureaucrats cloud the vision. However, all of the delay and politicking eventually led to a scaling down of the initial scope of the project from three potential sites to one.

The great lesson learned from this experience is best expressed by a quote from Machiavelli.

> *There is nothing more difficult to take in hand, more perilous to conduct, or more uncertain in its success, than to take the lead in the introduction of a new order of things.*

We found that good things can be done, but not easily. The cultivation of multiple power/resource bases is necessary to ensure success, a total quality process sometimes referred to as an *integrated deployment* or *consensus management*. The goal must be capable of exciting enthusiasm and must be matched with the practical game plan for achievement—both quality principles.

Failing Forward at a National Policy Level

People like me who have been involved in these and other lessons have taken them back to the Hill. It is not surprising, therefore, that Congress, at least now and then, develops quality programs with these lessons in mind. One of the most successful, in my opinion, has been the passage of the Intermodal Surface Transportation Act (ISTEA) of 1991. ISTEA is not so much a fixed program of projects or a narrowly defined avenue for funding them as it is a flexible policy that seeks total quality empowerment of people at the local level while building in means and methods for ensuring that quality factors are adhered to. It attempts to avoid the waste that comes with highly structured remedial programs, minimize fraud, and promote appropriate alternative uses of federal funds.

Transportation policy impacts our quality of life by shaping the physical environment in which we travel and live. Over the course of the last four decades, our society has paid a high price for the mobility purchased by our society's huge investment in the interstate highway system (and its state and local tributaries): urban sprawl, divided neighborhoods, and spoiled rural landscapes. But nowhere has that price been higher than in our urban cores. Despite the unquestioned economic efficiencies and benefits bestowed by modern highways, poorly planned roads have impacted many urban communities in ultimately damaging ways. Too often highways have been built with insufficient thought given to how they would impact the communities they cross. Alternatively, the legacy of poor highway planning has also often been an arid one for poor urban neighborhoods—diverting people, economic opportunity, and hope for the future to more favored communities and locales.

Historically successful in its own terms, national transportation policy was nonetheless ill equipped to meet the challenges caused by its own success, leaving it in serious need of a quality overhaul as we entered the 1990s. But while a growing number of observers saw the imperative for change, the increasingly ossified program was well-defended by powerful groups with a vested interest in the status quo, ardently championed by senior patrons of the halls of Congress. Aligned against this old guard were new forces struggling to have their voices heard and working to get their issues on the transportation policy agenda.

In 1991, the national highway program was due for one of its periodic statutory renewals, called reauthorization bills. Moreover, the interstate highway system was at long last nearly complete—a point of closure that encouraged an assessment of where transportation policy should be going as we approached the new millennium.

This legislative opening afforded critics of established policy an opportunity to leverage change—an opportunity to reconnect national transportation policy with the communities it was meant to serve and shape. Coming off the previous year's battle over the reauthorization of the Clean Air Act, a broad coalition of environmental, planning, and other public interest groups, including the AIA, turned their attention and focus to transportation and the 1991 reauthorization bill.

Gathered together in umbrella organizations like the Surface Transportation Policy Project (STPP) and the Campaign for New Transportation Priorities (CNTP), these groups challenged the hegemony of the traditional highway lobby. They found kindred spirits in the then-chairman of the Senate Subcommittee on Water Resources, Transportation, and Infrastructure, Senator Daniel Patrick Moynihan of New York, and his Republican counterpart, Senator John Chaffee of Rhode Island. In the House of Representatives, those visionaries often found support from the new activist chairman

Large transportation programs bring work to many communities through which they pass and, upon completion, provide improved transportation options. Although a transportation project can be a major inconvenience to the traveler during construction, it is usually a major source of federal dollars for the region and can be a key part of a city's urban revitalization program.

of the House Public Works and Transportation Committee, Bob Roe of New Jersey, and the intellectual author of much of the House bill, Surface Transportation Subcommittee Chairman Norman Mineta of California. Both of these latter men (now gone from Capitol Hill) hailed from heavily urban districts and shared a strong commitment to mass transit.

Assisting these Congressional heavy hitters were legislative rookies like me and relative newcomers like Frank Pallone of New Jersey and Peter DeFazio of Oregon. We introduced bills that attempted to stake out new policy parameters and inject them into the policy debate. Mine was the Transportation for Livable Communities Act (H.R. 2279, introduced in May 1991), parts of which ended up in the final bill. These bills, while having no chance of passing as stand-alone legislation, helped shape the debate on the massive legislative reauthorization bill and, I'd like to think, gave folks like Roe and Mineta some ammunition in heading off the vociferous counterattacks of the highway lobby. Pointing to us unreasonable young "whippersnappers," Roe and Mineta could cite countervailing demands when the concrete or asphalt lobbies pounded on their doors.

All of these legislative efforts—much sound and fury, but hopefully signifying quality in the making—culminated in what became known as the Intermodal Surface Transportation Act of 1991. ISTEA was an attempt to meet two challenges: first, finding the resources necessary to maintain and improve our infrastructure, and second, wisely allocating those resources. In this manner, the act differed from previous transportation bills that attempted to legislate specific projects rather than providing guidelines for local initiatives.

In terms of its distribution of federal transportation dollars, ISTEA reversed a decade of decline in funding for mass transit. Driven by the energy crisis and the oil embargo of the 1970s, the federal government had made a substantial commitment to funding mass transit. But in the 1980s, the federal government reneged on that commitment. Between federal fiscal years 1981 and 1992, federal funding for transit—in real dollars—declined by 50 percent.

ISTEA, in contrast, allocated vast new sums to transit. The prime beneficiary of those newly focused dollars, obviously, would be large urban areas that had suffered badly from the earlier retrenchment. The legislation also equalized previously skewed matching fund percentages. For instance, prior to ISTEA, the federal matching share for transit capital projects was 75 percent, as compared to 90 percent for lane additions to existing highways. Under ISTEA both percentages were moved to 80 percent, thereby ending a built-in incentive for states to choose highways over transit when looking for federal transportation assistance.

Even more important in the long run, ISTEA included new funding flexibility mechanisms that allowed state and local transportation agencies wide latitude in spending federal highway dollars to meet local needs. Put simply, federal highway dollars in the past were divided into segregated categories of funds that could not be intermingled or moved around. Highway moneys, for instance, could not be spent on transit projects. Under ISTEA, in contrast, categories of highway funding were reorganized in such a way as to grant states and localities unprecedented flexibility in deciding whether a new highway or a new transit system was the best way to solve a traffic congestion problem.

In addition, the planning requirements that states and localities need to meet to obtain federal dollars for transportation projects have been significantly strengthened under ISTEA. This translates into more thoroughly justified road projects. State highway officials have to meet a higher burden of proof before they build an ugly, unnecessary, or ill-planned highway. The new planning provisions were designed, in short, to make it easier to stop bad projects and initiate good ones.

Among the multitude of forward-looking policy changes contained in ISTEA, perhaps my favorite was the establishment of a small but important new funding category for "transportation enhancement activities" such as the construction of pedestrian and bike paths, scenic landscaping, preservation of historic transportation facilities, acquisition of scenic easements, buy-outs of unsightly billboards, acquisition of abandoned rail corridors for conversion to bike paths, and the like. Moreover, ISTEA requires public input as to how states spend these new moneys. These moneys can thus be spent on initiatives that, in the past, have never been eligible for federal transportation dollars.

In summary, ISTEA's changes have given valuable leverage to those who wish to move to a better-planned and saner transportation policy. State transportation officials have been given the authority to respond more flexibly and creatively to their state's transportation problems. By extension, they can expect to be held accountable if they do not.

The Challenges of Change

How have things been working out? As one might expect in the real world of government, ISTEA's full potential has yet to be realized. State governments and transportation departments have been slow to implement the newer and more progressive of ISTEA's provisions. Sometimes it hasn't been their fault. The federal bureaucracy was slower than it should have been to formulate and publish the necessary implementing regulations. In other cases, state officials have been reluctant to move quickly on new programs. As the director of the STPP testified before a subsequent oversight committee hearing, "The whining noise you hear is the sound of change." Perhaps most disappointing was the slow start made in using the funding flexibility provisions of the legislation.

But Rome wasn't built in a day—and look how long *their* roads have lasted! The lesson learned is that ISTEA is not the end of the battle for a better national transportation policy. What it *did* do was change the old rules of engagement under which that battle is fought. ISTEA does not guarantee good projects—projects sensitive and responsive to the needs of urban centers struggling to revitalize themselves. But it does provide new tools and leverage for those who care about making the right choices.

And many of those who fought the good fight in crafting ISTEA have stayed involved, working to educate and mobilize citizens who share their concerns. ISTEA is designed to draw ordinary citizens into the transportation process, particularly in urban America. But first they need to find out how they can get involved. Toward that end, STPP followed up its exemplary efforts in pushing for the legislation with a series of 11 regional conferences on "Transportation for Livable Communities," spreading the word in the year following the enactment of ISTEA. The STPP also set up a speakers' bureau to provide ongoing support for local groups seeking to work ISTEA's levers to their advantage. The Bicycle Federation of America, to give one example, committed $700,000 to a two-year advocacy campaign with the goal of getting more people involved in the ISTEA-mandated transportation planning process.

It is safe to say that the success of ISTEA is, in part, a measure of the quality principles that are integral to it. The legislation empowers people at the local level and requires consensus among state and local authorities. It is a highly flexible program, fostering better and more appropriate uses of resources. It encourages paradigm shifts in the way transportation projects will be viewed. And it passed largely because of the quality tenets of leadership and commitment.

The Challenges of Tomorrow

The playground and ISTEA examples give ample evidence of the challenges faced and the lessons learned in the public arena and the need for a total quality approach. Making our urban areas livable again will require quality initiatives and innovation in both our federal and local government spheres. More importantly, it will require cooperation between the two. While the federal government has often been accused of simply throwing money at modern urban problems (usually to little avail), its more fundamental failure has been its inability or refusal to encourage and leverage local participation in our urban cores.

Whether it be in the form of tax incentives or enterprise communities/economic zones, redevelopment authorities, or subsidized financing, the federal government addresses our urban problems best when it enlists the resources and creativity of the local constituency, especially today when so many cities are themselves entering into unique and fruitful partnerships with the private sector. Moreover, in an era of federal budget tightening and depleted local tax bases, there is really no alternative to this approach. This position is not a back-door desertion of federal responsibility. This is not a retreat, under the cover of rhetorical darkness, from very real public obligations. It is simply an acknowledgment of reality.

Total quality efforts like these must continue if the promise of urban revitalization is to be realized. There are no final victories in the political realm. Success will require significant reservoirs of patience and commitment that can be tapped over time to preserve our gains and move an integrated urban redevelopment agenda forward. As frustrating as this process will be, we desert the field of battle at our peril. There are no guarantees—the American political process, like our Declaration of Independence, promises us not happiness, but only its pursuit. But if we want to leave our children with better communities that enrich rather than impoverish their lives, we have no choice but to continue to fight the good fight. To close, let me quote Robert F. Kennedy.

> *If we fail to dare, if we do not try, the next generation will harvest the fruit of our indifference: a world we did not want, a world we did not choose, but a world we could have made better by caring more for the results of our labor.*

Otherwise, we will be left only with the hollow apology of T. S. Elliot.

> *That is not what I meant at all.*
> *That is not it at all.*

Chapter 3

The Crisis in Human Capital Development in Distressed Urban Communities

William H. Brown

> *A man's life is subject to inner storms far more devastating than those in the physical world.*
>
> —A. Yusuf Ali

A national debate has raged for several years over what to do about revitalizing America's urban centers. Issues have included the physical rebuilding of decaying and deteriorating areas, poverty and welfare reform for America's urban poor, the physical clean-up and environmental restoration of areas now known as Brownfield sites, and the crisis of the urban family and the need for a restoration of family values. In many instances, the antidotes for solving these problems include a call for economic growth and development.

To many persons, urban economic growth and development (or more aptly, urban economic redevelopment) will bring about both a physical and a sociocultural revitalization to distressed cities. If one looks into the issues and problems confronting urban America, however, a seeming reality is uncovered: In general, urban America is not really doing all that badly. At least that's how it may look on the surface.

Wasting human capital.

Urban America, as defined today, is not simply a core city with an overwhelming population of poor and needy people who require some form of public welfare transfer payments to subsist. Urban America is a group of sprawling megalopolises that also includes growing urban suburbs with healthy industries and well-heeled communities set in enclaves that contain upper-income families and solid economic foundations such as good school systems and healthy financial institutions.

Defining the Distressed Neighborhood

Given this reality, it becomes necessary to give some definition to the terms that are used to describe the process of decision making surrounding the rebuilding of America's cities and urban areas. While this may appear trivial to some who argue that the problems of poor and needy people should not be minimized by trite linguistic issues, the problem of concretely identifying and clearly defining targets for public policy is real. This is due to two ever-looming realities: first, the conceptual problem of ever-scarce economic resources, and second, the practical problems of creating working public policy in a political world.

The state of Illinois found this to be true in attempting to determine how to tackle the problems of cities under financial duress. In October 1988, Governor James Thompson established a 24-member Task Force on Municipal Bankruptcy to study the financial problems confronting the poorest of Illinois' cities. As a result of the efforts of the task force, the Illinois Distressed Cities Act became law in 1991. This law defines a *distressed city* as one that has acute problems as measured by several indicators. Additionally, a *severely distressed city* is, by further definition under this act, one that certifies that it is among the highest 5 percent of all home rule municipalities in terms of the aggregate of the rate percent of all taxes levied upon all taxable property and also in the lowest 5 percent in terms of per-capita tax yield.

The definition of a distressed city, as codified in Illinois law, provides for the development of public policies that redirect state resources to help bring financial relief to these communities. However, this definition, while serving as a solid point of departure, merely touches the surface of the conceptual issues that must be addressed. Upon further examination of distressed cities, one will find that a duplicity of sorts exists there too.

Just as the notion of urban America reflects two opposing sets of considerations—often brought together by forces that will be discussed later—the notion of distressed cities actually reflects a hodge-podge of human realities. These include neighborhoods where professionals with good jobs and salaries live; neighborhoods singularly comprised of the unemployed, the underemployed, and those who are no longer considered part of the labor force; and a smattering of both of these types of local communities. In the more affluent neighborhoods, the stereotypical picture is of people getting up and going to work on weekdays, taking their families to church on Sunday, volunteering for civic and community organizations, and living the "American way of life."

In the latter communities, however, a very different culture exists. One might call this a *culture of desperation* or a *desperate culture*. Pockets of desperate culture exist throughout urban America; they exist in most suburban growth areas as well as in America's distressed cities and decaying central core communities. The question is: How do we help solve the problems of human beings who survive in desperate cultures, no matter where they are?

Issues of a Desperate Culture

To better understand the issues confronting those who live in these urban pockets of desperation, I interviewed three individuals in three different cities located in three separate states. All spoke to me under a guarantee of anonymity. According to the first "survivor,"

> *Although I am young by some peoples' views, the reality of how crime had surrounded me never took hold until I found myself owing a "g" [gangster] some money. I had borrowed $20 and forgot about it. About a month later, I was sitting in my car when my "g" friend pulled up alongside me. He asked for his money, which I, being unemployed, did not have. Suddenly, another window in his car rolled down and a glass of ice water was thrown in my face. It was a warning and a threat, which I took seriously because I knew I had to. I then realized that to these guys who were dope pushers and hardened criminals my life meant absolutely nothing.*

In a separate discussion, a mother who was a single parent and the head of her household eloquently described how drugs had taken hold of her son and the effect it had had on her life.

> *We live in a housing project, so there were a lot of boys his age. At first, it was just smoking cigarettes and drinking beer with the other teenagers. Then*

> marijuana came in along with opportunity to make a little money selling crack cocaine. Soon he was staying out two, three, four days at a time, carrying guns, and . . . he had just changed. My nice, quiet little boy had become an uncontrollable angry member of the Crips gang, and I lost my son (along with a piece of myself) to this whole drug thing. It really hurts . . . it really does hurt. But I still love him and I am his momma, and I know that he still loves me.

And finally, here are the words of a middle-aged African-American male who told me how he gets electricity and heat in the winter months while unemployed and with little available government assistance.

> I originally bought this house when I had a good job in the factory, and I worked and eventually paid for it. Then the downsizing came, and I lost my job. It's been several years now since I've had work. You know, I mean other than odd jobs here and there. Last week, when the temperature hit below zero, I was ready, though. About two months ago, I took the wood-burning stove from a recently abandoned house and put it in my bedroom. Every day I would go out and collect wood from abandoned houses to use as firewood. I chopped it up with my ax. I also do a little work for the old man next door, so he let me run an extension cord from my house across into his back porch socket. So I had both heat and lights when the winter storms came.

The three examples of what people endure in desperate cultures reveal some common threads: a prevalence toward crime, a bleak view of the future that society offers, and a preponderance of poverty. Of these three threads, the problems of poverty seem to predominate and appear to be the root cause from a total quality

Some people have more coping skills than others. Few would argue that it is far more difficult for the undereducated and the underemployed or unemployed to cope in our society today.

perspective. Many have suggested that there is a correlation between poverty and crime. Furthermore, there appears to be a strong correlation between poverty and joblessness. Whether it is an unemployed male unable to pay his debts, a teenage youth who sees his only real economic opportunities in joining a gang and selling drugs, or a dislocated middle-aged worker attempting to survive on a daily basis, the issues of poverty can be directly tied, in many instances, to the problems of joblessness and unemployment or underemployment. The question of surviving in a desperate culture is often the question of living in an urban environment without a meaningful way to subsist.

Statistics Do Not Tell the Story

Given this rather grim reality, it is little wonder that economic determinists and other policy gurus might often suggest that economic growth is the answer to reducing poverty at an acceptable rate. Studies have shown a strong inverse correlation between the extent of poverty and gross domestic product per person. But statistics alone are not enough, and neither are policy models that merely aggregate statistical data or information.

The poor are a heterogeneous group. Some have better coping skills than others and often find a way to eke out a meager subsistence through a variety of short-term cash jobs. Others are less able to cope and tend to live on the edge, suffering from mental as well as physical disorders. Many of the poor are children, often from single-parent, matriarchal households. Many poor people are illiterate, unable to read a newspaper or complete the barrage of paperwork that government solutions often require.

In short, summary economic data (or attempts to reduce the study of human beings to a strict "scientific" approach) have not and will not change the conditions of poverty and despair in which the poor often find themselves immersed. And policies and programs formulated as the result of such summary data collection efforts will not lead to economic growth that reduces real poverty.

Human Capital Development: A Total Quality Idea

Some policy advocates, in considering these members of the underclass, have promoted strategies designed to increase employment, meet basic needs, increase productivity, and reduce income inequities through some form of income maintenance. This combination of approaches has been woven together under the terms *human resource management* or *human capital development*, a basic criterion of the Malcolm Baldrige National Quality Award.

The case for human capital development is hardly a simply economic one. Less crime, less hunger, fewer infant deaths, and more taxes paid by more productive citizens are important goals to be achieved. In American history, we have evidence of the stark debate that has raged over the need to increase the human capital in our society. The strongest evidence of the forms of antagonism at work in this debate can be found in the penetrating research of scholars such as Herbert Gutman, Eugene Genovese, and John Hope Franklin as they considered slavery and the education of slaves (whom many considered to be chattel in the same sense as an ox or simple farm equipment such as a plow).

The laws of states such as Virginia and Maryland gave slave masters the widest possible power, which often resulted in the codification of laws that prohibited the education of slaves. It has been repeatedly shown, however, that the importance of educating slaves resulted in valiant efforts to do so. It was not just slaves who sought and fought for these opportunities. Illegal schools were established and taught by whites as well as blacks, and self-teaching methods were led by sympathetic whites. In many respects it was the fruits of the heroic efforts of both black slaves and white nonslaves that led to the establishment of Negro schools and colleges and the migration of blacks to urban areas seeking a better quality of life. Even today, it is that spirit of determination, which has its roots in the period of American Negro slavery, that often generates a fresh wave of optimism we hear and see in urban African-American communities when the contribution of education to improving one's standard of living is discussed.

Yet in spite of the proven importance of education in changing the conditions that people survive in, searches of the periodical literature reveal that very limited efforts have been made during the past 50 years to truly consider the role of education in economic development. And even fewer efforts have been undertaken to create a practical theory of using public policy as a primary tool to establish a comprehensive strategy for human capital development.

During the 1950s and early 1960s, there was a surge of optimism in this regard. It was in the early 1980s, however, that real interest in the contribution of education to economic productivity began to catch the public's eye, fueled by the news that more than 25 million Americans were illiterate. It has been noted that human capital formation is one of the direct determinants of economic growth potential. In addition, it has also been determined that past investments by a society in educating and training its members have often allowed for the proper and appropriate exploitation of the potential for regional economic growth.

Again, however, I must point out that conventional approaches to examining the gross national product or gross domestic product fail to account for the role of human capital with regard to our economic productivity. Only two detailed attempts have been made in recent years to construct measures of human capital development, and both centered on factors other than the contribution of education and training to real economic growth and development.

Quality Factors: Taking the Whole into Account

To further elaborate on the question of what we can do to help poor people survive in desperate cultures, it makes sense to now address a point raised earlier: the fact that in urban society, one often finds two opposing sets of forces brought together by external circumstances. In urban society, we often find very exclusive enclaves within minutes of the worst public housing (Washington, D.C. is a case in point), or we find sprawling growth areas such as those near O'Hare Airport in suburban Chicagoland within a short drive of high areas of unemployment such as the Cabrini Green housing projects. What role does this play in the development of policies and programs that will help poor people meet their basic needs while giving them greater access to jobs and opportunity? To answer that question, let us look at two different elements: the role of developers in urban design, and human capital as an entity.

In great measure, it is the activities of urban planners and private developers that lead to the uniting of diverse and differing cultures. Urban history shows that cities have been designed and redesigned continuously. These efforts, usually the actions of government development professionals and private development entrepreneurs working in concert, are the normal, incremental efforts taken by everyday citizens, government officials, and businesspeople. Cities, communities, and neighborhoods are often the result of natural, evolutionary decisions made by people competing for individual properties in accordance with their own uniquely tailored plans for profit and progress.

Inside these geographic areas that have been targeted for change by some force (governmental, nonprofit, or private), however, people living in these communities are often not at all part of the incremental change process. These residents have diverse backgrounds, education, and family and consumer spending patterns. The only thing they may have in common is that they live within a certain distance of each other, for instance, and this (through the efforts of the planner and the developer) often leads to their existing in the same geopolitical structure. As a result, these very diverse humans now have the same governmental units, the same tax structure, the same road and highway system, the same water and waste treatment systems, and so on.

Often they react to this situation in very different ways. While they all have the same right to vote in a particular election, some will vote and others will not. Of those who do vote, their individual voting preferences will be different. It is these daily decisions, often made in the millions when we consider the behavior of a specific geographic entity such as a city, that create the uniqueness of communities and the unique set of problems generally facing each community. And it is the study of these citizens, who are making these thousands of decisions each and every day, that must guide the development of policies and programs that will truly address the problems found by those who are surviving in desperate cultures. Thus, it appears that the roles of urban planners, private developers, and the architectural/engineering and construction community as a whole must be incorporated with any practical theory of human capital development for distressed cities or desperate cultures.

While little attention appears to have been devoted to the development of a practical theory of quality human capital development, much has been written recently on human capital and human capital formation. Corporations have begun to consider investigating the barriers to learning and developing strategies to exploit learning.

Internationally, leaders in other countries are becoming convinced that they must improve their educational systems. Studies are now beginning to emerge that examine patterns of income inequalities and how they tie into the lack of human capital development. Other studies are examining how educational level, quality of education, and degree type affect financial success. The effects of government investments in training are being examined. And research has been undertaken that develops theoretical models for optimizing growth when continuing technology changes are anticipated. Human capital development approaches have been considered supply-side approaches that pay far too little attention to the environments and conditions that face those who form the workforce. It is this notion of human capital development as merely a supply-side consideration that must be challenged.

The Need for a Theory of Quality Human Capital Development

In conclusion, it is important to point out that addressing the problems of people surviving in desperate cultures is, in reality, addressing the problems of America's poor and truly needy. How do we go about changing a desperate culture into a culture of continuous learning—a culture in which every individual is dedicated to increasing his or her own capacity for quality corrective action? This is a cornerstone question that we need to ponder briefly. Let me submit that the answer lies in the creation and development of policies and programs that increase the human capital value of our labor resources by addressing the practical and concrete problems confronting people and communities and, indeed, our society as a whole every day.

Our point of departure for changing how America's urban poor cope with their day-to-day problems must begin with considerations regarding what their daily conditions actually are. Considerations about the physical and environmental conditions that exist in desperate cultures must be incorporated somehow with a model for human capital development.

A total quality theory must recognize that the problem of physically cleaning up an environmentally unsafe public housing project can and should be tied to training for the unemployed or long-term underemployed in environmental remediation. It should then be extended further such that the human capital investment needs of that community clean-up are linked to the financial capital and business start-up needs of that community. The expenditure of public sector dollars to assist the community in a clean-up effort should involve a coordinated and well-orchestrated new federalism that vertically links federal, state, and local governments and horizontally links community-based organizations, private sector resources, and nonprofit entities such as schools.*

As we move forward in discussion of these and other questions that may arise, we must immerse ourselves in not only the political and economic policy issues that must be addressed, but in the day-to-day struggle of those who must survive in these pockets of poverty and despair. Not only should we address the linkage between employment and economic growth, but we should examine our expectations regarding the multiplier effect of government expenditures in a municipality or community through minimizing financial leakages and maximizing local expenditures. We must also address total quality approaches to the social, political, and human issues that confront the at-risk child, the single woman on the public welfare rolls, and the dislocated worker who needs retraining in order to fit into tomorrow's workplace.

In a world of ever-tightening resources, governments and elected officials (as well as corporate leaders) must ask and answer tough questions about how best to balance these scarce economic and social assets so as to achieve competing goals. One way to do that is to better use the most valuable asset of our society—the people that comprise it.

---

*Editor's note: For ideas on how this might be achieved, see Chapter 7.

Chapter 4

The Lack of a Quality Focus in Urban Education Sanctioned by Government

Wilbur L. Campbell

> *It is doubtful that any child may be reasonably expected to succeed in life if he is denied the opportunity of an education.*
>
> —*Brown v. Board of Education,* Topeka, 1954

Education in the cities of the United States is grossly unequal to the education in the suburban and, in some cases, rural areas of America. The many reasons have been spelled out in detail over the years. But the underlying factor is governmental attitudes toward or sanctions of these inequalities. We tend to forget that schools are, of course, units of local government and are regulated and controlled by local, state, and federal agencies of government. There is a clear lack of a quality focus in education in the inner city, and it is sanctioned by all levels of government.

This chapter describes the many challenges facing urban education and, in particular, those that have faced the city of East St. Louis, Illinois, at one time considered one of the most blighted communities in the nation.

Some children express their creativity in nonproductive ways.

Education Is the Key to Urban Revitalization

As education is the key to urban revitalization, attention must be given to problems facing urban education. Urban revitalization requires a well-educated workforce with employees possessing skills needed by industry. A real understanding of these challenges is the prelude to developing economic solutions that will be meaningful and successful.

Governments control schools in ways that often seem transparent. Locally, they hire teachers, approve budgets, and develop rules that cover everything from eligibility for after-school activities to dress codes. And while curricula tends to be based on accreditation standards, local school boards encourage or discourage departures from the norm. State governments also play a role through the standards they develop that provide formal recognition to a school, thus making it eligible for federal funding. Additionally, at the tertiary level, states govern public universities and other state-run educational facilities. The federal government supports excellence in the schools through funding for programs such as Head Start and the Carl Perkins Vocational Education Program. The federal government also supports tertiary education through grants and programs such as those designed to encourage minority participation in the system.

Governments at all levels, therefore, are responsible for ensuring quality and equality in education. It is reasonable to assume that they must bear at least part of the responsibility to improve urban education and apply a quality approach to it.

The Role of Education in Sustained Economic Growth

The development of competent workers at higher skill levels must be truly integrated with any economic strategy for a city. The building blocks of this strategy include assumptions that

- Economic regions are critically important.
- Skilled labor, technology, and capital are key elements of advantage.
- Competition coexists with cooperation within industry clusters.
- Government's role is to support economic foundations.
- Global corporations as strategic quality partners play a key role.
- Creation of a more level, consistent, and predictable playing field is essential.
- Success is measured as a sustainable, improving standard of living for all citizens.

Urban plans developed on the basis of these holistic assumptions link education to economic development. The failure to do so in the past continues to hurt both education and the cities.

Poor Business and Labor Linkages

Educational programs in many major cities lack strong business and labor linkages. Business advisory committees often exist, but they meet as little as once a year, and then only for compliance purposes. Few preapprenticeship programs organized in cooperation with labor are available to students.

Schools are run by school boards and educators, often with little input from the private sector.* Apart from what they bring with them from their own experiences, the members of these governing bodies may have few business management skills or lack the appropriate total quality atmosphere in which to initiate them. School board members need to learn business practices and quality techniques; they need to know how a private sector board of directors operates. They must learn how to develop systems that foster the segueing of classroom instruction into real-world job training in relevant preparation for entry into the nation's competitive marketplace. The development of total quality goals and objectives to meet these needs provides the framework of the kind of quality approach that must be embraced in order to begin to solve the inequalities of education in this country.

The lack of linkage to business and industry hurts students, particularly in areas of urban blight where few work-based learning opportunities exist. Cooperative education coordinators and placement coordinators in the secondary systems have a difficult time finding jobs for students in communities where few good jobs exist. Students in distressed neighborhoods are unable to obtain the kinds of work experience that employers want. They cannot get the experience needed to qualify for union apprenticeship programs. The failure of business and labor linkages is costly over the long term.

---

*Editor's note: For alternative approaches, see the details of the ASQC Koality Kid program. For more information, contact ASQC at 800-248-1946 or 414-272-8575.

Business and industry pay for their failure to work cooperatively with education. Employers fail to help create a globally competitive workforce when they are uninvolved in education. They fail to have access to entry-level workers with good communication skills, industry-specific skills, general knowledge, and a fresh view of the work process. Because of this, urban employers face an inadequate pool of qualified applications from which to select employees. Costs for employee training increase when industry does not work closely with education.

By failing to work with education, employers do not get the kind of workers needed for today's jobs. The jobs of the 1950s were primarily unskilled jobs, but many of today's jobs require significant technical skills. Even cash registers are computerized. By the year 2000, 65 percent of all jobs will require skilled workers, according to the U.S. Bureau of Labor Statistics. Figure 4.1 shows the changes over the years in the skills required for employment. The problem is that urban schools are not producing graduates with the skills required by industry.

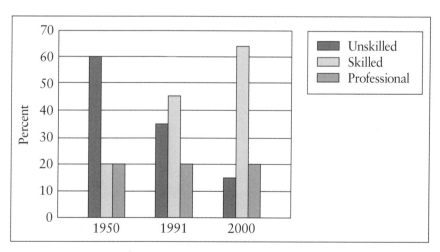

Source: U.S. Bureau of Labor Statistics, 1989.

Figure 4.1. Job skill level changes.

Employers contribute to education when they are involved. Specifically, the lack of employer linkages deprives urban schools of quality features like mentoring, field trips, job shadowing activities, work-based learning opportunities for students and instructors, input on school curriculum development, identification of education and skill requirements, and updates for educational systems on new and emerging technologies. Employers often serve as an important linkage in the development of community support for education.

Lack of Evidence of Institutional Effectiveness

Schools, particularly in K–12, lack evidence that they are doing what they say they are doing, whatever that is. Schools define their own mission and purpose and establish their own goals and objectives. They fail, however, to establish measures of any institutional effectiveness. The failure to employ or develop appropriate measuring tools and strategies leads to fuzzy evaluations of performance by school boards and administrators. The public is confused and unsure as to how well its schools are performing. Diminished public support is the outcome of the failure to produce evidence of institutional effectiveness.

It is important for all schools to prove their effectiveness, but perhaps nowhere more so than in the inner city, where the community's reputation hinders a student's ability to enter the job market. These students will have a better chance of obtaining employment after graduation if employers and the public have that proof. Additionally, studies show that employers are more willing to relocate to particular communities when they were convinced that the schools in the area are effective in what they do.

Lack of Technology in Urban Schools

The blackboard and overhead projector are still the primary instructional tools in too many classrooms as the nation approaches the new millennium. Many students are taught by teachers who are using the same techniques their parents were exposed to decades earlier. Most schools are planning to have a computer in every classroom, when what is really needed is a computer for every student. Urban schools often lack access to the information superhighway.

Occupational programs have suffered in the drive to offer students world-class training. State-of-the-art technology and equipment are not found in many K–12 and post-secondary institutions in urban areas. Schools often have to rely on hand-me-down equipment donated by businesses. One may argue that a 486 computer in the age of more powerful microprocessors is acceptable, but one is hard pressed to support the training of students in vocational skills with tools and machinery that are no longer on the market.

Science laboratories are hard to maintain, given the costs required for modern labs. It is no wonder that students in this country lag behind other industrialized nations in math and science test scores. Many urban students do not have access to the things that make science and math come alive in the classroom.

Inefficient and Costly Local Organizational Control

The organizational schematic for schools in this country is a monumental mess. Thousands of local school districts and local governmental units in each state fail to provide quality education in a cost-effective manner. The decentralized system of local control has resulted in too many school boards, too many bureaucracies, and too few economies of scale. Would McDonalds be where it is today if it had started as thousands of independent stores instead of organizing as a franchise? While each school system needs to remain autonomous in terms of its decision-making powers in order to provide the kind of education most appropriate to its population, in many instances the results of these decisions can be better managed within a larger regional framework of support, assistance, and quality control. Perhaps we need to "franchise" education in order to derive the quality benefits that come from greater efficiency.

In all fairness to state and federal agencies governing education, it is difficult to expect them to meet the needs of thousands of individual school systems, each managed by a board that operates in its directors' spare time (for the most part) and whose decisions are subject to being overturned as a result of routine school board elections. And while schools may vary significantly from region to region, overall they tend to operate in synchrony throughout much of the geographic area they share.

The relatively few class A and B schools (schools with larger populations) operate in much the same way in Iowa, Nebraska, Oklahoma, Kansas, South Dakota, and Missouri—the Plains states. And the hundreds of class C and D schools throughout these states work to offer not only the same academic excellence but many of the same extracurricular options as their larger counterparts. Again, each school is different, but taken as an aggregate, they operate in much the same manner. Economies of scale are possible.

Inequality in Funding

Public K–12 educational funding relies heavily on local property taxes. The use of property taxes by government to pay for schools means that educational quality is determined by the market value of the property in the school district. Suburban districts have more income because of higher property values, while many urban districts have less income because of lower property values. It is hard to build quality without dollars.

The inequality in funding means that urban schools have fewer resources to buy things that students need to improve their ability to learn. Student support services, counselors, tutors, adaptive equipment for special needs students, placement coordinators, computers, labs, occupational equipment, Internet access, modern libraries, and competent administrators cost money. The old adage is true: You get what you pay for. How can inner-city students be expected to compete with suburban students when the funding playing field is out of whack?

The neglect of our schools is obvious.

Jonathan Kozol graphically describes what is happening to children from blighted areas in *Savage Inequalities: Children in America's Schools*. The inequalities include building conditions, class size, dropout rates, funding, educational materials, teacher qualifications, health hazards, violence, and drugs. Kozol believes that government is responsible for the problems challenging inner-city schools. He states that the government perpetuates compulsory inequity by requiring attendance in public schools without requiring equity in public schools (Kozol 1991).

The constitutionality of unequal funding has been challenged in court. Many believe that students in this country are entitled to an equal education, but there is no equality when one district spends $3000 per student and another district spends $8000 per student. If separate but equal is unconstitutional, surely unequal funding is questionable. The U.S. Supreme Court must rule on this issue and guarantee a quality education for all students.

Jim Palos, a member of the Illinois State Board of Education and executive director of Midtown Educational Foundation, recommends that plans to attack problems with the school funding system in Illinois address erasing "unconscionable spending disparities" between rich and poor districts, establishing a "rational funding formula that includes defining a foundation level or the minimum dollars needed on a per-student basis to provide a quality education and determining the percentage of the foundation amount that the state will fund," and relieving the dependence on local property taxes (Voice of the people 1996).

Lack of Appropriate Government Support in East St. Louis: A Case Study

Education in the East St. Louis, Illinois, area faces many of the problems seemingly inherent in urban education in America today. The challenges here were so pervasive that a state oversight panel was created by legislation to control the elementary and secondary school district and the state ran the local community college (the only state-run college in Illinois). Until recently, the problems at the local community college were bad enough for the state to consider its dissolution. Only within the last few years has the school seen a significant change in the quality of the education it provides and the quality of the environment in which it provides it.

The elementary and secondary district continues to encounter difficulties. A diminished tax base, a declining population base, and the bureaucracy and inefficiencies of state officials cause problems for local educators. Charges of political control of the district and an inflexible union contract are heard around town. Many believe that students are deprived of an adequate education because of the incompetence of the adults in control.

The buildings in the elementary and secondary school district are typical of many found in urban areas: old, unattractive, and difficult to maintain; decorated with graffiti; afflicted with broken windows; plagued with broken furnaces; pitted with leaking roofs; and cursed with sewer problems. Several area schools now face a new challenge as a result of severe flooding in May 1996 that placed many of the buildings under several feet of water.

Select demographics of State Community College, as outlined in Table 4.1, are indicative of the urban problems of the entire community. The reader will note that the education level among this population is lower than that of the population of Illinois in general, that more people hold lower-paying jobs, and that the value of the community, as rated by housing prices, is exponentially lower ($29,646 per average home versus $102,759 per average home). While this last figure is skewed by the exceptionally high prices of the Chicago housing market, the $29,646 is low by any standard. These statistics reveal much about the challenges facing families who are undereducated.

The problems at State Community College were startling. Why did the state run it? Because no one else elected to serve the East St. Louis area when community college regions were voluntarily formed in the late 1960s. The rich industrial neighborhoods in the

Table 4.1. Profile of State Community College population (based on 1990 census).

	State Community College	Illinois
Household type		
Married	41.4%	78.8%
With children	18.3%	37.4%
No husband	51%	16.7%
With children	31.3%	9.2%
Household income		
Under $10,000	40.6%	14.2%
$10,000–$25,000	29.0%	24.1%
$25,000–$50,000	21.6%	34.6%
$50,000–$100,000	0.6%	4.9%
Average	$20,888	$40,885
Other income measures		
Average/family	$23,169	$47,259
Per capita	$5,792	$15,445
Below poverty line	43.6%	11.9%
Education level		
Below 9th grade	17.6%	10.3%
9th–12th grade	27.0%	13.5%
High school graduate	26.8%	30.0%
Some college	17.5%	19.4%
Degreed	8.3%	19.3%
Advanced degree	2.7%	7.5%
Occupation		
Manager/professional	17.1%	26.5%
Technical/sales	28.5%	33.1%
Service	25.8%	12.6%
Agrarian	0.5%	1.8%
Housing value		
Average cost—owned	$29,646	$102,759
Average cost—rented	$343/month	$471/month

Source: U.S. Bureau of Census, 1990.

larger community elected to become a part of the neighboring Belleville Area College district. The residents of East St. Louis were left without a local community college to serve them, so the state was petitioned to operate one. Illinois opened State Community College as an experimental college in 1969; thus the state operated the college. The governor appointed members of the college board of trustees, and two of the board members had to live outside the college district. The state wrote checks out of the state comptroller's office in the state capital. The college was audited by the state auditor general. The college had to meet two sets of recognition standards; one set of standards because it was a college, and another set of standards because it was a state agency. The State Community College Board approved all contracts, job titles, and curricula, and was responsible for determining college recognition status. Many of the failures of the college can be attributed to the entity in charge: the state of Illinois.

The school developed a reputation at the state level for high unit cost compared to other colleges, high administrative turnover, failure to comply with state business procedures, failure to implement changes recommended by state audits, inability to use new programs, inability to effectively manage federal and state grant or appropriation funds, declining enrollments while maintaining staffing levels, and general incompetence. The legislature grew weary of facing a request each year for budget appropriations for an experimental college it viewed as a failure. But it failed because these issues were not addressed as part of a holistic quality approach. Few quality measures were taken.

Meanwhile, the college president did not have the power needed to effectively operate the institution. The office could not spend more than $500 without board of trustee approval. The president could not hire faculty and staff. Minimum-wage student workers could not be hired without state board approval (State Community College 1992). The board of trustees, appointed by the state governor, was accused by the regional accreditation agency of micromanagement (North Central Association of Colleges and Schools 1990). The board members failed to understand the difference between policy and operations (a basic total quality precept), interfering in college operations and bringing politics into the educational decision-making process.

Evidence of lack of appropriate government support and interface was rampant and affected all areas of campus life. Even basic support provided to all other Illinois state buildings, such as custodial, landscaping, and facility maintenance services, were absent at the college. Meanwhile, getting approval to address these problems involved more time and effort than should have been warranted. Because these services were important but not of top priority, and because priority items were even more time-consuming, the college suffered in terms of physical decline. Students learned and instructors taught in dirty, inadequate classrooms. Administrators worked with outdated equipment in less-than-adequate facilities. It was just one problem the school faced that, when under the administration of the state, should have been administered by the state with the same attitude toward quality as other state buildings.

A Failure to Focus on Quality and the Results of That Failure

A quality approach to education must embrace many of the themes espoused by the private sector. Educators need to focus on doing the job right the first time, developing quantifiable methods to solve recurring problems, empowering people at the local and regional levels, providing long-range quality strategic plans, developing true leaders, and focusing on the students (the customer). Many problems facing education could be solved through a total quality approach. The failure to focus on total quality is tolerated by government without regard for the impact on students, employers, and the community.

Government entities servicing education in urban centers must take a primary role in developing holistic, measurable, practical systems—total quality systems—to improve educational standards for all students today. To fail to do so will jeopardize the future of our country as no other factor will. If we are to be the number one nation on the face of the earth, we must provide our students with the number one educational system in the world. And we must do it before it's too late.

Chapter 5
The Family in Crisis
Sheryl L. Cooley

> *The root of the kingdom is in the state. The root of the state is in the family. The root of the family is in the person of its head.*
>
> —Mencius

Danielle Cerone is a 23-year-old single woman with a four-year-old daughter. She is going to school to become a teacher; she works part-time in the day care facility her daughter attends. Her ex-husband acknowledges their daughter, but provides little in the way of financial support. Neither do her parents. Cerone was highlighted in an article in a local Southern California newspaper because she is a welfare recipient (Weston 1996).

Journalist Bonnie Weston goes on to outline the family's monthly budget. Cerone limits the amount of time she works at the day care, because if she earns any more her Aid for Families with Dependent Children (AFDC) checks will shrink; instead, she uses what little extra time she has to study. She receives food stamps, but less than the maximum, because she works. Her food budget hovers in the $135 bracket monthly, meaning there's that often no meat on the table. She has an old car that requires continual repair; but in Southern California, where mass transit is hardly adequate, it is nearly impossible to get around without one. "'The thing is, we just don't have a sense of community anymore, where neighbor helps neighbor and we all pitch in,'" she said in the article. Living in a single-parent family is tough.

The Demise of the Family and Its Support Structures

In American society today, where two-income households are the norm—where, in fact, average income families *require* two salaries just to maintain their middle-class lifestyles—it is no wonder that a disproportionate number of single-parent families live below the poverty line. The same social changes that have allowed women greater freedom to choose marriage (rather than being virtually forced into it for reasons of financial security and social acceptability) have also led men to take a different attitude toward their roles as husbands and breadwinners.

There is an entire culture of homeless families—men, women, and children.

At the same time, the past 30 years have seen companies move their employees willy-nilly across whole continents, causing the break-up of the extended family: that of parents, children, grandparents, and/or other relatives who have lived together or in close proximity to one another for generations. As a consequence, neighborhoods of strangers have erupted with little or no commitment to one another other than that demanded of common courtesy.

The pressures on the American family to cope without traditional extended family support structures and the subsequent backlash, which has resulted in a me-first generation, combined with women's ability to survive on their own for the first time in history, has led to a huge increase in the divorce rate. People who stayed married because of need or a sense of duty no longer feel obliged to tolerate such a relationship at the expense of their own satisfaction. While it appears that two people can raise a child better than one, we no longer require families to reside in pairs for legitimate acceptance into society. In addition, we no longer expect women to remain sexually inactive unless they're married, and we seldom look down on single parenthood, however achieved.

At the same time, we no longer ask the neighbor down the street to watch our kids while we run to the store. We no longer trust others to feed our pets when we take a vacation. We no longer expect the local banker to consider us as individuals when it comes time to foreclose on our houses. These social changes have expedited the demise of the traditional family, the extended family, and the community as a family.

The Rise of the Single-Parent Family

Fifteen years ago I taught high school, both in the United States and overseas. I taught in small towns in backwater communities where many of the kids went on to some sort of post-secondary education, even if it was only a vocational/technical school or apprenticeship program. They lived in relatively nice homes, went to fully accredited high schools, and could look forward to a reasonable chance of success in their lives. But even there, where their futures loomed bright if they could just keep out of trouble, the peer pressure to drink heavily and to have sex on a regular basis was tremendous. Every year we would lose one or two students—the boys would die, drunk, in car accidents; the girls would get pregnant.

It was as if two opposing forces were in play. Their upbringing demanded abstinence. But the boys had to get their notches in their belts; the girls had to lose their virginity. It was a status thing on both sides. And it was particularly true among my vocational education students, as if getting drunk and having sex somehow made up for their inability to compete in other ways with their peers, as if it somehow made them better or more worldly. It was as if they had made up their own rules and were determined to live by them.

But why is it that more teens get pregnant out of wedlock today than 15 years ago? Sociologists and social psychologists have developed numerous theories.

- Sex outside of marriage is de rigeur for most consenting adults who are dating today; children take their lessons from them.
- The media promotes this behavior more blatantly than in the past.
- Young females still have trouble getting birth control pills or are afraid to try.
- Men still hate to use condoms (although this is changing with the onset of AIDS).
- Young people are left to their own devices more often these days as both parents work.
- Children born out of wedlock are no longer doomed to life as second-class citizens.
- Saying no is more difficult than ever before.
- Society no longer compels young men to marry the women they've impregnated.

- People are no longer ostracized by their families, churches, or communities if they become parents outside of marriage.

Against this background, it is not so surprising that the rate of teenage pregnancy has increased dramatically and that the number of single-parent families is so high.

The Rise of the Single-Parent Family in the Inner City

Although the rise of the single parent in the inner city has been well documented, the surge in teenage pregnancies has not been limited to areas of urban blight. In fact, studies show that, while a large number of African-American teens who give birth do live in our nation's poorest urban sectors, statistically, the increase in pregnancy among white teens has outstripped that of African-American teens within the same age groups (Edelman 1987). However, just as there are greater safety nets for all persons living above the poverty line, so are there greater nets among pregnant teens above the poverty line. Their chances of initiating or continuing the cycle of poverty are fewer.

Additionally, in the inner city, which tends to be made up largely of African-Americans, single mothers for the most part are more likely to remain single. Marian Wright Edelman, in her book *Families in Peril: An Agenda for Social Change* (1987), attributes this to a number of factors: more young African-American teenage boys than Caucasian teenage boys are incarcerated or are homicide victims, more join the military in order to get out of the ghetto, more have substituted gang life for the family, and more live in a culture that accepts denial of any responsibility for the child.

The inner city has already bred a generation of single-parent families trying to cope with family life. Unlike their counterparts in the more affluent suburbs, many of them are crowded together in small geographic areas where support services are fewer, less affordable, and in greater demand due to the sheer number of parents who need them. While pregnant teens in higher income brackets may find themselves somewhat stigmatized by the system

Poverty creates stress that breaks down family values.

that supports them, there *is* a system in place for them. Their access to prenatal information, proper diet, and good health care is taken for granted. The safety nets are in place. But not so in the inner city. There, young parents-to-be, struggling to cope without these supports, often snub the system that barely provides for them. With poverty, lack of education, lack of maturity, and lack of security comes anger, attitude, and apathy, none of which is a positive driving force in the promotion of the family unit.

Traditional Family Structures Break Down Under the Stress of Poverty

The opportunity to operate in a traditional family setting assumes that certain systems are in place. These include job opportunities; affordable, livable housing; and safe neighborhoods—little of which is available in these distressed communities. It assumes that a decent education has been offered and that people have availed themselves of it. It assumes that the majority of the people who make up the community can succeed if they just try, that community services are for the few who have fallen between the cracks, and that our welfare system is sufficient to sustain these few. But in the inner city, as the tax base shrinks, so do public services, including education, crime prevention, and public beautification projects. Industry moves out. And young people, most of whom have never seen past the borders of their own neighborhoods (except through the distorted media of television and movies) are left to their own devices. No education, no jobs, no services, no support—none of the traditional footings that make the family unit self-sufficient. The traditional family crumbles in the face of poverty—or never forms at all.

Perhaps the greatest determining factor is education, for the educated can more readily afford the traditional family lifestyle. But society as a whole tends to underinvest in education,* and what it does put into the system in terms of monetary support comes in the form of property taxes. In the inner city, where the tax base has eroded, where there's not much to be gotten from property taxes, the educational system literally falls apart. As a result, the culture of the inner city has evolved to accept without disdain the undereducated. The problem, however, lies in the view from the outside world. In the United States, a high school diploma is nearly always a prerequisite to any full-time employment.

Additionally, a lack of parental support, a lack of preschool opportunities, a lack of school-sponsored extracurricular activities, and ultimately, a lack of good teachers have left children in distressed neighborhoods without the basics they need to succeed in school. Add to that drugs, guns, and racketeering in the schools, and it is not difficult to understand how it is that kids can be undereducated, virtually from the beginning of their school careers.

On top of that, there are the lessons learned out of school. Children learn through imitation. They tend to follow in their parents'

---

*Editor's note: Refer to Chapter 4 for a more detailed discussion of this subject.

footsteps, at least while they're small, developing a sense of right and wrong based on the training they receive in the home. For reasons that no one has yet fathomed entirely, some children stray from their teachings; others cling to them. But experts agree that what they learn in the first few years of life stays with them forever. For that reason, children need appropriate role models, nurturing adult caregivers, and an environment that makes them feel safe. In the inner city, where good role models are often absent, day care facilities are at a premium, and violent drug-related crime is common, these children are often traumatized well before they can develop appropriate coping skills. Education within the home and the community forms the foundation upon which the inner-city child grows to adulthood. For that reason, nurturing the family is essential to the health of the inner city in general.

Rethinking Traditional Family Support Arguments

Proposed quality solutions to family problems tend to operate from two very different camps. Today politicians, backed by whatever moral majority makes up their constituency, espouse the belief that the traditional family exists thanks to traditional moral values. They insist those values have been lost (not submerged) in the inner city and must be reintroduced in order to raise the phoenix of the traditional family unit. Somehow we must *teach* moral values. Never mind that we can't decide among ourselves just what those values should be or who should instill them. Forget the rhetoric that asks if we have a right to impose our values on others. Ignore the problems that are inherent in the traditional family—one that has tended to disregard the needs of the woman, undermine the rights of the children, and lay the financial success of the unit on the man. From the righteous across the nation comes a call to inculcate people into the mores of our society, whatever they might be.

Against the backdrop of those intent on a return to the traditional family are those who look at the statistics and foretell the end of the family as we know it. Catherine Ormell, in her article, "The Decline and Rise of the Family" (1995), says,

> *But however these new-style families operate, they will certainly be vastly different from the family as we know it today. Some sociologists believe—or just hope?—that institutions, employers, and neighbours and friends will take on roles once dominated by relatives. In the 21st century the blood bond will no longer be one of the strongest links between people. (p. 4)*

Here the call is for external sources to take the place of the missing spouse. Federal, state, and local governments, for the most part, have attempted to do that by providing funding for programs aimed at supporting the family. The federal government supports a single parent who has at least one child with AFDC, food stamps, and Medicaid. But not only does the welfare system allow these parents with young children to stay at home (a debate in itself), but it actively "disincentivizes" them for working if they make anything close to minimum wage by lowering their AFDC payments and food stamps proportionally. The adult has a choice: stay home and depend on a particular income each month, or work and depend on nearly the same income. Additionally, government efforts have been made to provide low-cost housing, although public housing has limited success. State and local governments have also tried to provide webs of support in the form of public/private programs; but the waiting lists for admission to these programs are often long.

The Community as a Village

Interestingly, the only organized groups that seem to be able to answer the call to arms are the community's formal religious organizations. Lawsuits have tied teachers' hands; today they live with such rules as "never touch a child in praise or punishment." We no longer expect our neighbors to correct our children; instead, we

Part of the success of revitalizing a community lies in supporting the family unit.

insist that they mind their own business. And we, the parents, leave latchkey kids to function largely on their own, befriending those we don't know and watching television we don't like but cannot keep out of our living rooms in our own absence. Numerous nonprofit organizations parade a variety of programs, but they tend to be scattered and of varying quality.

Only the churches and other organized religious institutions tend to offer a message of appropriate behavior on a consistent basis. For most of them, it is part and parcel with a belief in the achievement of life after death. The problem with the these entities is that they are there not only to indoctrinate children into the proper mores of life, but into their particular religious beliefs. This tends to disenchant those without any particular religious learnings. And even in a community that can agree on basic values teachings, organizations with religious affiliations struggle as the constitutional separation of church and state limits their ability to receive public financial support. Many communities struggle to find ways to provide a bridge between them as it becomes clear that places of worship are, in many communities, the glue in otherwise disintegrating neighborhoods.

For years Kent Amos, a former Xerox executive living in Washington, D.C., has provided additional parenting time for a number of his children's friends. Now head of the Urban Family Institute, he is a strong advocate of the "village" concept as the surrogate parent. Amos believes that good schooling must be supplemented by after-school programs that encourage studying, limit television intake, and provide alternatives to the street. His program is not directly linked to the preservation of the family unit itself, but rather offers an alternative "family" for at-risk children.

Hillary Rodham Clinton picks up on this theme in her book, *It Takes a Village and Other Stories Children Tell Us*. Her book is a folksy compendium of how to raise children, what the federal government has done to help children, examples of local support programs for children, and an exhortation for every American, as part of a community, to create a neighborhood environment for them (Rodham Clinton 1996).

The point is that piecemeal programs are not enough—a whole *quality system* must be developed to provide the support needed. Again, Amos describes it as a village approach. In a *Washington Post* article, it was noted that Washington, D.C.'s Shaw area had, according to the article, 8000 children, three high schools, four junior high schools, at least 19 churches, Howard University and Howard University Hospital, two Boys and Girls Clubs, a YMCA, and several economic development programs and social services agencies. "But they don't operate as a continuum," Amos was quoted as saying. "There's no synergy, no relationship between them, except physically." The article went on to say that Amos was working to get the institutions within communities like Shaw to operate together, in support of one another. He envisioned a "nurturing village" (A whole village 1994).

Other Quality Suggestions

We must look to a reasonable, flexible approach to helping families survive that gives them the resources, the skills, and the encouragement to be self-sufficient. Somewhere along the way, we must find a better way to predict the *kind* and *amount* of support that should be provided to families in crisis. No one expects the underclass to live the middle-class life, but for those who are trying, we should provide enough support to allow them to pull themselves up into the ranks of the middle class. The springboard should have some spring.

We must find a way to measure whether taxpayer and private help is being put to good use or is being used, instead, to put off shouldering the responsibilities of self-sufficiency. Additionally, for those who are not using their support wisely—who, in fact, seem to think that the world "owes them a living"—we must find other means to modify behavior. But somehow, we *must* find a means to distinguish between those are using the system to hoist themselves into a reasonable standard of living and those who are looking for a free ride.

Danielle Cerone, the welfare mother introduced earlier, considers herself lucky. She has a job. She has her schooling. She has finally found an apartment where, thanks to a public/private partnership arrangement, the rent is subsidized and fireworks, not gunfire, light up the night sky. The place is hers for up to five years. Because she's on welfare, her daughter has free day care on campus. Most important, she has a goal—and the means to support both that goal and her family.

But the Cerones of this world are not well publicized. Instead, it is the deadbeat families who draw media attention. As a result, the nation turns its collective back on support programs. In the last four years alone Cerone has seen her AFDC check shrink 30 percent in buying power thanks to cuts in the program and inflation. Now the California state legislature is looking to reduce that aid amount nearly 12 percent (The case for welfare reform 1996).

Summary

We must support systemic quality approaches to ridding the community of poor role models by providing adequate and appropriate public services. We must see to it that children are not caught in the crossfire of the latest gang activity and that the siege mentality is minimized. We must provide adequate housing. We must see to it that those who are struggling out of poverty have the wherewithal to buy groceries and heat their homes in the winter. They must have basic health care. If they're working, they must have affordable child care. And an area that is often overlooked, but according to marriage counselors is often a major reason for breakups in marriages—means must be found for families to have fun on occasion.

There is a reality that needs to be accepted here. It is one that Americans find difficult to accept: Not everyone can be helped. Every society carries a few of its fellow citizens; not every problem can be overcome. But in our culture, to fail to help those who are trying is unconscionable. The trick is to figure out who can be helped to become self-sufficient and who cannot. It's a prognosis we have been unwilling to make, but by refusing to do so, we risk spreading our resources too thin with too little result. We risk failing to help those who would best benefit by it—those striving to become contributing members of our society.

This is where an effective total quality system can be made to work. We need to do more than cobble together disparate programs of support for the family unit—whatever its makeup. We need to cherish the family and to give it the means to become self-sufficient, the assurance to live without fear, and the time to nurture its members. We need to provide those new and innovative ways to clone the traditional underpinnings that have fostered families of the past. Otherwise, we risk losing the institution of the family altogether.

Part II
The Vision

Chapter 6

The Vision of Urban Revitalization

Roger D. Hart and Sheryl L. Cooley

> *We are a nation of communities... a brilliant diversity spread like stars, like a thousand points of light in a broad and peaceful sky.*
>
> —President George Bush

The vision is clear: Revitalize today's crumbling communities. Recreate the vibrant neighborhoods they once were. Make them contributors to the economic and social fabric of the nation. Make them safe. Make them inviting. Make them self-sufficient. Reverse the trend of decay.

Background

The concept of urban renewal as addressed in the mid-1990s finds its roots in Lyndon Johnson's "Great Society," in part with the Demonstration Cities and Metropolitan Development Act of 1965. The act was passed as a result of recommendations prepared by a nongovernmental task force composed of representatives from both public and private industry, labor, and minority organizations. It was approved by the National Association for the Advancement of

Colored People (NAACP), the Urban League, the U.S. Conference of Mayors, and the National League of Cities. Known as the Model Cities Program, its objectives were to

- Provide financial and technical support to cities intent on rebuilding or revitalizing blighted areas.
- Generally improve living conditions for people living in those areas.
- Effectively concentrate and coordinate public and private efforts on behalf of those citizens.

Unfortunately, the program itself was not well spelled out, especially in terms of qualifications for recipients. As a result, members of Congress cornered funds for use in their own districts. Need was not so much a determinant as legislative clout. Additionally, the budget allowed for 75 cities to become Model Cities; however, by the time legislation had passed, 150 communities had won eligibility (eventually that number became 225). Meanwhile, funding remained static until, eventually, it ceased altogether during the Nixon administration.

Numerous other bills passed through Congress. One of the most important was the Community Reinvestment Act of 1977. It was designed to ensure that banks provided equitable loans to middle- and lower-income people. The law attempted to curtail what appeared to be blatantly greedy and prejudicial practices on the part of the nation's major lending institutions.

In the interim, local communities were developing grassroots programs to address the deterioration of their neighborhoods. It was during this time that Community Development Corporations became key players in the fight on poverty. Their primary purpose was to build or renovate homes, the theory being that every person deserved a reasonable minimum standard of living. Local Initiatives Support Corporations (LISCs) appeared on the scene in 1979, the outgrowth of less formal private/public partnerships at the national level. Basically, LISCs provided funding for housing development.

Interestingly, a presidential commission launched near the demise of the Carter administration recommended that urban blight not be fought, because there was no help for decaying urban centers. The commission recommended, instead, that urban entities continue to spread to greenbelt areas and that urban blight be ignored.

Title VII, Enterprise Zone Development, was part of the Housing and Community Development Act of 1987. It authorized no funding, but did provide for coordination of existing federal programs and regulatory relief in areas that would be designated by the U.S. Department of Housing and Urban Development (HUD). The words *economic zones* became a key phrase during the Reagan years. Several bills were brought before Congress, but none of them passed. Part of this had to do with partisan politics. Touted as part of the supply-side economic platform, the Democrats wanted nothing to do with the bills.

President Bush had no better luck. Although in favor of measures that sought to initiate these zones, he continued to veto them. They were always tied to bills that included tax increases, such as the Tax Fairness and Economic Growth Act of 1992, and Bush was already getting enough heat on that issue. It wasn't until after the civil disturbance in Los Angeles, a result of the Rodney King trial verdict, that the Empowerment Zones and Enterprise Communities (EZ/EC) Program was born in the passage of President's Clinton's economic package as part of the Omnibus Budget Reconciliation Act of 1993.

On the Quality Front

Urban planners have long expressed the notion that urban revitalization must involve a broad base of private and public support. In 1991, the U.S. Army Corps of Engineers Construction Engineering Research Laboratory (USACERL) proposed to work with HUD to modify management and assessment technologies that the Department of Defense (DOD) employs in managing its nearly $500 billion inventory of roads, bridges, sewers, buildings, transportation systems, training land, public housing, fire stations, planning offices, and security response teams for civilian use on a test bed basis. It was also proposed that this test bed city demonstrate the use of DOD-developed environmental programs for remediation, restoration, waste reduction, and regulatory compliance. The proposal was rejected by an in-house evaluation team because it was believed that a strong commercial advocate—an architectural, engineering, and construction (A/E&C) partner—was needed.

When ASQC's national Architectural, Engineering and Construction Division executive roundtable convened in 1993, the same theme was proposed. Key executives, representing nearly two dozen A/E&C firms (and accounting for nearly $40 billion in worldwide construction that year), discussed the need to support a national urban revitalization program.

In their discussions, urban revitalization programs for the future would not look like urban renewal programs of the past. Conference participants suggested that wholesale dislocation of urban populations and community clear-cutting was neither financially feasible nor socially acceptable. It was understood that urban revitalization needed to involve an integration of economic development and educational and infrastructure improvements. It was noted, however, that to carry out cost-effective urban revitalization efforts, firms might be asked to shoulder an inordinate financial burden.

As an outcome of the ASQC roundtable, a collaborative organization was proposed. It was intended to loosely follow the corporate models of US Car and Semitech under which competing commercial firms could jointly develop or prove out urban revitalization programs in partnership with communities, government, and, perhaps, each other. The concept raised during the 1993 conference was a corporate consortium to be named *US City*. The term has been federally trademarked.

Two subsequent ASQC national conferences addressed the issue of urban revitalization. Key leaders from academic institutions, the

Urban revitalization—buildings, people, jobs, and education.

American Institute of Architects, and the American Society of Civil Engineers, major urban design firms, state and city officials, many of the largest A/E&C firms, the U.S. Army Corps of Engineers, and leaders from both the materials and insurance industries discussed the special requirements of urban revitalization. The conclusion was the same: America must create new vehicles though which multiple organizations can partner to bring about urban revitalization.

The Many Quality Issues Associated with Urban Revitalization

The urban revitalization process is a messy topic for a number of reasons, and for the mere mortal can appear overwhelmingly difficult to navigate and fruitless to pursue. Like a cancer that invades the entire body, eating away at vital parts, urban decay can seem unstoppable. And as with any diagnosis, the extent of the disease and its measure is a combination of test results and intuition. Consequently, the program of cure is based on the best guesses of experts and incomplete evidence. Such is the "science" of urban renewal. Issues surrounding the process of urban revitalization quality planning include the following.

• Determining the *amount* of urban renewal required by any distressed neighborhood is difficult. While the general populace screams that their tax dollars should go to help the poorest in our nation, critics point out that the areas just beginning to fall into disrepair should be attended to first. The blight isn't as bad, they concede, but it will get worse if left to fester—better to stop it now.

• There are many social issues to address: poverty, crime, education, job opportunities, motivation, and health care, to name just a few. What programs are available? What ones work? What ones will work in a particular community with its particular mix of determination and despair? What programs need to be developed? Who should do it? Who should pay for it? The list goes on and on.

• Opinion plays an important role. Nationally, there must be a call for urban reform from politicians who, as representatives of their constituents, take up the cry. This, in turn, is predicated on the attitudes of the general populace. Some believe in providing social support programs to the underprivileged; others feel that the poor can only help themselves. Additionally, within a given community, attitude plays a key role. There must be a consensus of will at the grassroots level before the kind of master plan required of an urban revitalization program can succeed.

- The interrelationship, interdependence, and interface of all issues relevant to urban revitalization make it difficult to develop programs and practices that do not overlap—duplicating processes, eating up resources, and wasting funds. For example, educational programs in our schools must go hand-in-hand with job opportunities, which go hand-in-hand with the schedule for rebuild of physical structures, which must go hand-in-hand with the allocation of funds.

- Regulatory issues cloud the picture. Often public dollars cannot be given to religious organizations, and yet the church is often the primary stabilizing factor (and the only avenue of hope) in a blighted area. In terms of infrastructure, federal and state-related Superfund laws that establish "joint and several" liability for any person or organization that has ever owned a piece of property now requiring environmental remediation severely restricts reconstruction activities in older urban quarters.

- Finally, political issues not only muddy the waters, but sometimes change the course of the river over and over again in frighteningly short periods of time. It is difficult to build on "here today, gone tomorrow" government opportunities.

The Illness of Despair

The root of urban blight lies in the move of the United States from an industrial giant toward service-oriented industries. High wages and the increased cost of technology upgrades led many manufacturing industries to look outside the United States for cheap labor, lower taxes, and less insidious regulation—or face certain death. Whether one argues that self-serving capitalists abandoned ship for personal gain or that they were forced out by an inability to make a reasonable profit, the fact remains that they could compete better elsewhere. With the dawn of the computer age, in which America had the lead, and with the large number of college graduates coming out of the 1960s and 1970s, successive decades of businesspeople have found a future in service industries. Unfortunately, that industry has offered little for the poorly educated and even less for the highly skilled manual laborer.

For those who had lived through the Great Depression, the loss of jobs was not a new concept. But as one man put it, "My family was poor; we were all poor. We just didn't know it." Perhaps the 1930s was a era of great naiveté. With few social programs, nothing was expected. Without television, there was not a visual stick by which to measure the national norm. And for a long time after, a person could survive on the federally established minimum wage. People could take pride in being a dishwasher or a doorman or a janitor or a short-order cook. With the current cost of living (groceries, food, clothing) and the high cost of transportation, insurance, and day care, it's nearly impossible to make a decent living in a minimum wage job today.

The intelligent alternative is to accept welfare, food stamps, and handouts. Intelligent—but not self-motivating. As even more invasive programs behind what was once the Iron Curtain have proven, handouts often breed laziness, self-contempt, and despair.

The psychology of despair is difficult for most Americans to understand at a community level. Yet it is nothing more than an extension of personal despair. Think about a recently widowed woman who has spent her life as a homemaker, whose children have left the nest, whose knowledge of the world beyond her borders is limited to the evening news. She has no place to go, nothing to do, and no will to do it. Relief comes in the form of friends and family and, sometimes, professional help. Relief comes in the knowledge that the fabric of her life will mend in time, that eventually the future will be bright once more.

Sometimes, that future never happens. The sorrow overwhelms, worms its way into the spirit, and brings the woman to her knees. She starts sleeping late in the mornings and drinking highballs at night. She stops eating well. Her dress becomes sloppy, as does her house. She rails of the unfairness of life, and the hope for death and the abhorrence of it play fearsome games in her mind. People whisper behind their hands that the woman is "not quite right—never really got over it." They gaze in pity and try to stay out of her way. The eventual loss of her partner combines with the loneliness of her ostracism, and sorrow turns to despair.

The psychologist Abraham Maslow described a theory of need based on a pyramidal structure. At the base, he listed physiological (food and shelter) and safety needs. Psychological needs rested on top of these—the need to belong, to be loved, and to have self-esteem. At the pinnacle was self-fulfillment needs or self-actualization. According to Maslow, people struggling to survive cannot move on to the higher needs associated with achievement.

Failing to meet these levels of need leaves little room for hope. If there is no perception of light at the end of the tunnel, or worse, if the light is an oncoming train, there is little impetus to struggle forward. The pleasures of the moment, the euphoria or oblivion of drug- and alcohol-induced states, the lust of sex, the security of gangs—these provide instant gratification. They are the symptoms of despair. As we did with the widow, we ostracize these people from our world—the festering begins, the disease spreads, and the decay begins in earnest.

Physical Property Issues

One of the key elements of urban revitalization is the effective repair or replacement of physical structures. For some urban areas, this in itself breaks the cycle of decay. Many cities around the nation have redeveloped old and crumbling communities made up primarily of commercial/industrial infrastructure with an eye toward industrial renewal or tourism. This has several advantages, including a relatively straightforward plan for renovation, the creation of new jobs, the encouragement of small business entrepreneurism, and the generation of cash within the zone of renewal. The renewed area, in turn, affects the surrounding neighborhoods, often with the fringes becoming more upscale as young urban professionals move in seeking lower-cost housing. As these neighborhoods are being established, community leaders work to partner with one or two large-scale businesses to help cement the tax base and supplement a program of economic diversity.

On the surface, this system of urban revitalization appears to work well. However, it often leaves the community with two kinds of users—the daytime workers, and the scum of the night. This is particularly true where housing is not an integral part of the revitalized area, but exists only at its edges. Cities have found that they must expend as much effort and support in developing an appropriate night life as they do in creating one for the daytime. Restaurants and coffee shops, legitimate businesses that run multiple shifts, colleges and universities with strong evening curricula, upscale multiunit housing—these types of entities must be made a part of the revitalization program as well if an urban area is to experience true renewal.

Sometimes simply repairing buildings and creating a "village" community can stop the cycle of decay.

For communities in which blight is deep-seated and geographically large, the development of tourism or industry may not be an appropriate first step. Here neighborhoods must start with life safety issues. Communities can expect major setbacks in the beginning as contractors are brought in to alleviate the worst of the life safety problems. With no sense of ownership in the effort, the community will be hard-pressed to maintain facilities once initial renovation has taken place, as those who have owned the streets and held a choke hold on its populace fight all efforts to undermine their power. Since the work of repair will likely not be the result of local labor, and as violent crime will still be evinced, it will be difficult to maintain the initial level of rework. But life safety issues cannot wait, and the means must be found to maintain the facilities once they are repaired.

In the case of severe urban blight and despair, every effort must be made to lure businesses and educational facilities into the area as soon as it is physically inhabitable. Many experts today espouse the concept of making the physical rebuild effort itself the economic catalyst to urban revitalization. After life safety issues have been addressed, a program of infrastructure repair and replacement must be developed in conjunction with a training program for the trades. This means that the master plan and a strategic quality plan must include a budget and schedule dependent on qualified local help.

Nonprofit organizations and government support vehicles for infrastructure rebuild are well entrenched. Several systems are in place to help a community replace its decaying urban areas. However, one issue clouds the horizon: environmental remediation. Under current laws and with current technology, the cost to remediate a site is often greater than the anticipated value of the property after remediation. And it is not unusual to find that a great deal of the property in the older, industrial urban communities needs remediation before reuse. To use or purchase such a piece of land means becoming liable for its wastes. Few small businesses can afford the remediation, and few large ones can be enticed into the area with that specter hanging overhead.

There is some discussion about turning this challenge into an opportunity by training and certifying the local residents to remediate the area. This is one of the recommendations made by USACERL. Just as the U.S. government trains its personnel in remediation, so can they train the civilian population. In theory, then, these highly trained personnel could find employment outside the community when the work within it has been completed, providing remediation for the government at numerous sites across the country. The idea has value, although private contractors willing to manage the actual remediation efforts (many only want contracts to conduct the studies) are few today because of the high risk involved in terms of worker liability. These issues will have to be overcome through government support.

Not all remediation is related to the soil or water under a building. Asbestos abatement also accounts for much of the renovation problem. Again, local personnel can be trained, but liability here is particularly sticky. It would not make sense to develop a local business that would have to bear such risk. Nor would "rip and skip" contractors provide stability in the scheme of economic revitalization.

Social Issues

The social issues that affect the success of a physical renewal program are so plentiful and diverse that it is difficult to get one's hands around them: prostitution, drug trafficking, "gang banging," teenage pregnancies, poor education, poor diet, poor hygiene, poor medical care, few job opportunities, poor-paying jobs, and unproductive workforces top the list. However, they boil down to three categories of concern.

- Crime
- Lake of education
- Lack of income

Crime. Part of the difficulty in developing appropriate programs to combat these ills lies in their interconnectedness. For example, crime is largely born of greed, desperation, boredom, or the lack of a sense of self-worth. Measures can be put forth to drive crime from the streets through physical confrontation and massive arrests. Often, however, this type of action only moves crime underground or into the next neighborhood. Not only must the violent be taken out of the community, but efforts must be made to keep from growing another crop. It goes back to building a future that provides motivation for rational behavior in the present.

Studies show that an increase in visibility of local police curbs crime (Williams 1985). Cops who walk the beat and get to know the people of the neighborhood are in a better position to foster peacekeeping than those who do not. In part, this is because they know the people and can determine the source of trouble and how best to deal with it, and in part because the community has a chance to become less suspicious of what is, in effect, grassroots

Security is an essential ingredient in the renewal of communities.

authority. This is quality empowerment. Additionally, local police can support local community leaders as they develop appropriate school programs on such topics as child molestation and kidnapping, saying no to drugs and sex, and AIDS. They can also help neighborhoods set up community watch programs.

Moving the pimp off his corner will not end prostitution, however, because underlying factors will continue to put women in the position of selling their bodies. They either need to earn money, or they will seek to make it easily. Forcing the local drug dealer out of the neighborhood will not end the practice of abusing drugs. Others will come to take their place as long as there is a market. Covering the graffiti on the wall will not stop the gangs or modify their behavior as long as children need a surrogate family, breaking rules is an accepted (sometimes admired) practice, and teens feel alternately that they are invincible and that life isn't worth much. The roots of criminal activity, especially juvenile delinquency, must be dealt with if the chain of criminal behavior is to be broken.

Lack of Education. Most decaying urban communities must upgrade their educational programs. Educators must stop thinking of themselves as academic teachers who are responsible only to hand out instruction within a certain time period of each day. In all fairness, most educators enter the field as idealists, and many would do more than they do if they had the resources. But schools, one of the great influences of each generation, are depressingly underfunded in areas of urban decay, primarily because funding comes from an ever-shrinking tax base.

Like police forces, schools must be well funded and run by well-trained administrators and teachers. To do less is to cheat a child of one of his or her most basic inheritances—the opportunity to learn, to better himself or herself, and to be better equipped to deal with life's problems. That means that children who come to school tired or hungry or hung over or suffering from abuse should find refuge in the school—there should be programs to keep them from falling into the abyss of despair. That means before-school programs, after-school programs, and community centers where children can go to study, get tutorial help, learn a skill, or just play.

One must always walk carefully through a discussion of craft training—that is, training men and women to perform skilled manual work. After decades of watching so many of our children graduate from college to become white-collar workers, to suggest that the urban poor might do any less is to risk being labeled as prejudiced. After all, many of the urban poor are African-American or Hispanic, and people of these races have traditionally been relegated to manual labor.

However, to ignore the undereducated adult who will never go to college and to snub our collective noses at the craftspersons of the world—the bricklayers and retail clerks and firefighters and paramedics—and think only of the architect or doctor or engineer is to do any number of people a great disservice. Plumbers, carpenters, electricians, mechanics, and roofers can make a decent living with sound training. And in these economic times, they can make better money than some of their white-collar counterparts. In the long run, both trade and university training options must be open to those who want to work. Additionally, trades programs must be instituted if the neighborhood's residents are to help in the rebuilding efforts.

Lack of Income. Lack of income is largely a result of lack of job opportunity. Lack of job opportunity is the result of a shift in the economic base out of the community—companies move to the suburbs or industries die. Without a solid tax base, other support mechanisms founder. Lastly, as poverty breeds despair, it also breeds a lack of will.

Without motivated employees and a neighborhood that supports a good quality of life, it is difficult to entice businesses into the decaying urban community. Experience in some states has shown that near-term incentives work better than long-term incentives—that investment-related incentives work better than their labor-related counterparts (Rubin 1994). Basically, the firms that can be attracted to the area must believe firmly that they can make a profit as a result of the move. The greater the area of urban decay, the greater the profit potential must be (Porter 1995). Few companies can afford to exercise philanthropy in these economic times.

Although many smaller businesses start up as service providers to their larger counterparts, others serve the needs of the community. Barber shops, restaurants, and grocery stores rely on the neighborhood populace to purchase their products and services. Efforts should be made to identify businesses that are particularly appropriate to a community and to foster their growth.

Through the community revitalization model that involves intense use of local labor, it is envisioned that numerous businesses will develop as a result of the physical renewal of the area. Materials and services purchased to address life safety issues may have to be brought in from outside the community. But the master plan must include a program to foster a system of local vendors. At the same time, it must ensure that regulations are not enacted that would create unnaturally high prices for these goods and services.

Quality Paradigm Shifts

If the vision is to succeed, there must be paradigm shifts in our thinking. If the axiom of "If it ain't broke, don't fix it" does not apply (and it certainly does not in the atmosphere of urban decay), then the opposite must be true: "If it's broken, fix it." If the old ways don't work, don't use them.

For example, HUD Secretary Henry Cisneros has proposed to renovate public housing facilities to become life-long learning campuses. The theory is that people who want to learn can have access to public housing and that public housing facilities will primarily become academic centers—self-contained, state-of-the-art "colleges." As long as learning continues on an individualized basis, the participant can live in the structure. On the surface, the program seems to be no more than another handout doomed to fail. People will move into the center, take a few courses on a continuing basis, and laze around letting the federal government take care of them. And true, this is exactly what must not happen.

But Cisneros is trying to get at the root of educational problems facing the poor. Transportation to school can be difficult and unsafe. For the most part, traditional teaching methods do not allow learning to take place at the student's pace, but must aim for the middle, pulling some children down and dragging others along. The curricula is usually cast in stone. And few teachers can handle 40 students at a time, no matter how good they are. Discipline is always a problem.

Cisneros' view is not one of allowing participants to "slouch toward Bethlehem," but providing alternate learning environments in areas where the traditional ones just don't work. It attempts to keep people safe, provide them with the latest technology, give them day care, offer personalized tutorial help, and create motivation. Much like the "School of the Air" in Australia, it has the potential to work if curricula criteria are set out clearly, qualified personnel are made available, offenders are systematically routed, and the community supports the effort. It is another attempt to create the paradigm of a village atmosphere.

On the Quality Front (Again)

For too many years, quality has been seen as a by-product of expense. If one had enough money to "do the job right," the result was a quality product or program. One *affected* quality by using top-notch materials and equipment and by hiring master craftspeople to do the work. The concept of quality evolved, however, as automation and standardization led to higher standards of performance and superior products on a much broader basis. Manufacturers found they could produce better products at lower costs if they optimized procurement, equipment, labor, and performance. *Effecting* quality meant developing quantifiable measures to determine optimal levels of production.

The age of nuclear engineering catapulted quality to center front stage as procedures were written to ensure that every step of the design, construction, and operation processes was evaluated according to a standard process of review and documentation. The process was cumbersome but effective. And the idea of quality control seeped into the entire A/E&C industry. However, as America faltered and the gross national product fell, increased productivity became the mantra of the day. While work processes were scrutinized for improvement, the focus shifted to downsizing personnel and cutthroat competitive pricing at the expense of all else. *Quality* was an adjective, not a noun. Quality referred to a level of excellence (or lack thereof), not a process to ensure excellence. Projects and programs were executed quickly and cheaply, and quality—or the lack thereof—again became a by-product of such activity.

Meanwhile, experts in the field of quality assurance and quality control continued to fight for the ideas of *quality management,* defined in general as the management of all things related to quality and usually spelled out in a plan designed to effect (not affect), monitor, and ensure quality products, work, and work processes. But the concept lost favor in the eyes of those who saw quality as an impediment to low cost and accelerated schedules. People wanted quality results, but they felt they could not spend the time or money to implement any but the most basic quality policies, especially when they could not show a direct link between them and the bottom line.

Today, the pendulum again is shifting as companies begin to view quality as a competitive advantage and governments, mindful of waste (or the perception thereof), seek to improve their systems of management. Today the word *quality* is beginning to be recognized as a force, a means to derive improvement in services and optimization in processes. It is what gives companies a competitive edge. The pendulum has only begun its trek through its swinging arc, but indications are that it is on its way.

All of which means that there is a shift toward thinking of quality as the base of the equilateral triangle whose sides are labeled "cost" and "schedule." The problem, of course, is that quality is a concept—an intangible object. It is more than procedures and inspections and tests and measurements; it embodies the best of the human spirit and skill and knowledge and forethought and will.

The Role of Quality in Urban Revitalization

The role of a quality system is to keep the vision alive, carve out the details, allow for flexibility, manage the process, measure the achievements, and effect excellence in the process. It is estimated that $160 billion are wasted in the A/E&C industry alone because of rework—the result of poor upfront decision making and project mismanagement. This is because quality fails to be the framework upon which project development and execution is hung.

A solid urban revitalization plan, then, is one that is based on quality factors: a good plan, sound management, and adequate resources. This implies the following.

• A program of renewal that addresses both physical and social issues in a timely and holistic manner. Long-term goals are not lost in the desire for short-term results. The plan is strong enough to stand the test of time but flexible enough to allow for change. It's life cycle costing and more on a grand scale.

• National/state/regional/local and public/private partnerships that operate within a single organizational structure. This implies empowerment at the local level, while assuring that anarchy doesn't take hold and destroy the entity and the whole plan. It implies an outstanding communications program and network. And it implies strong and capable leadership willing to act in the best interest of the people. It requires men and women of great strength, tenacity, skill, humility, and foresight.

• Access to initial sources of funding and hands-on support. Urban plans and exotic organizational charts are of no use if there is not money and appropriate human resources to get the program off the ground. (The plan, described in the first bullet, should take care of developing additional funds, services, and support both within the community and outside of it.)

- A test bed approach. Quality management means making sure new ideas work with a minimum of risk before spending great amounts of capital to launch them full scale. This quality tenet is often overlooked in the hurry to complete a program or launch one. Impatience with new systems also keeps people from change; the old methods are proven, if not optimal.

- Long-term commitment. Too many efforts die in political cross fire. Because public support will always be liquid, long-term commitment must be found among other constituents (which is part of what makes public/private partnerships so palatable). Somehow the program must be designed to succeed in spite of dramatic changes in the political climate of the moment.

- An honest quality assessment of the program and its parts on a routine basis and a quality plan for emergency review, when necessary. Results must be quantified where possible—statistics reviewed in light of the total program. Critical milestones must be met, or else plans to put the program back on track rapidly must be implemented. All aspects of the program must be reviewed in terms of a schedule of commitments and viability.

- Recognition for the deserving—even if it's the community itself. Too often urban revitalization programs do not include public relations plans except as parts of other development efforts. Outstanding individuals need to be recognized. And the community, if it hopes to throw off the stigma of urban blight, must develop a plan to keep more than just itself and its neighbors abreast of its struggles, developments, and, most of all, its accomplishments.

Much will be lost in urban revitalization if quality is not the driving force behind the renewal process. Quality is not only a systemic approach, but a process of interface. It is the glue that makes a program whole. A focus on quality will ensure a focus on means and methods, cost, schedule, measures, and excellent results. Slapdash won't do; foot dragging won't do; short-sightedness won't do; nor will power plays, nay-saying, or ineptitude. With quality as the fulcrum, programs are balanced between want and need. The hand is on the tiller at all times.

The Vision Burns Bright

In America the vision is the same as it's been for more than two centuries—to create a good life for ourselves and a better one for our children. For that reason we try and fail, then try again: failing forward, ever hopeful of a better future—and with hope, creating the vision anew.

Chapter 7
Democracy and Total Quality
Roger D. Hart

> *The central theme in our American heritage is the importance of the individual person.*
> —President's Commission on Civil Rights, 1947

Total quality (TQ) is an extension of the concept of democracy: consider the quality tools of empowerment, teamwork, and consensus management. International proliferation of quality means the international proliferation of democracy.

The Roots of Our Country

With so many problems facing our cities and the nation, the effort to rebuild them can seem mind-boggling. It is, perhaps, worthwhile to take a deep breath and look at all these problems from the 50,000-foot level. Is there any common thread that runs through the concerns, problems, or ideas that can be recognized when addressing the reconstructing of a nation? Because, truly, rebuilding our cities means reconstructing our nation.

A key aspect of a TQ approach to solving problems is to objectively look at them and honestly, as well as pragmatically, find their root cause. This is sometimes referred to as *root cause analysis* (Russell and Regel 1996). Root cause analysis looks for a common denominator among the problems. Is there something that crosses over all of the seemingly independent problems of education, politics, crime, and strife? The answer clearly is yes. There is a common denominator that crosses over all of these types of problems—people. *We the People* cross over all of these boundaries.

Our culture and people have to get back to the roots of our country. The nature and effect of people on all societal systems have to be changed in order to meet the significant challenges of our nation. How can these challenges be met? The U.S. Constitution says many things, and most people agree that it is morally sound (Peasle 1970). It was written and ratified 208 years ago and has been amended numerous times. However, the Constitution has never been revised. Why is this the case? *We the People* tend to hold this document sacred, almost to the point of giving it religious connotations. Is this how George Washington, James Madison, Thomas Paine, Thomas Jefferson, and other founders desired the Constitution to be held? I do not believe so. They were fed up with tyranny, monarchs, excessive taxation, and the denial of certain rights that they thought were inalienable.

If our founding fathers were living today, they would be the first to say, "Let's make the Constitution and the laws user friendly. The Constitution should be a living document. The government described in the Constitution should be reflective of, sensitive to, and easily usable by the citizens of the United States of America." The writers of the Constitution provided considerable foresight into the mechanics of government during that period of history and well into the twentieth century.

Reflecting back on the ideas of root cause analysis, maybe these mechanisms are in need of change due to our present day society and technology.

The Third Wave

Some believe today that the United States and the world are undergoing a third wave of revolutionary change (Toffler 1995). They maintain that the first was the agricultural revolution 10,000 years ago and the second was the industrial revolution some 300 years ago. Further, they also believe that this third wave has been caused by such forces as

- Economic labor
- Capital based on intangible assets

Sophisticated technology will play a major role in the third wave.

- Electronic monetary systems
- More creative and less interchangeable work
- Working in the home, on the road, and in the air
- Small business replacing big business
- Creation of the virtual corporation

While you might argue the pros and cons of a third wave, clearly with the evolution of technology and culture, significant manifestations of change are in the making.

Our governing institutions must reflect and support matching proactive and positive change to our society. On the other hand, they must protect the principles of life, liberty, and the pursuit of happiness that have made the United States great, based on sound and practical moral principles. How do you serve both of these masters? Is there really a way to do both? I believe so.

The U.S. Constitution: A TQ Strategic Plan

Before this question is answered, let's further reflect on the U.S. Constitution, which describes our government structure. Does the Constitution really require a revision? To answer that, let's consider the following list of sentences from the Constitution, to which I have applied editorial comments. I would like you to read them, keeping in mind one of two general questions: Is there a better way of doing things based on today's readily available technology? Or, on the other hand, do some parts of the Constitution still make sense given today's environment, particularly relating to the problems of our cities?

- *Our government is based on the separation and balance of power among the legislative, executive, and judicial branches.* Is this really conducive to working together, or should cross-functional teaming be used to solve important problems?

- *Based on the Magna Carta idea of natural rights, our Constitution sets a defined zone of freedom to protect individual rights.*

With the present government gridlock and mega-multinational corporations, is this protection truly being preserved?

- *The trial of all crimes except impeachment are to be held by jury.* Is this actually the case? Or does our judicial system run more smoothly because other means of justice (for example, arbitration) are employed? Should the Constitution be changed to reflect this?

- *All accused individuals have the right to a speedy trial and defense.* Is this the actual practice?

- *Election of the President and Vice President is by and determined from the Electoral College chosen by the states.* Is this the most effective way today to reflect the will of the people, or has the global-village potential of today's communications changed that?

- *No member of the House of Representatives shall be less than 25 years of age. No member of the U.S. Senate shall be less than 30 years of age.* These are essentially the only job requirements for members of Congress. Is this enough, given today's changing environment?

- *The number of representatives in the House is determined by a ratio of 1:30,000 based on population.* Is this appropriate based on today's technology, that is, the "lot size of one" concept (ASQC 1996)?

- *The Congress shall assemble at least once in every year.* Why should they ever "unassemble," given today's readily available communication mechanisms?

- *Each House shall keep a journal of its proceedings.* Should this be a journal, or a home page on the Internet? Communication mechanisms are very different today.

- *The Congress shall have the power to coin money, regulate the value thereof, and of foreign coin and fix standards.* Such monetary basis is projected to be obsolete by several futurists with the advent of international electronic banking. Should this statement be clarified?

- *The Congress shall have the power to define and punish piracies and felonies committed on the high seas and offenses against the law of nations.* Should not this be rewritten to reflect other methods of transportation today, given world problems such as terrorism and drug trafficking?

- *No title of nobility shall be granted by the United States and no person holding any office of profit or trust under them, shall, without the consent of the Congress.* This can reflect many issues, but certainly one might agree that this needs to be made more current.

- *No state shall, without consent of the Congress, lay any imposts or duties on imports or exports, except what may be absolutely necessary for executing its inspection laws.* This can also reflect many issues that may be desirable to be clarified.

- *Each state appoints its members of the Electoral College.* The method described in the Constitution is nebulous and subject to interpretation. Should this also be revisited?

- *The judicial power of the United States shall be vested in one Supreme Court, and in such inferior courts as the Congress may from time to time ordain and establish.* Should this be practically clarified, based on the original intent of the Constitution?

- *A person charged in any state with treason, felony, or other crime who flees from justice and is found in another state, shall on demand be removed to the state having jurisdiction of the crime.* Should this be practically clarified in this document, given today's actual practice as it relates to the powers of the governor in each state?

- *In suits of common law, where the value in controversy shall exceed $20.00, the right of trial by jury shall be preserved, and no fact tried by a jury shall be otherwise reexamined in any court of the United States, than according to the rules of the common law.* Is this the case today? Obviously not. Should the Constitution be updated to reflect the effect of long-term inflation on property values?

- *Involuntary servitude, except as a punishment for crime whereof the party shall have been duly convicted, shall not exist within the United States, or any place subject to its jurisdiction.* Should this be clarified, particularly as it relates to crime and punishment in rebuilding our nation today? Is this not an available labor pool?

I realize that any one of these subjects can bring up very controversial responses, and there are lower-level government interpretations to each of them. Wouldn't it be nice to openly and in a positive manner bring several people together to perform structured total quality management brainstorming (Hart 1994) of new ideas at this level of government to rebuild our cities? This was done once before. Innovation and proactive leadership were running rampant once before. It was a revolutionary thought, but it was accomplished. It was accomplished during the Constitutional Convention, concluded on September 17, 1787, and ratified by the states a year later. Now may be the time for a second Constitutional Convention, using TQ to solve our cities' problems.

Quality has to start at the top, but it directly affects the bottom.

Total Quality: The Heart of Our Country

The current fundamental concepts of TQ reside within the heart and roots of our country. Contrary to many popular beliefs that total quality management is foreign to our culture, I assert that this is, in fact, the basis of the United States of America. (I further assert that the concept of TQ was initially quite foreign to the Japanese, and that it has changed Japanese culture over the last 40 years.) Based on the analysis of the U.S. Constitution, I hope you can gain an intuitive appreciation of this fact: TQ is very American and democratic in its nature. It is very American to have governance to rebuild a nation with the following attributes.

- Effective leadership chosen by *We the People*. The key to a quality system lies in providing quality leadership and organization and in defining responsibility. The term *leadership,* in this book, refers to a take-charge attitude to determining and implementing quality work. It is not reactive but proactive leadership that enhances quality effectiveness through democratic means. For leadership to be translated into every aspect of a quality strategic plan, there must be the support of *We the People*, adherence to quality guidelines, proper advisement by quality organizations, and the empowerment of every person to contribute to quality.

- Futuristic and practical strategic planning. If we desire a long-standing initiative to improve and rebuild our cities and to use TQ in a participation management philosophy, we must develop a TQ system. It must incorporate successful techniques from the variety of elements within our democratic society that lend themselves to a quality improvement process. This method has become popular with the advent of such quality advocates as W. Edwards Deming and the phrase *total quality management.*

- People empowerment, recognition, and reward. An important element of the TQ system is human resource management and development. The best-written and best-documented system is of no value unless *We the People* are informed, trained, developed, and empowered with positive incentives, recognized for our work, and truly rewarded. The human factor is an effective element of any quality system in our communities. Most organizations involved in urban revitalization clearly need this idea of empowerment. This is one of the most important elements of an effective system.

• An effective governing process that uses the latest technology. During a complete revitalization effort, we must be responsible for the quality, coordination, and technical accuracy of services. In a global world and competitive marketplace, the consequences of deficiencies, even ones that a few years ago would have been called insignificant, can be disastrous, both economically and legally. Therefore, the revitalization effort should strive for flawless documentation, which simply assures uniform adherence to time-tested processes and procedures. These processes and procedures should be established, documented, and maintained on all projects involved to ensure that the design, construction, or implementation will comply with requirements.

• An ability to produce measurable positive results for the people. It is important in any revitalization effort to measure results. Results are project-by-project or program-by-program measurements identified and factored into an automated mechanism, which highlights successful processes for use in future projects and is documented for easy access. For example, the use of quality cost analysis is one of the most effective tools for this purpose. Costs are somewhat universal and uniform within a particular type of project and can be measured from project to project.

• Governments directly focused on their customers: *We the People*. Sometimes in the day-to-day activities of an urban project, customer focus and satisfaction can get "lost in the woodwork." However, it should be one of the most heavily weighted factors. Let it be clearly understood that this does not necessarily mean *We the People* are always right. What this means is that all people must have a clear understanding of the program's true value to our country, focus on the program's value to the whole, and satisfy *We the People* in more of a long-term effort. Keep in mind people know more than government gives them credit, but they simply do not have the resources to communicate effectively. Keep in mind that we must, indeed, look at the end user to understand the conceptual criteria of the project. In every quality system, customer focus and satisfaction are paramount to project success.

Rebuilding Through Quality Champions

This idea of revising the U.S. Constitution by holding a second Constitutional Convention may sound very noble it its effort, but can this practically be accomplished? Even if you believe that this is impractical, we offer you a relatively simple idea for making significant differences in the operation of governance in the United States that could greatly affect rebuilding a nation. This is the idea of quality champions. I have discussed previously the ideas of determining root cause and common denominators as a part of the democratic process. This common denominator was determined to be *We the People*.

Perhaps it would make sense to address the subject of people directly. Almost everyone would like "life, liberty, and the pursuit of happiness." Almost everyone would agree that they want to find a method for achieving those ends. A fundamental factor of TQ is education. When people are educated and enlightened, they endeavor to strive hard to obtain a desired result. I would assert that TQ education is the key and first step toward obtaining life, liberty, and happiness, a metaphysical rebuilding of our nation.

There are many forms of education available in today's world. They include formal schooling, on-the-job training, the media, seminars, books, the Internet, and so on, all of which have value to one degree or another. Using these forms of education, and with the support of the government, my vision is to hire, train, and staff total quality champions throughout our country in order to provide TQ advice and counsel to the leaders of our many institutions.

Trainers would coach cross-functional teams and lead efforts only until TQ methods had been fully deployed. Like a rock dropped into a still pool whose waves radiate outward in endless undulations, TQ training in our nation's institutions would continue until TQ reached all levels of management and organization in both the public and the private sectors.

In an effort to better describe the quality champion and how quality championing might be deployed in society/government institutions, I offer Figure 7.1. The diagram has two portions. The top portion is a Pareto diagram in which the electorate can determine the "statistically significant few" concerns to which to apply the concept of quality champions. Data points to the left of the tangent intersections of the exponential curve represent the "significant few." The bottom portion of the figure is a illustrative diagram on how to deploy the concept of cross-functional teaming, further explained as follows.

Cross-Functional Teams: Business, Government, and Institutions

An important aspect to TQ in rebuilding a nation is the creation of cross-functional teams among business, government, family organizations, and religious institutions. According to Sheila Kessler (1995) in her book, *Total Quality Service,*

> *Cross-functional teams are quality improvement teams that consist of representatives from different departments and/or layers of the organization. Many functions . . . cross departmental lines and need to involve various functions to analyze problems and achieve goals. (p. 144)*

This is the core of solving the concerns of the nation's cities. There are primarily two types of challenges associated with our nation's urban areas, as detailed in the bottom portion of Figure 7.1.

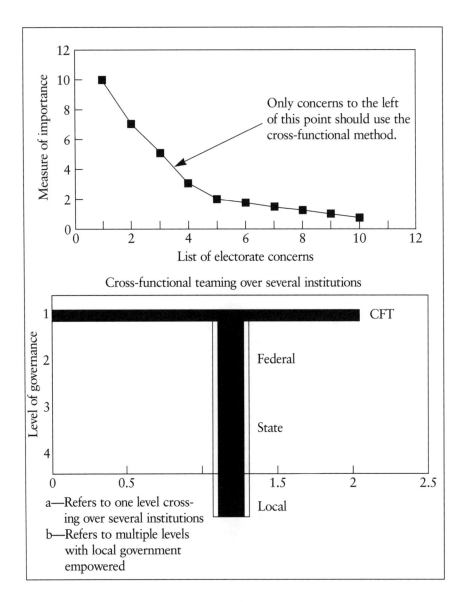

Figure 7.1. Quality champions and cross-functional teaming to break down institutional gridlock.

- Type a problem: The source of one type of problem deals with various business and government institutions at a particular level (for example, federal or state, but not both, designating a horizontal management matrix).
- Type b problem: The source of the second type of problem deals with multiple institutions on several levels (for example, federal, state, and local—a vertically arrayed matrix) normally associated with a problem of high priority at the local level.

Once the "significant" problem or concern has been identified using the criteria described in the top portion of Figure 7.1, it should then be categorized as demonstrated in the bottom portion of the figure. This is when the concern gets categorized as either type a or type b. If the significant problem or concern has a broad scope (for example, K–12 school funding in the United States), then a type a team, crossing over several institutions, should be deployed. If the significant problem or concern has a narrow scope (for example, making East St. Louis a test bed for urban renewal), then a type b team, crossing through various levels of governance—federal, state, and local—should be deployed.

Kessler (1995) further describes strategic quality goals as key to deploying such cross-functional teams. Questions (problems in urban cities) can only be solved by identifying them at the "top" (on a national scale) through setting strategic quality goals. On the other hand, she goes on to say that, 80 percent of the time, the true solutions to these questions come from the "bottom." In this case, the effective deployment of both horizontal and vertical team strategies should solve 80 percent of the problems of cities.

Studying the history of federal, state, county, municipal, and city operations can teach us several things about political and alternative motives, human jealousy, regulatory stalemates between political parties, lack of ability and desire to understand true costs, lack of working together, and the like. For quality champions to succeed, they must develop or ensure that they are working with cross-functional teams with the following attributes.

- Fair representation from all interests and parties
- Clear checks and balances on team member selection
- Clear checks and balances on the division of responsibility within the team
- Clear and strong responsibility and authority to do what it takes to achieve the desired solution

These teams should have strong, empowered authority in matters of funding, law or regulatory change (when necessary), organizational change, and, in general, working directly with the root of the problem. I realize that these are strong words when taken literally; however, appropriate controls can be established (such as two-thirds vote overrides).

Remember that an important element of TQ is human resource management and development. The best-written and best-documented constitutionally based governance system is of no value unless the people are informed, trained, developed, and empowered with positive incentives, recognized for their efforts, and truly rewarded. In today's society, a cross-functional team that truly embodies TQ is particularly important.

The human factor of a TQ system in our nation's communities cannot be overemphasized. Most government organizations involve serving the people of our communities; they clearly operate as service organizations. In a service organization, people are the products. Therefore, the human element of an effective TQ system is probably the most important factor in urban revitalization.

All elements of a TQ system deal with the human factor to one degree or another. What attributes of an effective cross-functional team should be enhanced to directly affect the quality of rebuilding a nation? They include the following:

- Facilitating and focusing early in the life of rebuilding

- Benchmarking against world-class comparisons, no matter where or in what country
- Ensuring the qualifications, education, and training of the cross-functional team empowered to solve such urban problems
- Empowering team members to use their true capabilities through innovative technologies to solve problems associated with jobs, education, and economic well-being
- Creating solutions to the problems of our cities that are correctly focused, effectively using the people, and motivating them through recognition and reward, along with increasing their technical excellence

According to J. M. Juran, much of history deals with recurring cycles of events (Juran 1995). A new force comes over the horizon: Is this third wave of change in our society this new force? In order to meet this third wave challenge and to rebuild our nation, many "givens" will have to be changed. They include

- Laws that can only be understood by attorneys
- Regulatory guideline upon regulatory guideline upon regulatory guideline
- Discussing what to do rather than actually doing anything
- Governmental gridlock that occurs whenever a matter of importance must be addressed immediately
- Government run like a group of self-serving small businesses, year by year
- Mega-multinational corporations left unchecked
- Putting "band-aids" on problems rather than deploying permanent solutions

Effecting New Programs

The problems that affect the rebuilding of our cities can be changed. This change can occur by empowering cross-functional teams to tackle national-scope issues (see Figure 7.1). The work of such teams partnering with business can be both difficult and yet tremendously rewarding. Our country is proud of its grassroots citizenship efforts. We are proud of the planning and strategic efforts in cities such as Los Angeles, Detroit, Atlanta, and East St. Louis. These sustained efforts have included support of Empowerment Zone/Enterprise Community revitalization efforts, the intended use of a learning campus concept for revitalization, and the comprehensive planning of large-scale public/private partnerships to revitalize many cities.

In addition, we recognize the need to continue to grow and learn within our distressed neighborhoods and to implement at the local level those programs that are spawned through true cross-functional relationships. We also recognize the need to take successful local accomplishments and apply them, as appropriate, on a national scale. This is the quality key to rebuilding our nation.

New programs resulting from cross-functional teams can be established. These programs would take into consideration the role of state governments in support of what are known as *vital economic foundations*. These are the following:

- Human resources—developing competent workers at higher skill levels
- Financial capital—developing a strong capital base
- Technology—developing basic and applied research capabilities at the regional level
- Tax and regulatory issues—improving the business climate and removing the obstacles and burdens to business
- Physical infrastructure—developing long-term planning, using revenues for expansion as well as maintenance
- Quality of life—eliminating the growing gap between the "haves" and the "have nots;" supporting cultural arts, recreation, and tourism as well as promoting a healthy environment

The result could be a unique framework for economic development that consists of a series of key program elements designed to be implemented at the local level. These could include the following:

- Establishment of industry-focused training programs that help workers gain new skills to meet changing industry needs and employment opportunities
- Expansion of adult education programs in basic skills needed to function in a more complex and technical work environment
- Increased emphasis on vocational and technical training for non–college-bound students in the K–12 system, including regulatory changes to permit effective internship and coeducational programs; and better motivation and support for training in basic skills within the present education system
- Expansion of small business assistance programs with the participation and support of private, cluster-based coalitions
- Encouragement and support for venture investments and local small business with high growth potential and strategic cluster importance through networking and catalyst initiatives
- Better education and training opportunities for potential entrepreneurs and managers of small businesses in the fundamentals of planning, starting, and managing small technology and cluster supplier businesses
- Greater cooperation and coordination among government agencies at the state and local level in definition, planning, and action to strengthen foundations
- Greater involvement of the private sector in planning and implementing foundation improvements, and support and leadership for privately supported initiatives
- Economic development goals that emphasize creation of higher-quality jobs to drive strategies that focus on improving specific economic foundations and support the competitiveness and growth of industry clusters

- Cooperation and coordination among all state agencies involved with economic competitiveness as well as between state and local agencies
- The involvement of industry to leverage limited but important state resources in effective economic development through public/private partnerships and industry coalitions that can plan and support an overall program and specific cluster-focused initiatives

All of this can be accomplished with the right TQ system and quality champions to move it forward.

Total Quality to Build Belief in One World Community

Using TQ is a unique way to build a belief in the American people that they are truly part of and one with a world community. With the breakdown of European communism and the shifting of world powers, global society is changing drastically. This change has taken different forms; both good and bad. Economies are rebuilding themselves in other images, clan-type disputes are rampant, and technological revolutions are occurring every day. To rebuild our nation and remold it into the economic and political giant it once was, it is imperative that *We the People* must not only find a niche in today's world, but proactively affect the world of tomorrow. This proactive stance should take the following forms:

- Leaders elected by the people who have tremendous strategic vision
- Our governance having clearly established systems of technologically advanced data and analysis
- Clear strategic quality plans dominating all aspects of the rebuilding effort
- The people of our nation managing by self-determination and developing their skills through education with rewards and recognition

- The process of our government being directly controlled by the people at the lowest possible level through use of the latest technology
- The results of rebuilding being measured and continuously improved
- The overriding focus and weight of this rebuilding effort being on *We the People*

You will note there is a strong parallel between the vision of this chapter in rebuilding a nation and the U.S.'s efforts from 1776 to 1787. I hope the reader will continue to think about this parallel and build on what we may have started here in some small way. For as Thomas Edison once said,

> *If we all did the things we are capable of doing, we would literally astound ourselves.*

It is up to you.

Chapter 8

Financing and Restructuring Debt in the Inner City

Ishaq Shafiq

> *Of the maxims of orthodox finance, none, surely, is more antisocial than the fetish of liquidity.... It forgets that there is no such thing as liquidity of investment for the community as a whole.*
>
> —John Keynes

Politicians and managers of governments, public agencies of all sorts, and communities face difficult challenges in the years ahead. Components of these challenges include a myriad of municipal fiscal problems, high property taxes, industrial job losses, demographic changes, shifts in property values, unfunded federal and state mandates, shifts in federal and state responsibilities and funding priorities, a volatile global economy, declining retail sales, and high unemployment rates.

Many of our once financially and economically vibrant cities are now near bankruptcy. In the spring of 1975, New York City was unable to market its debt because the bond market discovered that New York had, for more than 10 years, been using questionable accounting and borrowing practices to eliminate its annual budget deficits. In 1978, when the Ohio state auditor discovered the city of Cleveland had overdue accounts in excess of $36 million and a large general fund deficit, a state of emergency was declared. From 1972 to 1992, 103 municipal bankruptcies were reported.

More recently, Washington, D.C.; Philadelphia, Pennsylvania; Chelsea, Massachusetts; South Tucson, Arizona; East St. Louis, Illinois; Wellston, Missouri; Bridgeport, Connecticut; Bay St. Louis, Mississippi; and Orange County, California (the wealthiest county in the United States) have called upon the federal bankruptcy courts for relief or asked their respective state governments for financial and management assistance.

At the same time, confidence in government has declined to record lows. Government is being viewed as ineffectual, corrupt, bloated, and incompetent. Tax revolts have emerged throughout the government sector, and politicians are debating the issues of taxes versus quality of service nationwide.

Since the 1980s, austere funding has also provided an impetus to change, challenging government organizations to increase productivity and cope with shrinking financial and economic resources. The shift from manufacturing and distribution activities to administration, information, and other services has left a profound mark on many of America's urban areas. Mass transit, the growth of suburbs, the erosion of the family structure, population shifts, and the proliferation and decline of particular governmental services has left major urban cities increasingly occupied by a significantly higher proportion of mainly poor, diverse, and unskilled citizens (Bluestone and Harrison 1982; Stanback and Noyelle 1982).

By the late 1980s, nine large cities had predominantly African-American majorities: Atlanta, Georgia; Baltimore, Maryland; Birmingham, Alabama; Detroit, Michigan; Gary, Indiana; New Orleans, Louisiana; Newark, New Jersey; Richmond, Virginia; and Washington, D.C. In 13 other large cities, African-Americans made up 22 percent or more of the population. By 1988, African-Americans made up 57 percent of central city populations throughout the United States; the proportion was more than twice that of whites (27 percent). William J. Wilson, in his book, *The Declining Significance of Race* (1978), finds that this has led to various social issues—female-headed households, crime, and joblessness in the inner cities have further widened the gap between fiscally and economically depressed cities and those that reflect strong, vibrant fiscal economies.

In addition, the emigration of businesses also leaves behind depreciated or obsolete buildings and infrastructure that impede the development of new industry and new service employment and hinder the delivery of government services to the citizenry. Bluestone and Harrison (1982) note,

> *The primary effects are, of course, visited on those closest to the production unit when it ceases operations. The unit's own employees lose salaries and wages, pensions, and other fringe benefits; supplier firms lose contracts, and the various levels of government lose corporate income and commercial property tax revenue . . . these events produce tertiary effects in the form of increased demand for public assistance and social services, reduced personal tax receipts, and eventually layoffs in other industries including the public sector. By the time all these ripple effects spread throughout the economy workers and families far removed from the original plant closings can be affected, often with dramatic consequences. (p. 67)*

Moreover, the local public sector must maintain or upgrade the public infrastructure to attract new firms. The United States boasts the most extensive and sophisticated public works system in the world. Estimates are that the United States has more than 3.8 million miles of roadways, 565,000 bridges, 1000 public mass transit systems, 1600 airports, 25,000 miles of inland and intercoastal waterways, 70,000 dams, 900,000 miles of pipe in water supply systems, and 15,000 wastewater treatment plants provided mostly by municipalities and other political subdivisions of the states.

All of these factors have led many public officials and administrators to begin embracing total quality (TQ) processes as a means by which progressive government management practices can be implemented to impact cost efficiency and quality of government services.

East St. Louis: A Case Study

First, I have chosen East St. Louis as a case study because I know it well and have been involved in its revitalization. Second, East St. Louis makes an excellent case study because of its pressing municipal fiscal problems; the economic and social challenges of poverty, crime, and high unemployment; a deteriorated physical infrastructure; severe environmental concerns; significant decline in manufacturing and retail activity; and intergovernmental turmoil. Third, because the political and community leadership of East St. Louis implemented a unique collaborative effort among various government entities, private businesses and residents have been able to begin addressing the city's fiscal, economic, and social challenges. Fourth, it lends itself to discussion of the ways in which a TQ approach is appropriate to the management process of municipal governmental entities experiencing challenges similar to those of East St. Louis.

Historical Summary of East St. Louis

East St. Louis is located in the western urban core of St. Clair County, Illinois, which includes the municipalities of Belleville, National City, Fairview Heights, O'Fallon, Centreville, Alorton, Brooklyn, and Sauget, all east of downtown St. Louis, Missouri. It occupies 13 square miles on the shore of the Mississippi River. Since East St. Louis was incorporated as a municipality, it has been a significant factor in the St. Louis regional economic base.

Most communities in the Midwest began as agricultural centers. East St. Louis went on to become a regional magnet for the meat packing and manufacturing industries.

Early historians reported extensive development in manufacturing in industries that produced trucks, car springs, steel cars, stoves, locomotives, spikes, nails, enameled ironware, machinist tools, frogs and switches, glassworks, and aluminum; there were two machinery forges and two rolling mills. There was also a stockyard packing plant. From the 1890s to 1960, East St. Louis was the location of 55 of the region's 70 largest industrial firms. During this same period, East St. Louis became the western terminus of 27 major railroads. These factors contributed significantly to the influx of thousands of immigrant laborers from the rural areas of the region, the south, and southern Europe. The first wave arrived from 1840 to 1880 and included persons of English, Irish, German, and Scandinavian extraction. The second wave ran from 1880 to the first decade of the twentieth century. During this period, African-Americans also migrated to East St. Louis in large numbers.

Industrial firms in St. Louis and communities adjacent to East St. Louis provided the local economy with more than 45,000 jobs. But when industrial employment in the St. Louis region declined, important local industries such as primary steel, railroad cars, brewing, stoves and ranges, auto carburetors, electrical machinery, and motor vehicles saw the closing of key factories. Manufacturing lost 10 percent of its share of total regional employment between 1950 and 1970, according to the U.S. Bureau of the Census (1967, 1972). During the mid-1950s, industrial firms provided 33 percent of the city's employment and 30 percent of St. Clair County employment. When plants began to close during this period, employment reductions resulted in a loss of 25,000 jobs in the East St. Louis area by 1970. The number of manufacturing firms declined from 79 in 1967 to 58 in 1972. They included such companies as Intercoastal Corporation, Swift Armour and Hunter Packing, Aluminum Company of America, Alcoa Research Laboratories, American Zinc Co., Hill Brick, Ober Nester Glass Co., American Steel, Moss Tie, Walworth Valve, Socony Mobil, Phillips Pipeline, Continental Can, and C.K. William & Co.

Retail firms that were major employers also closed their local operations and terminated thousands of workers. Included were such companies as Sears Roebuck & Company, W.T. Grant, SS Kresge, and Woolworth. In the food line Kroger, A&P, National Tea, IGA, and A.A. stores closed all of their outlets. They experienced competition from regional shopping malls. Largely a post-war invention, these malls are generally located close to the intersections of major highways and built with the latest customer amenities. Thus, they combine easy automobile access, protection from inclement weather, and variety of selection, which historically were the exclusive prerogative of the city.

This factor also had an impact on the revenue flow to the city from sales taxes. By the mid-1970s, Walgreen Drug Company was the only national retail business that remained in East St. Louis.

Retail businesses for the same period declined from 860 to 462 according to U.S. Census information. In a 15 year period from 1960 to 1974 the volume of retail sales in Illinois increased by 75 percent in constant dollars, while total sales in East St. Louis declined by 31 percent (Illinois Dept. of Revenue 1969–74).

Total employment for manufacturing and retail declined from 9618 to 5685. Unemployment in East St. Louis rose from 10.5 percent in 1960 to 21 percent by 1980. In contrast, unemployment in the United States during the same period increased from 5.5 percent to 7.1 percent.

Population

This pattern of rapid decline in the economic base and municipal revenues affected the city in several ways. First, the population drastically dropped when highly skilled, employable, and taxable residents emigrated to other areas. In 1950, East St. Louis reached a population of 82,295 residents. By 1990 the population declined to 40,944.

The Neighborhoods

Businesses left behind depreciated or obsolete buildings and infrastructure. Large sections of the city's neighborhoods became riddled with abandoned, crumbling, and fire-scarred buildings. The blight extended from East St. Louis' downtown to its neighborhoods, with block after block of substandard homes and vandalized projects reminiscent of wartime's aftermath. Streets, buildings, educational facilities, and recreational buildings were also allowed to deteriorate. As a consequence, the residents received less adequate services; unemployment continued to increase, as did the high dropout rate among the youth; and East St. Louis's social environment became consumed by crime.

Poverty

The exodus of business, industry, and skilled workers left East St. Louis with a primarily low-income population whose major predicament was joblessness. The rise in joblessness in turn helped trigger an increase in the concentration of the poor, a growing number of poor single-parent families, and an increase in welfare dependence. Median incomes were extremely low compared to other adjacent cities. By 1990, the city had one of the lowest per-capita incomes ($6621) in the United States for a city its size. The percentage of families with income at or below the poverty line in 1970, 1980, and 1990, respectively, was 22.4 percent, 40.1 percent, and 51.4 percent.

Housing

Available housing units in the city declined from approximately 26,000 units in 1960 to fewer than 15,000 in 1990. In 1972, Judd and Mendleson wrote,

> *Housing reflects the low family income of the community. Existing housing is not being replaced, and large segments of the housing inventory are beyond repair or rehabilitation. (pp. 20–21)*

They reported that a 1966 housing study conducted by Southern Illinois University estimated that about 1300 new or rehabilitated units were needed annually for five years to correct serious deficiencies in the city's housing inventory. In the succeeding two-year period, 35 new housing units were built while 670 vacant, vandalized, and substandard units were demolished (Judd and Mendleson 1972, 20–21). During the same period, the number of vacant units in East St. Louis rose from more than 4 percent to more than 9 percent. By 1990, the number of housing units had declined to 13,057 with a vacancy rate of 10.3 percent. Moreover, approximately 18 percent of East St. Louis residents lived in public housing (U.S. Bureau of the Census 1990).

Financial Difficulties and Fiscal Mismanagement

Throughout much of its history, East St. Louis has experienced financial difficulties with fluctuating revenue sources and fiscal mismanagement. The decline in the manufacturing and retail base and the decline of private housing contributed to a decrease in municipal revenues. Elliot Rudwick, a noted historian, and others stated that, as early as 1917, municipal employees were paid with devalued tax anticipation warrants in lieu of salaries, which conversely could not be redeemed at face value (Rudwick 1982; Franke 1906; Illinois Department of Transportation 1982).

Until 1990, East St. Louis funded its daily municipal operations from a process known as *judgment funding*. Under this technique, creditors, with the approval of the city, brought their bills to court for payment and obtained a judgment against the city. The city then issued and sold bonds to satisfy vendor judgments. These bonds represented the full faith and credit of East St. Louis and were amortized over a two- to 10-year period. As a consequence, a considerable amount of property tax revenues were allocated to principal and interest payments for judgment bonds. For example, in 1972 the city was forced to spend almost half of each dollar received to retire bond debt service charges (Morton Hoffman and Company 1973).

Meanwhile, East St. Louis' real property tax assessment base declined every decade since 1950. By 1990, the property tax base was down to 47.1 million from an assessed valuation of $187.6 million in 1960. Table 8.1 illustrates this point. Erosion of the local tax base diminished the city's ability to generate revenues.

The situation became such that a large portion of the major local East St. Louis employers relocated outside the city boundaries in National City, Sauget, Venice, Brooklyn, Granite City, and other small jurisdictions. As a result, East St. Louis derived no tax benefits from the industries, even though it supported and continues to support the health, welfare, and other social service needs of many of the employees. At the same time, it also provided a viable

Table 8.1. Assessed valuation of property in East St. Louis, 1960–1990.

Year	Total Assessed Valuation (in millions)
1960	$187.6
1968	$168.8
1975	$108.7
1980	$ 58.3
1990	$ 41.7

infrastructure—roads, sewage, garbage disposal, and so on—for its residents. Meanwhile, uncollected tax bills totaled 4 percent in 1969. By 1983 the figure was up to 21.2 percent.

Only an increased infusion of federal grants from Model Cities, revenue sharing, the Comprehensive Employment Training Act (CETA), and Community Development block grants enabled East St. Louis to avoid bankruptcy. In 1975, approximately $12 million of the city's $20 million budget came from the federal government. Additional federal outlays—which included public assistance, job training, and highway and public works programs—increased from $52 million in 1970 to $95 million in 1976. The U.S. Department of Housing and Urban Development (HUD) provided another $131 million in aid during the fiscal years 1974 through 1985 which included $30 million in Community Development block grants, $67 million for public housing, and $12 million for urban renewal projects. About 80 cents of every dollar of K–12 school district revenue came from state and federal sources.

In 1985, HUD took over the city's public housing efforts and appointed a private company as property manager. The action was prompted by allegations of fiscal mismanagement and theft by local government administrators. In addition, there was evidence of a high incidence of deferred maintenance as well as serious deterioration of housing units. A trash collector discontinued providing garbage collection services because East St. Louis failed to pay five months of fees amounting to about $262,000. Garbage got piled throughout the city on vacant lots and around abandoned buildings.

The city's financial crisis intensified in 1987. As revenues continued to decline, so did the quality of city services such as street repairs and public safety. Federal money no longer paid for any city services. A study of budgets over the past decade showed that, as revenue decreased, the city administration used the judgment bonds previously described to pay bills and create temporary cash flows. Financial experts estimate that this practice has mortgaged the city well into the next century and has cut operating revenues dramatically (M.M. Beal and Company 1990). City assets were frozen after East St. Louis failed to begin payment of a $3.4 million judgment arising from the beating of a jail inmate by another inmate in 1984.

Job vacancies in the police and fire departments were left unfilled, and half of the city's six fire houses were closed. Firefighters sued successfully to collect three years of back uniform allowances. A money shortage also meant that police officers sometimes bought their own two-way radios because the city was unable to pay for them. The fleet of police and fire vehicles suffered severe maintenance problems.

To further complicate the city government's financial woes, a proposed riverfront development became embroiled in lawsuits and government probes. Due to project inaction, the city was notified on February 19, 1991 of the pending cancellation of its Community Development block grant because of financial mismanagement. All of these problems left the city administration incapable of providing even a minimum of services.

Approaches to Resolving the Fiscal and Mismanagement Crisis

In December of 1988, the governor of Illinois appointed a financial task force to review East St. Louis's fiscal affairs. In January 1989, the Governor's Task Force on Municipal Financial Distress submitted its final report. The report recommended a series of actions to address the problems of municipalities nearing financial insolvency throughout the state. In addition, the task force attempted to provide specific guidance for how the state might address the serious financial problems experienced by East St. Louis. According to the report (East St. Louis Advisory Board 1990),

> *Given current revenues and obligations, the City is incapable of providing even a minimal level of services within the constraint of a balanced budget . . . At present, services are grossly inadequate and the budget is not balanced.*

Based on this report, the city of East St. Louis and the state government took steps that resulted in East St. Louis losing total control of its fiscal and internal management. First, in 1990 the city applied under the state Financial Distress Act for designation as a financially distressed city to qualify for state financial assistance under this act. The city further certified that it met the following provisions of the statute demonstrating financial distress.

> *That the City of East St. Louis is among the highest 5 percent of all home rule municipalities in term of the aggregate of the rate percent of all taxes levied upon all taxable property; that is in the lowest 5 percent in terms of per capita tax yield; and that it has requested by ordinance adopted by the City Council that a Financial Advisory Authority be appointed for the City.*

East St. Louis became the only city in the state of Illinois to receive such designation under the newly enacted statute.

Second, the governor appointed a five-member financial advisory oversight panel. Third, the citizens voted by referendum to restructure the city government. This action resulted in transforming the government from a strong mayor/alderman form of government structure (with members elected from city wards) to a city manager/city council government (four members and a mayor elected citywide). Fourth, these changes provided an energizing stimulus to the hundreds of city employees who had endured payless paydays, political beggaring, and citizen contempt, and who needed assurance that management reform free from political influence would be implemented.

The city's first priority was to stop its fiscal free fall by stabilizing its current operations through actions using remedial quality techniques. This required a significant improvement in the tools, procedures, and people skills employed to plan, control, and report the city's revenue and expense flows. The financial management infrastructure was characterized by

- Systems and record keeping that were in disarray (including a nonoperational general ledger)
- Inadequate quality control and incomplete information that made it difficult to establish integrity of collected data
- Limited technical or quality skills among present staff
- Ill-defined roles for key financial managers, particularly the city treasurer and comptroller

A second pressing need for the stabilization was for the city to reduce the current cost of servicing its debt obligations and contain the growing cost of outstanding claims against the city. Debt service and pension obligations cannibalized the major revenue streams represented by property and utility taxes.

The focus of the second stage of the plan was on maximizing the revenues the city realized from the sources over which it had the most control: permit, license, and franchise fees; wheel taxes; and fines. Improved enforcement of the city's health, safety, building, and traffic codes and systematic collection efforts could generate revenues well in excess of their costs. However, successful use of any plan of recovery for the city could only be achieved with

- Political and civic unity and leadership
- Elimination of deficiencies in quality systems and procedures

- An injection of emergency and bridge financing
- An injection of technical and quality management skills
- Time (an estimated five to seven years)

Upon the recommendation of the city manager in March 1993, the mayor and city council authorized the development of a policy known as the Debt Restructuring Plan Without Bankruptcy and the recruitment of a cross-functional debt restructuring team. East St. Louis recruited a group comprised of people from the private investment banking sector, the mayor, the city manager, the city's finance director, the city attorney, and representatives from the state oversight panel. The initial focus of the team was to develop a strategy to address the city's major creditors, which were

- The Internal Revenue Service (IRS)
- The U.S. Department of Labor, under CETA
- Fire and police pension funds

The IRS's claim arose from an arbitrage rebate that was estimated at $14.5 million. The arbitrage arose out of East St. Louis' issuance of $223.7 million in Port Facility Development Revenue Bonds on December 31, 1985. The IRS had demanded a rebate on the grounds that the issuance date of the Port Facility bonds should have been disregarded for federal income tax purposes and that 148(f) of the Internal Revenue Code applied since the Port Facility Bonds were not issued until October 1986.

The CETA claims arose under grants given the city from the federal government totaling $22.3 million. On March 23, 1983, the Labor Department issued a Final Determination disallowing $4.5 million of the city's expenditures of the CETA grant. On February 5, 1987, the Department issued a second Final Determination disallowing an additional $651,354 of expenditures relating to the city's alleged improper use of CETA grants.

The firefighters and police pension funds are funded by the city through real property and replacement taxes. However, claims

Financing and Restructuring Debt in the Inner City 127

Quality partnerships have to be created between federal, state, regional, and local governments and with business leaders. Mayor Bush has worked diligently to cultivate such relationships for the city of East St. Louis.

arose from the city's failure to levy sufficient taxes to make its annual contribution since 1987. The amounts of the liability were $16.1 and $9.7 million dollars, respectively.

A major concern that the cross-functional debt restructuring team had to address was how to minimize the city's cash outlay to liquidate these claims. As a consequence, I recommended that legal counsel pursue a structured settlement arrangement. Under this financial arrangement, the city would make a lump sum cash payment into an investment fund designated by the particular creditor. The objective that we attempted to achieve through this technique was that within 5 to 10 years the monetary returns from the investment fund would amortize the city's financial obligation to that creditor.

The second option was to sell fiscal responsibility bonds. However, to sell fiscal responsibility bonds in the public municipal markets, it would be necessary for the city to have some form of credit enhancement for the securities. Such credit enhancement usually takes several forms, as follows.

- *Bond insurance or letter of credit.* It was doubtful that the city would be able to obtain a letter of credit or insurance on its own. Therefore, such enhancements could only be obtained with the state or some creditworthy body serving as the account party and payor under the letter of credit.

- *Debt service reserve make-up provision.* The state or some other creditworthy body could enter into an agreement under which the creditworthy parties would agree to make up any deficiency or shortfall that may occur in the debt service reserve fund for the bond issue. This form of support is commonly referred to as moral obligation bond financing.

- *General obligations.* The state or some other creditworthy body could issue its general obligations to use its full-force credit and taxing powers in order to meet the financial obligations.

- *Dedicated revenue stream financing.* The state or even the city may pledge a dedicated revenue stream to the repayment of the bond issue. In order to receive an investment grade rating, the revenue stream must be segregated from general city funds and must be isolated and secure.

Our efforts culminated in 1994 with the development of a common-law Debt Restructuring Plan. This legal alternative is an out-of-court disposition of the city's debts effected through voluntary settlements between the city and its creditors. This plan was executed in lieu of the more defined procedures followed under federal bankruptcy where plans are developed, subjected to creditor votes, and submitted for approval by federal bankruptcy courts that are empowered under certain circumstances to force creditors to accept them.

The most significant event that served as the catalyst for the successful use of the Debt Restructuring Plan occurred on March 24, 1994, when the IRS agreed to accept the city's settlement offer of $1.4 million to liquidate and discharge its $14.5 million obligation. Second, CETA shortly afterward agreed to discharge the city's $12 million obligation for a $1 million cash settlement. Third, the firefighters and police pension funds boards agreed to lump sum payments of $15 million and $900,000, respectively, and agreed to execute a three-year covenant not to sue. These four settlement agreements resulted in the liquidation of $46.2 million of the city's estimated $81 million of debt obligations. Additionally, with the successful operation of this entire process, in addition to the financial backing of the state of Illinois, the city reduced its debt obligations from $81 million to $22 million.

The process of financial recovery has not stopped at the financial liquidation of the city's debt obligations. The city has begun to implement the restructuring of its entire financial management system. This effort has culminated with the city receiving clean audit findings with minor recommended management changes that have further enhanced its financial management system.

Total Quality System

The goal of conscientious government sector managers is to produce better and more goods and services with the same or fewer resources. To that end, one of the appeals of TQ is that it provides a systematic process for energizing employees and improving the performance of delivering municipal services. V. Daniel Hunt (1993) provides a succinct characterization of quality management.

> *The essence of quality management is involving and empowering the work force to improve the quality of goods and services continuously in order to satisfy, and even delight, the customer. To achieve this goal requires identifying customers and their needs, having a clear idea of how the organization plans to go about meeting expectations, and making sure that everyone in the organization understands the customer needs and is empowered to act on their behalf. (p. 32)*

In East St. Louis, TQ methods were and continue to be employed as the city works to strengthen its financial base. Mainly through the efforts of public departments and agencies, but with the consensus of the community as evidenced by the support of the city council, a plan was devised to rebuild the financial infrastructure of East St. Louis. Having identified fiscal stability as the foundation for new and sustained growth, council members turned first to alleviating the worst of the fiscal distress, much of which has been described previously. Throughout the process they measured results in the most forthright manner: by developing a baseline budget for the city and tracking activities against it.

But the city's leaders looked to more than the bottom line. They sought consensus quality management—ways to empower the municipal service employees toward self-sufficiency by encouraging municipal agencies to develop appropriate quality work processes. Managers within the municipality then focused more of their attention on creatively developing quality strategies to incorporate those quality work processes into the city's overall mission and goals.

It should be noted, however, that the nature of the public sector environment potentially places certain constraints on achieving TQ objectives and implementation programs. These constraints can be somewhat different than those found in the private sector. Areas of challenge include the following:

- Working within a web of authority (also known as the bureaucracy)
- Managing consensus among exceptionally large numbers of people
- Working with government constraints on financial control
- Understanding power relationships in the public sector

These are discussed in more detail as follows.

TQ in the Public Arena

First, the public sector is webbed by multiple access to multiple authoritative decision makers, a phenomena designed to ensure that public business is examined from a variety of perspectives. This means several things for TQ applications. First, because of these multiple authoritative decision makers, multilevel accountability and reporting relationships often evolve, including such varied "supervisors" as the general public; other branches, levels, and agencies of government; special interest groups; and the media. TQ designs are thus frequently more difficult to guide to fruition because there are "so many cooks in the kitchen."

Second, it is generally more difficult to muster the support and gain the approvals necessary to enter into TQ activities in the first place—more votes are needed from a wider range of people. The public sector involves a greater variety of individuals and groups than the private sector, with different and often mutually exclusive sets of interests, reward structures, and values. Consequently, in the public sector we find, for example, inherent conflicts between interest groups seeking to reduce spending and those seeking to safeguard the public health or provide for more street repair. The TQ practitioner will likely spend more time building support, seeking consensus, and lobbying than would be needed in the private sector. Thus the need to use support-building activities against these impediments is greater than in the private sector.

Third, financial support is often more difficult to obtain for public TQ work, not only because funding sources have only recently begun to support TQ efforts, but because the public sector usually has more limited resources. In addition, because federal restrictions place limits on how much consultants can earn, the quality of help is often affected. Private enterprise is in a much better position to negotiate competitive fees. Moreover, in the public sector, funding is further complicated by the frequent need to have one branch of government administer moneys appropriated by a second branch. Quality control and program monitoring is frequently easier to maintain, therefore, in the private sector, where the same entity can both authorize expenditures and disburse funds.

Fourth, power relationships are different. In the public sector, where power is deliberately diffused and where the top-level appointees are subject to frequent change, it may not always make the most sense to start at the top. Additionally, sometimes it is more difficult to agree on just exactly where the top is, a problem complicated by the constitutional, historical, and political forces that tend to pull levels away from the political center. As a result, TQ must be mandated by that political center but, once in place, steered firmly by those in a position to foster the vision for the long term.

East St. Louis's approach to urban revitalization has sought to improve the city as a whole. To that end, we have identified the need for public funds in order to improve public services. It has not been an easy road, not always a straight path, not always a successful effort—and it is not yet complete. But the focus has been to provide quality services in all municipal arenas, relying on optimal use of city resources paid for through a holistic TQ program of fiscal responsibility. The restructuring of debt was just one project within East St. Louis's quality urban revitalization plan.

Chapter 9

Fighting Drug Crime in the Distressed City

Gordon D. Bush

> *If poverty is the mother of crimes, want of sense is the father of them.*
>
> —Jean de la Bruyere, *Les Characteres*

As is so often common in depressed urban areas of the United States, the illegal drug industry is the only business that thrives. Because it is illegal, it is clandestine. Because its products are habitual, it is insidious. A disease that starts with the weak and the desperate, drug abuse worms its way into the backbone of the community and sucks the marrow dry. Life, no longer precious, is no longer bound by the morals of common society. The disease spreads, the violence increases, and crime becomes a major issue in the declining city. Every good citizen lives in fear.

That was the condition of East St. Louis, Illinois, in the late 1980s. My hometown, which had been in decline while I was growing up there, had suffered a total meltdown in my absence. The demise of its local industries, the chaos of its city government, and the state of disrepair among its city services had reached such a point that the citizens had ceased to function as a community. That's when the drug dealers moved in.

I was born and raised in East St. Louis, worked in the meat packing house or the steel foundry while going to night school to earn a degree in urban planning. I served in the armed forces in Germany during the 1960s, rising to the rank of major. By 1989, I held a masters degree in city planning and had a beautiful wife and two children. After several years as a civilian, I had returned to the service. My family had come home to live in East St. Louis while I was stationed in St. Louis, Missouri (across the Mississippi River), at the 102nd Army Reserve Command; I was one of the few active duty officers there.

Seeing the city brought tears to my eyes. Clouds of dust and litter danced across the streets in the breeze. Shop fronts and industrial plants stood mute, their walls painted with raw graffiti, their windows broken or boarded over. Refuse lined the alleys like decayed mortise in old, gigantic cracks. Sanitation services were erratic; in the heat the town stunk; one could almost taste it in the air. Gunfire filled the night sky. East St. Louis reportedly had the highest homicide rate per capita in the United States. This was my hometown.

Of all the city's problems, it was the crime and thuggery rampant in East St. Louis that galvanized me to action. With my educational background, I thought of urban planning as the holy grail, the great solution. After much soul-searching (papers had been cut to send me to the Pentagon), I left the service and was hired as a city planner. They were good people, the city planners, and they had good ideas. But nothing we ever put before the board of aldermen ever went anywhere. Somehow our plans always seemed to get lost in the morass of the board's bureaucracy. Made up of representatives from each of the eight wards and chaired by the mayor, "business as usual" forged the politics of the day; it was as if the wards were little fiefdoms and the job of the board members was to maintain the status quo.

In 1975, I ran for and was elected as city treasurer. I thought that the person whose hands were on the city's till could effect change, but I was wrong. However, from that vantage point it became clear that the power came from the mayor's office—that a vast majority of decisions extended from that realm. In the early 1980s, I was appointed to the Real Estate Appeals Board and in 1985 was elected to a second term. After that, I returned to the U.S. Army. But in 1991 I left the service and threw my hat into the East St. Louis mayoral race.

The decision to run was not easy. By doing so, I was committing my family to life in this city on a permanent basis. By doing so, I would of necessity become a political animal, and I had never been overly fond of the type. By doing so, I was casting my fate to the wind. It was a frightful thought and posed an even more grave question: Could I do any better than the "professional" politicians who had preceded me?

But I have a deep and abiding faith in the Lord. I prayed for guidance, trusted that He would show me the way. In the spring of 1991, I campaigned hard on a platform of political and economic reform—and on April 21, I won. That night we celebrated. The next morning I got up, said a little prayer, and rolled up my shirtsleeves.

Crime: A Thread in the Pattern of Urban Decline

To revitalize a community is to wage war on poverty, violence, greed, ignorance, bad attitudes, and despair. Each comes with its own set of challenges so interrelated that to deal with only one is to invite defeat of the others. To take back an area of urban blight requires an overall quality strategy addressing all facets of each problem and prioritizing them for optimal results. Time frames must be set, budgets must be developed, resources must be tapped, and at the end of the day, results must be devised and documented; and honest, qualified, hard-working people with a quality vision must assure that each job is done right the first time, each time.

On the one hand, it seems overwhelming because the very interwoven nature of the social, political, and economic problems that

 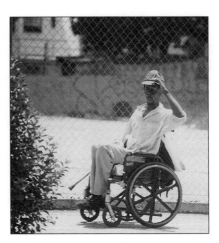

Crime, violence, and poverty have created a generation of need.

affect the inner city make them a nightmare to address. It is difficult to view them in terms of separate and distinct issues. Poverty is a result of lack of employment opportunities, lack of education, lack of good health, and political malaise. Poor education is largely the result of a shrinking tax base caused by the loss of industry. Poor health is the result of poverty, ignorance, and a dearth of social services. Add to that the fact that all of these problems themselves severely sap the resources available to suture them, and it is easy to understand how communities, once thriving, solid, and middle class, become drawn into the quagmire of indifference and despair.

On the other hand, the same problems that defy separation for easy execution also present unparalleled opportunities for success. Programs employed to address one problem will address many if developed as part of an overall quality strategy for revitalization and not simply as a means to alleviate the symptoms that define the single issue. It's a bit like killing two birds with one stone, multiplied tenfold.

Once problems and possible quality solutions have been identified, programs must be funded, developed, and implemented on a priority basis. In a speech delivered in Washington D.C. in May 1994 at the Federalist Society and The Manhattan Institute, U.S. Supreme Court Chief Justice Clarence Thomas (1994) said,

> *Young children cannot learn in schools if they are besieged by drugs and constant threats of violence. Nor, for that matter, can they lead normal lives if so many street corners, sandlots, and apartment buildings are fixed places of business for drug dealers and other criminals. How can the parents or older brothers and sisters of these children lead productive lives if economic and educational opportunities are stifled by rampant community violence and disorder? If they can't walk or drive down a street without fear of being shot or assaulted? (p. 515)*

My opinion exactly. No community can hope to draw industry, clean up its city, or give its children a future unless it first deals with crime—and in particular, drug-related crime. Why? Because drug crime is particularly insidious. It is well organized and well financed. It hooks its victims, often for life. It reaches down and touches our most precious resource: our children. And it is largely responsible for the explosion in teen homicides. Apart from serial killers or rapists, drug dealers are the most despicable of persons and the most clever. Like cockroaches, they breed rapidly—and like cockroaches, they are difficult to exterminate.

But to deal effectively with the drug problem means dealing with a any number of problems—gang activity, vandalism, violence, and fear. Only a community that is safe from these evils can expect to survive.

Dealing with Underlying Problems

In East St. Louis, we recognized that we had to fight the battle on two nearly opposing fronts: We had to find the resources to initiate

Realistic partnerships are needed to solve the root causes of crime.

an anti-crime program, and we had to curb crime in order to garner the resources. We began by identifying our greatest needs: (1) to improve services, especially police services; (2) to develop a grassroots program against drugs; (3) to convince our citizens that we were serious about ridding our city of crime; and (4) to find innovative quality approaches to funding.

We began by availing ourselves of whatever expert advice we could find. We reviewed our budget. We sought support from our neighboring communities, worked with the state, and applied for federal support. We found an industry that would cost us little to develop but would offer good returns almost immediately, and we adopted a plan to snag it. We sought out programs that would best meet our needs, and we worked—and continue to work—to avail ourselves of the best of them.

We began by looking in our own backyard. We had a problem with basic public services. Our police department was nearly nonfunctional, our fire department substandard, and other city services mediocre at best. The reasons why were many—lack of equipment, lack of resources, and lack of pride. Not only were we asking these and other city employees to operate without the wherewithal to do so, we were often asking them to do it for free. Simply put, we weren't meeting payroll.

Review of the budget led to the conclusion that city moneys were being mismanaged and misused; priorities were for patronage over public service. In a political climate reminiscent of Chicago, New York, and the Kansas City of Truman's youth, the fiefdom mentality of the ward-elected board of aldermen precluded significant change. However, our citizens were not so indifferent to the problem as one might think; within six months of the mayoral election, the residents of East St. Louis eliminated the board, replacing it with a smaller city council composed of officials elected citywide.

With these changes came others. Funds became available when city government was downsized. Many of the eliminated positions had belonged to political favorites. Others had simply become extraneous as the city had changed, but had never been reviewed for relevancy. We retired some jobs vacated through attrition.

The last opportunity for the city's survival was one that the previous administration couldn't see. A new Illinois state law called the Distressed Cities Act was passed for use by any city in the state, but was crafted for those such as East St. Louis. This act, if distressed status were applied for by a city, would provide approximately $4 million to stabilize city finances—but more than that, it would provide a governor-appointed panel with final authority over the city's budget. Considering the fact that the city had absolutely no alternatives other than bankruptcy, I didn't mind; I wanted a more stringent accounting of taxpayer/government moneys anyway.

In fact, now that the state was involved, we used its lawyers to break an old habit of the county court—seizing the financial checking accounts of the city. The state panel's presence also helped give me the leverage to fashion a budget that was more aimed toward citizen service with less politician serving. Further, it set the stage for a debt restructuring process that would come later as a riverboat casino poured funds into the city coffers.

Developing a Well-Trained, Well-Equipped Police Force

A direct assault on crime, especially drug-related crime, requires—at a minimum—a well-trained police force of adequate size with access to reliable equipment. In the summer of 1991, East St. Louis boasted 60 police officers, six of which were on disability. The average age of an officer was 48. Most of our police personnel were career officers, having joined the force 20 years previously, when burglary, family disputes, and disorderly conduct were typical crimes. Few had any extensive training in the crime of drug trafficking and its related problems—prostitution, aggravated assault, and murder. Statistics show that an urban police force should have three officers per 1000 population. In East St. Louis, a city of 42,000, we should have had a force of at least 126 officers.

The officers shared among them perhaps as many as a half-dozen police cars that ran somewhat; many other vehicles stood as hollow shells, stripped over the years for parts to keep the others running. Tires needing replacing. Some cars were without radios; the officers used portables when they were available. I met with police union leaders two months after I took office. It was a sweltering day, 101 degrees with 90 percent humidity that soaked through my shirt and tugged at my heels. Waves of heat shimmered on the horizon as I drove to work. The air smelled sultry, pungent with sweat. Not surprisingly, the union was demanding cars with air conditioning for the cops on the beat. To spend all day in those hot boxes was unconscionable, they contended. Sitting in my office, where the window air conditioner made the room just tolerable, I could hardly disagree.

We worked with the governor and the state highway patrol and, with federal funding, hired 13 officers to form an anti-drug team. They arrived with their own cars, their own state-of-the-art equipment, and considerable expertise. Known as the Delta Team, they focused on drugs and gangs. As the political winds shifted, the funding ended. But we kept the program; today this special cadre of officers, like all other East St. Louis police officers, draws its salary from the city's coffers.

Meanwhile, President Clinton's crime bill provided for the development of a program known as Community Oriented Policing (COPs). COPs focuses on placing police officers in local neighborhoods, teaching them to work together with the community and helping it develop neighborhood watch programs. Those in the program also provide referrals to other agencies, operating as an unofficial central source of information about the social programs available to the families on their beats.

Additionally, under the Distressed Cities Act, the city was eligible for special assistance from the state. I pleaded with Governor Jim Edgar for some relief. Within 10 months, we were given 17 used state police cars in good condition. They had about 50,000 miles and were normally sold to local police departments for approximately $10,000 each.

Sustaining the Momentum

Stop-gap measures and donations can be used to get a crime-fighting program started, but an expanded tax base is necessary to sustain it. Although not directly a program under the city's crime-fighting umbrella, bringing a major industry to the city, part of our economic program, was vital to the survival of many of our initiatives. After much thought, prayer, and public debate, we was decided to approach the state of Illinois and its gaming commission to establish a riverfront gambling casino.

One had recently opened with considerable success in Alton, Illinois, about 20 miles north of East St. Louis. The proponents of the riverboat casino plan felt that, if casinos worked well upstream, they would work just as well further south. Analysts told us that demand for this kind of entertainment had not yet peaked; therefore, we would not so adversely impact other riverfront businesses as to cripple them by starting one of our own.

For this effort, we put together a three-pronged program: one to "sell" East St. Louis to a dubious gaming commission, one to convince the governor that we needed the casino in East St. Louis

An expanded tax base is one of the roots of successful urban revitalization.

(at that time they were looking to put the facility in the river near the town of Sauget), and one to educate our local citizenry. In a community where crime was already a problem, gambling hardly seemed an appropriate business opportunity.

The story of our efforts is a book in itself. Suffice it to say that we were successful. The governor, who knew our revitalization program well, gave us his support. The gaming commission was given assurances that the crime on our streets would not extend to the casino, and we offered a program of support guaranteed not to burden the industry. In return, our residents would get 40 percent of the 1200 new jobs (which pay an average of $22,000 a year). A Casino Queen Foundation would be established to provide $2.5 million over a five-year period for low-interest loans to citizens who wanted to go into business or who wanted to expand current businesses. Also, priority for riverboat vendors would be given to East St. Louis businesses.

And finally, in a community that is nearly all Christian, largely Baptist, we worked closely with the churches to put in place a system of notification and to implement appropriate programs should it become apparent that local residents were having any gambling-related problems. After all, it would have done us no good to have exchanged one addiction for another.

The casino has been in operation for three years now. We have been fortunate; to date I have had few calls from the churches or other concerned groups. Our citizens have not fallen to the trap of the vice that this form of entertainment can generate. Nor have we seen any indication of a rise in gambling- or drug-related crimes.

Instead, we have created employment opportunities for a good number of our residents and have brought much needed moneys into our city coffers. Today we receive 5 percent of the revenues from this venture. When we had put forth our plan, we were hoping to generate $3 million annually; instead, we see $10 million. Twelve thousand people visit the Casino Queen Riverboat & Casino daily. To date, crime related to incidents at or on the approach to this gambling facility remains at zero. Our gamble has proven a success.

Seeking Alternatives to Expanding the Tax Base

Drawing industry into any declining community is a Herculean task. While waiting for the income that industry will generate, one must look to other means to expand the tax base. East St. Louis began by finding ways to restructure the city's debt.

East St. Louis has no high-rise office buildings, no sports stadiums or high school stadiums, no major tourist attractions—and never has had—yet in 1991 we were carrying $90 million worth of debt, a tremendous amount for a city of our size. Several million dollars were owed to the federal government, primarily to the Internal Revenue Service. We worked diligently to restructure this debt.* By doing so, we have "freed up" funding for numerous city

---

*Editor's note: For a more detailed account, see Chapter 8.

services and programs, much of which has been used to fight crime.

Fighting Drug Crime at the Grassroots Level

Fighting drug crime is not just a matter of apprehending criminals, particularly when it involves the illicit drug trade. On an individual level, it is a matter of moral rectitude, belief in oneself, and good decision-making skills. Inevitably, those who are "heavy into drugs" have little self-esteem, few positive role models, and, increasingly, are too young to really understand the issues regarding drug use.

Children do not begin to develop analytical skills until they are about 13 or 14 years old. If one asks most eighth graders why Harper Lee titled her book *To Kill a Mockingbird* as she did, one is likely to be met with blank stares. But if one asks those same children the question a year later, most will be able to answer. Because children lack an ability to analyze abstract ideas, they must be taught early, and in a straightforward manner, just why illegal use of drugs is bad. If the horrors of drug abuse have not been made clear to them, and if the paths to drug abuse have not been spelled out to them, and if they have not been offered clear alternatives, their curiosity and childish greed likely will override any vague admonitions they've received over the years.

The issues surrounding self-identity are complex and stem from a combination of experiences in the home, school, playground, and community. One cannot educate character or moral fiber; there are too many factors, and too many forces at work. And there is still the question of whether fortitude, goodness, and optimism are inherited tendencies or linked exclusively to environment. We only know that success in life, peer pressure, ingrained beliefs, naiveté, and parental love and guidance play key roles in forming our children.

The city's approach to stomping out drugs is twofold: do away with the supply and eliminate the demand. Since involvement in drug abuse often begins at an early age (when children are "recruited," say, as couriers), in East St. Louis we chose to target, and continue to target, the schools—particularly the elementary schools. In all of them, we have instituted the Drug Abuse Resistance Education (DARE) program.

Started in Los Angeles in 1983, DARE was brought to Illinois in 1986 when the state police piloted the program in East St. Louis. In 1990 the city introduced its own DARE officers, people who had completed the two-week training at the Illinois Police Academy (which trains all DARE officers within a 14-state area). Today, DARE in East St. Louis targets fifth or sixth graders with a program that runs one hour a week over a 17-week period. DARE focuses on drug prevention and violence resolution skills. Detective Sergeant Lencie Stewart, a 24-year veteran of the police department and head of the DARE program, tells me he has followed the development of "his" kids over the years. According to Stewart, only two of the nearly 3600 children who have gone through the program under his tutelage have been involved in any serious felonies.

As part of this program, I have been invited to many of the schools as a keynote speaker. Part of the strategy of DARE is to put appropriate role models before the children. The program officer feels I am a good candidate since I was born and raised here. My message is simple: Say no to drugs. Say no to drug dealers. Tell family members to say no to drugs. I tell the children to let themselves grow up in the sun, not in the shadows. I urge them to be strong.

In addition, we have worked hard to develop appropriate relationships with the churches of East St. Louis. Recognizing the constitutional mandate of separation of church and state, we have nevertheless sought to forge solid ties with an institution that, in our community, brings a large number of our citizens together and provides a range of individual programs to try to meet the needs of their congregations. Our churches represent the "last best hope," the one institution that is still treated with respect, where grassroots efforts are most likely to succeed, and where one-on-one communication with many people is a well-established tradition. The churches often function as our sounding board; they are quick to let us know when our ideas are stupid or won't work. We often seek their support in developing appropriate citywide services. They help us by running programs on a quality test bed basis. We learn from them the mood of the community. And they help us to get the word out against crime.

For this administration, crime is a priority. Criminals, especially drug dealers, are the scourge of the earth. Our job is to run the thugs out of town. Our churches help us convey those convictions and highlight our successes better than our formal public relations programs, our newspapers, our barbershop grapevines, or our over-the-fence gossip machines. We have crafted a separate but synergistic relationship with the most powerful institution in town.

Measuring Success and Quality Results

How successful have we been as a city? Today East St. Louis has 100 police officers and 60 fully equipped, properly maintained police cars. Our homicide rate has dropped from 68 deaths in 1991 to 33 in 1995. Since most homicides in East St. Louis have been drug-related, these statistics give testimony to our progress on that front. As mentioned, there have been no reported incidents of crime related to the riverfront casino. And while it is unfortunate, perhaps just as indicative of our success is the number of complaints we're hearing from the surrounding communities—Washington Park, Centreville, and Alorton. There the drug crime rate is rising; there the drug problem increases as the dealers find new niches outside our city.

We have also improved other services. We have 20 additional firefighters and a new fleet of fire trucks, including a new ladder truck. The public works department has been rebuilt and reequipped. The city sports new front-end loaders, vacuum trucks, weed-cutting tractors, snow removal equipment, and utility vehicles. Although we don't know just how it happens, we know that community pride resides in inverse proportion to the crime rate. We are working to make our citizens proud.

On a personal note, I go about my business every day like every other citizen. Unlike the previous mayor, who feared for his life, I have no need for bodyguards. The police do not drive me to work or around town. My family is safe.

East St. Louis continues to shed its cloak of despair. After four years of effort, we have received federal designation as an Enterprise Community, which makes us eligible for further government funding. It may be a bit simplistic, but we believe busy hands are happy hands. To that end, we have earmarked a majority of these funds for development of a unique and innovative educational program designed to get kids back into school and provide adequate and appropriate job training for other members of our community. Although crime is often the result of passion or greed, it can also be a result of need (survival), boredom, or ignorance. Our goal is to have a better-educated community; as with all our interwoven efforts, we expect it to lower our crime rate, as well.

There is no one simple answer to the challenge of curbing crime. However, an all-encompassing program of urban revitalization is required if crime prevention is to succeed. It cannot operate in a vacuum. Funding is required; human resource management and development are required; innovative quality ideas are required; as are community and political support. While not everyone may agree with me that the support of the Lord is required, today most experts agree that we must believe in some universal truth, even if it is only a belief in the philosophy of religion.

Today the city of East St. Louis still struggles to climb out of its poverty and to revitalize itself on many fronts. We still need better schools and better housing. We still need jobs and more opportunities for economic growth. We still need government financing and support. And our crime statistics still do not satisfy me. But we have turned the corner. We are headed in the right direction.

Once again, our people have reason to believe that tomorrow will be better than today.

Chapter 10

Solving Urban Education Problems Through a Quality Focus

Wilbur L. Campbell

> *Give a man a fish, and you can feed him for a day; teach a man how to fish, and you can feed him for a lifetime.*
>
> —Ancient Chinese proverb

The problems of urban education are numerous. Schools are plagued with inadequate private sector linkages, outdated programs, lack of community support, lack of technology, and an influx of crime and drugs. The subjects discussed in this chapter are diverse in nature, united only by their link to education and the quality processes they represent. However, each addresses a major educational issue: the revitalization of a school that has gone downhill; the development of curricula that prepares all students, not just the college bound, for life after high school; and the need to find appropriate alternative education means and methods in areas where the traditional ones do not work. The focus here is on solutions and the importance that quality plays in their success.

Quality Strategies in Social Programs vs. Construction Programs

It has been difficult for urban educational institutions in particular and social institutions in general to focus on the delivery of quality programs and services. It is a great deal easier to deliver quality products in the construction industry, for example. There are a number of reasons for this, including the following:

• Construction projects run for a finite length of time and (at least theoretically) within a well-defined budget. The labor hours required to build the structure wax and then wane. Eventually, the project is over. But many social programs run into perpetuity. As is seen with education, time and dollars must be continually poured into the coffers for the program to survive, regardless of the quality of the program.

• It is more difficult to fund social programs than construction projects. While this has evolved into a political issue, the fact is that people like to *see* the results of their generosity. Even at the grassroots level, it is easier to get a local donation for computer equipment than for operating expenses. Apart from money received from tax revenues and/or philanthropies, many social program organizations cannot get large commercial loans. Lending institutions require collateral; on the whole, social programs have little to offer in terms of physical wealth.

• The progress of a construction project is measured in percent of completion against budget and schedule. There is no such easy measure when dealing with people's lives. Social programs measure success one person at a time and, sometimes, in infinitesimal increments. Even in education, where we measure student progress routinely, the system is neither standardized nor applied equally. Additionally, seldom does a construction program fail so badly that a contractor has to start at the beginning more than once; one does not need to rebuild the foundation of a structure over and over. But some participants in social programs must continue to do just that, as the cycle of welfare and poverty tells. It drains the system, wearies the community, and fuels the fire of dissatisfaction with the program itself.

- On the whole, employees working in social programs are poorly paid except at the highest levels. Consequently, the programs offer little lure for the the nation's best and brightest. To exacerbate the problem, some programs are managed by political appointees with little experience in the field and, often, even less interest.

- The politics of change can seriously damage social programs, especially those that are government funded. Today some argue that many of the programs begun under the War on Poverty were just beginning to bear fruit when they lost their funding. True or not, until we as a nation make up our collective mind to help or not to help those in poverty and despair, we will continue to see the violent swings in social policy that so diminish the effect of social programs.

Perhaps most importantly, social programs operate outside the framework of formal quality techniques, because few formal attempts have ever made to institute them. Largely because quality methods have been preoccupied with ensuring that certain procedures are followed and physical tests and measures are undertaken, they have not been seen as relevant, appropriate, or practical in the social program arena. There is no direct corollary between a concrete stress test and an educational exam, except perhaps in a vocational educational setting, although the concept of nondestructive testing exists in both instances. On the other hand, many social programs have employed informal quality techniques for years. The following case study gives some examples of such efforts. The quality techniques used have been spelled out in each section so that the reader can better see how fundamental quality is to the success of any educational program.

Revitalization of a School: A Case Study

The problems facing State Community College (SCC) in East St. Louis, the only state-run college in Illinois, involved presidential power, board of trustees micromanagement, state recognition, accreditation, audit compliance, and transition to an independent college. The school had developed a reputation at the state level for high unit costs, high administrative turnover and unfilled positions, failure to comply with state business procedures, failure to implement state audit recommendations, inability to implement new programs or cut ineffective programs, and declining enrollments while maintaining staffing levels.

Many of these challenges were addressed through the use of quality approaches. These included the following:

- Instituting leadership
- Developing expectations of "doing the job right the first time"
- Developing quantifiable methods to measure quality progress
- Breaking down barriers between staff areas; empowering the staff
- Developing appropriate short-term and long-range strategic quality plans
- Creating consensus through local community involvement in the decision-making process
- Fostering an atmosphere of cooperation with local, regional, and state government agencies, including the state-appointed SCC board of directors
- Encouraging formal accreditation audits

Gaining the Authority to Act

Janet Finch, the new school president, arrived with extensive educational management experience as well as industrial management experience. Her private sector experiences, which included grounding in quality management, helped her guide the institution through a difficult period. Her goal was to correct the problems caused, in part, by the failure of the state to properly manage its own college.

The need for a short-term survival plan was obvious when the Finch administration took over in January 1995. There was no evidence of planning in the president's office. A short-term survival plan was developed that addressed the need for immediate action by the board of trustees. The plan requested an increase in presidential spending authority from $500 to $5000, the power to hire faculty and staff below the deanship level, and the authority to approve purchase requisitions. The bookstore presented another problem. The vendor threatened to withhold books for the spring 1995 semester unless the $75,000 owed from the previous semester was paid. Finch needed the authority to negotiate a settlement because the college did not have anywhere near the amount owed.

The board of trustees had been burned by previous presidents who failed to keep the board informed and spent funds without authority; they had to be convinced of the need for increased presidential authority. Finch planned and conducted a retreat for the board members to rebuild trust and to apprise them of her plans. Speakers from the state board, the state board staff, and administrators from other colleges participated in the retreat, along with the SCC administrators. The board was convinced that a focus on quality and change was needed and granted Finch increased presidential authority.

Implementing a Strategic Quality Plan

A strategic quality plan was designed to address the major challenges facing the college. It provided the means to meet state recognition standards, accreditation criteria, accreditation general institutional requirements, and accreditation patterns of evidence. The strategic quality plan focused on building quality through recognition, accreditation, and transition.

Meeting state compliance standards was the first major challenge to be addressed. Finch and the administrative team worked to implement changes at the college to meet state standards. The team sought to build quality and document the improvements in order to prove to the state that the changes were institutionalized and not just "band-aid" fixes. The state had given the college just six months to clean up its compliance disaster.

At one point, Finch was, all at the same time, president, dean of instruction, dean of finance and administrative services, director of personnel, and internal auditor. In those capacities, she was able to hire professionals with expertise (instead of political connections) and assemble a team capable of transforming SCC.

As a result of these hirings, the college was energized, and work was completed in record time. Finch submitted a draft report in three months. Unbelieving state officials visited the college and found five noncompliance items. The college challenged the findings, and additional visits resulted in only one noncompliance item: failure to hand in reports on time over a 25-year period. The state threat of nonrecognition (which would have made the college ineligible for accreditation) was eliminated.

Despite assurance of state recognition, accreditation remained a challenge facing the college. Not much work had been done to implement recommendations from the last accreditation team's visit. College committees were inactive, and faculty and staff were minimally involved in program and institutional improvement. Teams were organized to review each area of the college and to address the recommendations. These groups focused on meeting general institutional requirements and producing the patterns of objective evidence that would ensure accreditation. Such accreditation patterns of evidence required documentation of accomplishments, and the teams worked diligently to make quality improvements.

The college had been on probation in the past, and the team was determined to avoid backsliding. A self-study was completed that addressed the accreditation issues. Recommendations were made in the study that were then implemented. As a result, the college regained its former accreditation status. Meanwhile, the college and the state worked to make East St. Louis Regional

Community College District a viable entity. (All other Illinois community colleges are administered by community college districts). Plans were made to change the school from a state-run institution to one that was run at district level.

The objectives of the transition were to regain public support, develop a new image, increase enrollment, become more fiscally efficient and effective, and offer expanded and higher-quality educational programs and services through partnerships. Faculty, staff, and community members were empowered to participate in transition planning. They volunteered for committees that planned all areas of the new college. These committees were asked to identify transition issues, review the literature and visit other institutions, develop a model of their area, identify problems, and make recommendations.

Employees who had been quiet and unassuming proved that they were capable of good thinking and quality planning. Additionally, the state gave assistance by providing benchmark data for analysis. Enrollment, market penetration, student/staff ratio, program completion, instructional expenditure, and space utilization data were examined. Data were compared to the average of peer institutions, and targets were projected through fiscal year 2000.

Empowerment worked. Many employees seized the opportunity to demonstrate their abilities and produced reports with recommendations about their areas of expertise. Together, they painted a vision of success for the new college.

Meetings were held with neighboring colleges, business leaders, legislative leaders, students, and community leaders to obtain support for the transition and the new college. The result of the quality focus was successful transition legislation. Transition legislation was passed by the state legislature and signed into law in June 1996. The school has subsequently been renamed Metropolitan Community College.

Working with the Private Sector

Private sector support was obtained to help the college overcome a continuing problem, the bookstore. The college did not operate its own bookstore. Space was given to a vendor that delivered books to the college each semester, sold them, and pocketed the profits. As the fall 1995 semester approached, the vendor informed the administration that there would be no more books without payment of a previous debt. The college did not have the funds. Another vendor was approached, but declined because the college owed it money from a previous semester. School was scheduled to open in a week, and accreditation and recognition were in danger without textbooks for the students. Additionally, SCC had been criticized in the media the previous winter because textbooks arrived a few days late. The college faced a public relations disaster unless books could be obtained.

Fortunately, the college vocational director had established excellent linkages with a large private concern. The vocational director approached a company representative and pleaded for assistance. The firm's philanthropic arm responded by settling the $56,000 debt to the vendor. Books arrived in time, thanks to private sector support. Since then, SCC has opened its own bookstore, which it owns and operates for the benefit of the college, students, and the community.

School-to-Work Opportunities

Private sector collaboration and cooperation can lead to quality improvements. Education has the chance to learn from the private sector through the School-to-Work Opportunities Act (STWOA). Passed in 1994, the act provides federal assistance to states for development and implementation of statewide school-to-work programs that respond to regional economic conditions and labor requirements (see Figure 10.1). In 1994–1995, $345 million was apportioned to states and local communities, with $190 million

Solving Urban Education Problems Through a Quality Focus   159

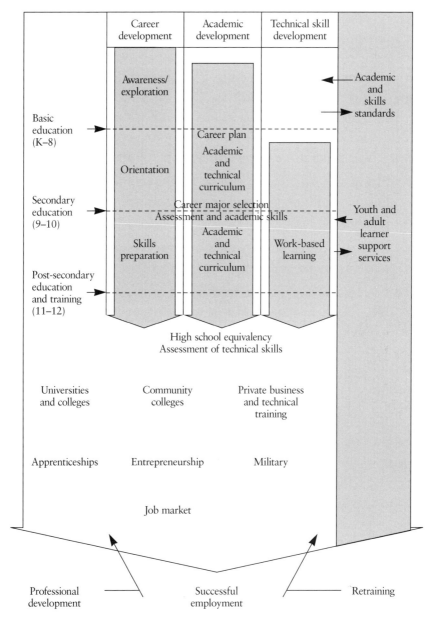

Source: Reprinted with permission from the Illinois State Board of Education.

Figure 10.1. Education-to-careers system.

appropriated for 1996 (Illinois Dept. of Education 1996). The legislation requires schools to organize STWOA committees to govern workforce education programs. It requires private sector control. Fifty percent of the membership in these committees must come from the private sector and labor.

Through STWOA, urban educators have the chance to work with the private sector to improve the educational quality in the cities. These programs can accomplish the following:

- Promote seamless transitions from secondary education to meaningful, highly skilled employment and/or post-secondary education.
- Directly engage employers in the process and use the workplace as an active learning environment.
- Give students exposure to a broad array of career choices in order to help them select academic majors that reflect their individual interests, abilities, strengths, and goals.
- Deliver enriched learning experiences to those considering dropping out of school, low-achieving youth, and youth with disabilities and assist them in obtaining good jobs and in continuing their education in post-secondary institutions.

STWOA programs have improved education in urban areas in Illinois, including the Chicago area. The Chicago system was established by Chicago Mayor Richard Daley in 1995. A steering committee was put in place composed of members from the city colleges of Chicago, the Chicago Board of Education, the Chicago Chamber of Commerce, a large local bank, and the mayor's office. After reviewing economic growth data, the committee determined that manufacturing, health/medical services, food service/hospitality, and finance were growth areas and targeted these industries for STWOA activities.

Mayor Daley sent invitations to thousands of employers to join the program. Hundreds of employers attended four recruitment meetings and signed agreements committing themselves to participate in collaborations among public and private sectors, labor and management, city and state government, agencies and educators, students and parents—all directed at the targeted industries. The overall partnership that developed improved transitions from school to work, strengthened the linkages between levels of education, and created support services. As of this writing, program participants plan to build on existing programs to further provide teaching, work experience, curriculum development, certification, counseling, support services, and funding. Chicago companies involved in the partnership include IBM, McDonalds, Helene Curtis, First Chicago Corporation, South Shore Bank, and Bell National Bank.

In Boston, Massachusetts, a collaboration among the Boston public schools, the Boston Private Industry Council, eight local hospitals, and Jobs for the Future (a nonprofit organization) led to the creation of the Project ProTech/Health Care apprenticeship program in 1991. The program combines classroom learning, clinical internships, and paid experience. It links the high school system and the community college system and provides a structured pathway from school to skilled employment. The program was so successful that ProTech/Financial Services was created for the banking and insurance industries.

Students benefit from school-to-work programs that combine career education with academic excellence. Schools that collaborate with the private sector in urban areas provide students with the following advantages (Illinois Dept. of Education 1996):

- Academic skills that meet the highest educational standards, applied in a real-world context
- New workplace skills, including analytical thinking, problem solving, and teamwork
- Career exploration, guidance, and planning
- Internships, apprenticeships, and other work-based experiences
- Credentials that are recognized nationwide
- Improved opportunities for post-secondary education
- Preparation for a wider range of occupations

- Understanding of the connection between academic performance and employment opportunities
- Flexibility to meet the needs of a changing labor market

Private sector involvement in education that can benefit any city is mandated in Goals 2000, the Educate America Act, which was signed into law in 1994. The act creates a framework to identify academic standards and measure student performance. Goals 2000 establishes the National Education Standards and Improvement Council, designed to enhance student performance and curriculum content and establish internationally competitive standards and assessment systems. The act establishes a national Skills Standards Board which develops standards for occupational clusters in industries and provides students with a skills certificate. Goals 2000 can improve urban education by focusing on quality, standards, assessment, and certification of skills.

Customized Occupational Programs

Occupational educators must focus on providing customized training programs for business and industry in order to better aid students entering the workplace. Colleges and schools must connect with employers to meet their specific training needs.

For example, if an employer needs 20 metal fabricators, an agreement can be negotiated with the local high schools or community colleges to offer a program for 30 students. The employer may commit to hiring the best of those who complete the program, assuming that they have developed the required skills. Students have an incentive to complete the program—the possibility of a craft or a profession. Employers work with the school to develop a customized curriculum and may provide instructors for the program. The program may be offered at the workplace using company equipment (assuming that liability issues can be addressed). Customized training programs have the potential to focus occupational programs on employer needs, not the needs of educators.

Technology-Based Learning

The East St. Louis (ELS) Regional Vocational System is using a learning-through-technology improvement program. The ESL system is made up of East St. Louis School District 189, Brooklyn School District 188, and Metropolitan Community College. The chairman of the regional board of control, Robert Isom, directed the region to implement technology-based learning and charged the system technology committee with the task of infusing such learning into the region.

Toni Perrin, director of instructional media for District 189, and her committee identified resources available to assist educators as technology is used to support instructional quality. They also selected an approach detailed in *Learning Through Technology: Study Group Framework and Profile Tool* (NCREL 1995), which was developed by the North Central Regional Educational Laboratory (NCREL) in cooperation with the Illinois State Board of Education, the 14 Illinois Technology Demonstration Sites, and the Illinois Mathematics and Science Academy.

The quality approach calls for using instructional models that feature engaging, meaningful learning and collaboration embedded in challenging and real-life tasks. It recognizes that technology can serve as a tool to support, enhance, and extend instruction, and can play a significant role in increasing student achievement.

Metropolitan Community College opened a Student Assessment Center that uses technology to help instructors and administrators improve student achievement. Among others, the center uses STAR 2010 and SkillsBank 96, two software packages. STAR 2010 adds, edits, and removes student/class information; assigns lessons and viewing prescriptions; views and clears student trouble spots; customizes information settings; records placement and testing results; and documents reading, mathematics, writing, and applied skills progress.

SkillsBank 96 is used for diagnostic purposes—testing students to pinpoint their weaknesses and strengths. The program then makes recommendations regarding lessons needed. The system also provides actual lessons, brief tutorials, examples, practice items, quizzes, and tests. A number of reports can be generated, including one that details a student's performance, one designed to inform parents of their students' progress, one designed to document overall class performance, and several others.

NCREL describes six indicators of high-performance technology.

- *Access.* A technology or technology-enhanced program has high performance in terms of access when it has connectivity, ubiquity, and interconnectivity.

- *Operability.* A technology or technology-enhanced program has high performance in terms of operability when it has interoperability—the capacity to easily exchange data with, and connect to, other hardware and software.

- *Organization of resources.* A technology-enhanced program has high performance in terms of organization of resources in response to questions about information and data storage, how resources are connected, how information is transmitted, and who is in charge.

- *Design features for engaging learning.* A high-performance technology program has design features that promote engaging learning. Engaging learning provides challenging tasks, opportunities, and experiences; allows students to learn by doing; provides guided participation, and provides information that is just in time and just enough for the student.

- *Ease of use.* A technology-based learning system has high performance in terms of ease of use when it features user friendliness and effective help, speed of processing, user control, training, and support.

- *Functionality.* A technology-enhanced approach has high performance in terms of functionality when it offers opportunities for students to use media technologies, use the diversity of tools that are basic to learning and working in the twenty-first century, develop programming and authoring skills, develop skills related to project design and implementation, and use tools that create new tools (NCREL 1995).

Business and industry partnering is critical to the infusion of technology-based learning. The region has developed partners through the Education-to-Careers partnership that will assist schools in the area develop technology-based learning. Together, they are developing quality approaches designed to lead to increases in the indicators of high-performance technology.

The regional system has submitted grants to state and federal agencies to fund the technology initiative, meanwhile proceeding to implement the project using funds available from existing resources. Administrators are committed to educating students through technology that will improve teaching and learning.

The vision of a technology-based learning system is shared by the community. The 1996 *Technical Blueprint for School District 189 Plan* states that "the community believes that students will be able to compete globally on an intellectual and technological basis" because School District 189 will provide the necessary technology to effectively meet the learning needs of the students (ESL Public School District 189). Through a school and community partnering, students and parents will be effective users of information technology.

Quality in Educational Training Programs

In fact, educational programs are better served if issues of quality are factored into the whole. Quality factors include the following:

- Creating consensus and consistency of purpose through public/private partnerships
- Adopting a new philosophy in terms of teaching and learning
- Using resources judiciously
- Providing guidelines for continued success

- "Doing the job right the first time;" addressing specific job skills
- Implementing methods to ensure improvement
- Implementing programs of education and retraining to meet tomorrow's needs today

Campus of Learners

The Campus of Learners concept represents a paradigm shift in the nation's collective efforts to provide quality education to all citizens. For too long, the emphasis was on the schoolhouse or the college campus: discrete facilities to which students came in order to be educated. At the same time, little emphasis was placed on the effect of the public housing environment on education. Public housing that had fallen prey to the worst that society could offer provided hard lessons that, in effect, negated the teachings of the school. In a world of guns and drugs and abuse, children and adults found the teachings of the school too foreign to understand, too naive to accept, and too shallow to be of much help in the struggle for survival. The projects killed the educational spirit and left nothing positive behind. The Campus of Learners concept seeks to rekindle that educational spirit while revitalizing the public housing system.

Urban education must take advantage of the opportunity to educate students wherever they live and to educate entire families. If students are living in government-sponsored housing projects, learning opportunities should be placed in the housing projects to create a Campus of Learners (HUD 1996). The Campus of Learners initiative gives public housing residents the opportunity to live in a campus-like setting that is focused on learning. Residents selected to live in public housing designated a Campus of Learners agree to enroll in and complete courses in computer technology, job training, comprehensive education, and support services. It is envisioned that the this approach will lead these "students" to self-sufficiency. Successful participants will find jobs, move to private housing, and leave the welfare system.

The Campus of Learners concept is an infusion of quality education directly into resident apartments. The Campus of Learners is envisioned to provide numerous services to public housing residents, as outlined in Figure 10.2.

Key principles that guide program planners include many quality factors, including a strategic quality vision for bold and ambitious change; adopting a new philosophy of education; driving out fear; education; training; and access to technology; and community consensus and support. While working within federal and local fiscal guidelines and formal building codes and specifications, the focus of the Campus of Learners is quality education, not the short-term bottom line. Here physical rebuild and social program development go hand-in-hand toward fostering the revitalization of distressed neighborhoods.

- Secure environment
- Computer training
- Workforce education and career training
- Adult basic education/general education
- Nursery and child care services
- Head start/preschool education
- Tutorial services for all family members
- Alcohol and substance abuse counseling
- Resident-based policing programs
- Personal hygiene and health programs
- Fiscal credit counseling
- Family savings incentive program
- Budget planning and training
- Training on how to start and operate small business
- Home repair and maintenance training
- Information on home purchases
- Senior citizen housing assistance
- Recreational services
- Public housing sports teams

Figure 10.2. Campus of Learners: Public housing resident services/educational opportunities.

Examples of Successful Campus of Learners Programs

Examples of model collaborative efforts are available from around the country. These programs are operated through partnerships that include public housing authorities, local businesses, computer consultants, and universities. The programs have a track record of success in helping residents and low-income individuals obtain employment.

South Bend, Indiana. The South Bend Housing Authority has established the South Bend Housing University to provide technology training for residents and teach job skills that lead to self-sufficiency. The housing university networks with area schools, service agencies, and community centers and works to provide a technology-enriched curriculum for residents. Each family develops a Family Empowerment Plan that features individual education and training plans for each family member. A community computer center is available for tenants through local technology partnerships.

Denver, Colorado. The Denver Housing Authority gives residents access to high-technology computer learning services. A public/private partnership with TeleCommunications, Inc., the Community College of Denver, Denver University, and the Denver School District provides a network of educational resources, family services, and employment and training programs for North Lincoln Homes public housing residents. All 206 apartments in North Lincoln Homes were designed with built-in computer wiring.

Hartford, Connecticut. The Hartford Housing Authority has taken a partially vacant complex and turned it into a comprehensive learning and living center. The mayor's office, Hartford school district, Trinity College, and the private sector have collaborated to computer wire all of the units in the Charter Oak development, offer adult basic education programs, and work with local elementary and technical schools.

East St. Louis, Illinois. The East St. Louis Housing Authority plans to use existing funds to create a Campus of Learners in cooperation with education service providers in the region, including Metropolitan Community College and Southern Illinois University at Edwardsville/East St. Louis Center. In East St. Louis, the Campus of Learners is seen as a solution to the educational isolation of public housing residents.

Quality Themes

The subjects discussed here are an eclectic collection of material, each with different points and thrusts, each with different solutions. And yet it is all part of the answer to the question of how to refurbish and reinvent a quality education system today that prepares people for the next millennium. If any common thread runs throughout these discussions, it is that of quality as embodied in vision, leadership, planning, review, cooperation, empowerment,

Providing computer technology training in public housing complexes is part of the Campus of Learners program.

and a willingness to step outside the norm. Perhaps in no other arena is it more important that quality operates as the underpinning of existing and proposed programs. Only through the kinds of quality factors outlined here can our educational institutions meet the needs of our children in the twenty-first century.

Chapter 11

The Economic Well-Being of the Inner City

Sheryl L. Cooley

> *The human imagination has already come to conceive the possibility of recreating human society.*
>
> —Edmund Wilson, American critic

Perhaps the need for total quality (TQ) is no greater than in the area of economic revitalization of the inner city. This is due in part to the fact that such a program of development is multifaceted, with many kinds of challenges and opportunities; that economic revitalization tasks can take years to create, fund, and implement; that the original excitement of the program wanes in time, portending obsolescence through loss of vision; and that shifting political winds can threaten recently established structures, dramatically affecting the direction of program initiatives. TQ management in this instance implies long-term management of a comprehensive urban economic revitalization program based on a systemic, but flexible approach not only to the issues of creating jobs but to the integration of other plans to create and sustain a sound economic base.

As cities across the nation can confirm, the resources to rebuild the physical infrastructure of an inner city can be found and, when properly managed, used well. Over the years, federal, state, and regional governments have worked to help the inner city, sometimes by providing funding sources such as community block grants, and sometimes by creating supporting management structures such as community redevelopment agencies. In the past 15 years both public and private entities within and surrounding the local communities have had considerable success garnering support for projects that produce evidence of success—buildings, streets, malls and transportation systems—tangible evidence to which they can point with satisfaction. In nearly all cases, it has been assumed that *that* success would prove the catalyst for further development, and the second step of development would be born of its own volition and proceed as an unfettered, natural outgrowth of the initial process.

But evidence has shown that, by the time the focal revitalization program has been completed, other businesses, thriving independently of this effort, must have been put in place to ensure the survival of the community. It has become apparent that economic revitalization plans must focus not just on the rebuilding effort, but on the kind of profit-making opportunities that will be left behind in the dust of departing construction trailers. Otherwise, the community, having trained only construction workers and encouraged entrepreneurs in businesses designed to directly serve this boon, will find a tremendous outflow of what has become their most valuable asset—their people, with their newly gained skills and experience, who will leave to establish themselves in other boom towns that have not gone bust yet again.

Over the years, numerous communities have successfully renovated the physical elements of distressed neighborhoods. But for all the fanfare accorded them, they have largely failed to revive the local economy. For example, Elliott D. Sclar, a professor of urban planning at Columbia University, and Walter Hook, executive director of the Institute for Transportation and Development Policy, contend in a contributing chapter to the book *Interwoven Destinies* that Baltimore, Maryland's efforts to revitalize its city have failed despite the well-documented renovation of a derelict wharf-side area of largely abandoned shipping warehouses to create the boutique atmosphere of Harbor Place. The authors note that there are still few jobs and "Baltimore still [has] classrooms without school books, let alone computers" (Sclar and Hook 1993). The jobs that were created during construction are gone, and there have been only so many permanent jobs created in the wake of construction. Baltimore did a good job of jump-starting a new economic era; it found a way to clean up a distressed neighborhood, improve its city's image, and expand its tax base. But the plan was incomplete.

Baltimore is not alone in its efforts to rejuvenate its city. East St. Louis, Illinois, has done much the same thing. The city has managed to induce a floating gambling casino to set up shop on its riverfront shoreline. Income from the city's percentage of profits has dramatically expanded the tax base. The community has also brought St. Louis, Missouri's metro link line to the east side of the river. This has provided a considerable number of construction jobs and, additionally, has given residents a means of mass transportation to reach the other side of the river—where most of the jobs are. Even then, however, many of those jobs lie in outlying communities, not in St. Louis' riverfront city center that, in itself, is still struggling with its own revitalization efforts. Operation of the mass transit line and work within the casino have also provided jobs. Nevertheless, the city continues to struggle with unemployment.

Omaha, Nebraska has also retrofitted its local downtown district. A few square blocks of old warehouses have been renovated. An immediate downtown area of derelict buildings, drug dealing, and prostitution has been bulldozed and a pretty little waterway created in its place. A new public library has been erected at one end of "the mall;" historic buildings flank one side, rife with cozy restaurants and numerous boutiques. New offices have been built along part of its perimeter.

Unfortunately, companies that were already part of the Omaha landscape or that brought in their own employees have moved into the new buildings; few new jobs have been created for those who need them. The expensive little shops struggle. Transients use the library more than any other group of people, especially during the cold winter. And the people on the near north side, an area that has been poor and predominantly African-American for decades, still struggle to survive. The economic base has shifted, but it has not changed much. The building of the physical infrastructure has had little lasting impact on the rate of joblessness.

As these examples indicate, economic revitalization must include the development of stable and appropriate long-term employment opportunities that pay living wages. But how do community leaders convince industry to open shop in a blighted area? How can they craft a deal sweet enough to bring in business without giving away the very thing they need the most—the taxes they will receive as a community and the wages they need for individuals? How do they use the best resources from within and without to write an economic success story?

To date, no one knows for sure.

Across the United States, cadres of experts, each with an agenda for success, have offered excellent ideas that, in the end, have not met the ultimate test of time: They have not brought the community out of poverty. Among the better-known efforts are those undertaken in the aftermath of the 1992 civil disturbance in south central Los Angeles. Rebuild Los Angeles (RLA) was born, headed by Peter Ueberroth, the former baseball commissioner who is best known for his role in the 1984 Los Angeles Olympics. His plan emphasized public/private partnerships, community empowerment, and neighborhood redevelopment. For a while, a spirit of optimism prevailed; a master plan had been developed that made Los Angeles truly the "City of Angels."

Except that it didn't happen. Eric Mann (1993), in an article in *The Nation*, noted,

> *Drive through South L.A. on any afternoon, and you will see thousands of unemployed men and*

> *women. Ueberroth was right about one thing: Joblessness is the greatest single material obstacle to rebuilding the inner city. A consultant hired by R.L.A. reported that 75,000 to 90,000 jobs are needed in South L.A. alone. Yet today not one major factory is under construction there, and the hard and soft pledges to Ueberroth involve fewer than 5,000 jobs. The growing perception is that the best jobs R.L.A. has created are its own P.R. department. (p. 406)*

These sentiments have been repeated, albeit more carefully, by others. A spokesperson for the Los Angeles Community Redevelopment Agency noted that Ueberroth's plan had great vision but had been built on the assumption that south central Los Angeles would develop once again as a major industrial base. The real problem, he said, is that there is no real impetus for heavy industry—the kind that would provide hundreds of jobs—to move into the area. California's worker's compensation and pension laws, the lack of large parcels of available land, and the environmental condition of the geographic area slated for rebuild, combined with state and national environmental laws, virtually prohibit the renaissance of a solid manufacturing base in the Los Angeles basin.

Over the long term, for many cities, the resources and incentives just haven't been there.

Public resources are notoriously finicky. As political parties and the mood of the nation changes, so does the availability of federal, state, and local funds. Jimmy Carter had trouble with his urban and welfare policy initiatives. Ronald Reagan and George Bush supported major cuts in social programs. By 1990, the budgets for urban programs were not a great deal larger than they had been in the early 1950s (Peterson 1993). In recent years Washington has cut the national budget by placing the burden of funding programs on the state. States, in turn, have been forced to eliminate local programs to pay for these others. Meanwhile, not only has funding to cities dropped, but cities have in essence become responsible for metropolitan areas well beyond their borders.

The alternative to public funding is private funding. However, in this day and age, where impersonal institutions carry large blocks of stock in publicly held companies, it has become policy for them to sell their blocks if these companies are not profitable in the short term. As a result, publicly held firms can afford to be philanthropic only when their businesses are thriving. Thus corporate philanthropy cannot be counted on any more than can federal resources.

To date, public/private partnerships for inner-city economic development have focused on the use of public funds as seed money to bring a business or industry into a distressed community while private, (usually) local organizations manage them to best meet the needs of their communities. Tax breaks are provided as incentives to relocation. Those incentives are phased out over the space of a few years, with the business expected to begin operating profitably by that time. History has shown, however, that often the incentives are not great enough or that communities often expect too much from their new business "partners," in terms of job training and the like, to sustain the system. While the incentives are not bad in themselves, perhaps it is time to look at new and innovative quality ways to use those public and private moneys that can be made available to help the inner city.

In the Short Term

In the short term, of course, considerable opportunity may be found in the revitalization effort itself. For all of the shortcomings of work that is not expected to exist past the life of a particular project or program, it must be recognized that such efforts provide a catalyst to further economic growth. Often, too, short-term projects leave behind them the legacy of experience and the taste of success. No community can accurately predict whether the short-term opportunities of which they prevail themselves will plant the roots of sustainable growth in future years or will simply count as a blip in the slope of economic decay. But only pumps that are primed deliver gushers of water. Without the initial effort, the pump remains dry.

Construction Work

Construction work typically pays decent wages, and apprenticeship programs through the local schools and unions can be put into place with relative ease. (That is, suitable programs have already been developed and political and community consensus is relatively easy to obtain.) If any paradigm exists here, it is that of developing large numbers of women into the workforce. While it can be argued that men who can support their families won't abandon them, women must not be forced to rely on such an argument—it may prove false. Additionally, studies show that proportionally larger numbers of single-parent, female-headed households reside in the inner city (Edelman 1987).

Cities can sometimes use construction as the first step in urban revitalization.

The idea has already been tried in Indianapolis, Indiana. There the city gave a developer a prime parcel of land on the edge of a distressed neighborhood, requiring that the developer employ a large proportion of people within the neighborhood. Much of the neighborhood was made up of single-parent households headed by women. The developer successfully trained the women and developed the infrastructure (sewers, streets, and utilities), as contracted. Afterward, he sold the land and made a profit in the process.

Federally Funded Projects

Often with the building of new structures comes new or improved infrastructure systems—roadway, sewerage, and communication systems. As part of a regional system of infrastructure development, this can provide employment opportunities for many years. In fact, these kinds of developments offer significantly more opportunity for smaller firms, as it gives them more time to get up and running and more opportunity for professional training. However, again, it is likely to breed more infrastructure-oriented firms than the community can support once the major infrastructure program ends. These people, too, will be forced to find other niches, turn to other jobs, or leave the community in search of work.

"Brownfield" site work offers similar opportunities. Too often, new business cannot be enticed into the inner city because the land requires environmental remediation. Abandoned buildings, relatively simple to demolish, often stand over the toxic waste of a bygone era. Federal efforts have been underway to waive the laws governing egregious environmental statutes in distressed neighborhoods, and, in some cases, moneys have been made available to help with the effort. For high-density neighborhoods, then, identification, remediation, and demolition of these Brownfield sites will provide jobs and job training in the short term.

Another look should be taken at job opportunities on other federally funded projects. While WPA-like programs might be a godsend to the urban poor, other programs, never designed to create jobs, may be appropriate venues to employment. For example, while Superfund site cleanup may bring the specter of exposure to nuclear contamination, remediation of recently closed military bases does not. And while the *planning* of remediation work on our nation's bases—much of which involves cleaning the soil of spilled jet fuel—takes considerable expertise, much of the actual work does not, although a 40-hour safety training course is required.

In the Long Run

As with most urban problems, inner-city employment must be dealt with in both the short term and the long term. Although it is true that teaching in a dump is not conducive to learning, it is also true that new or renovated schools are not the solution to the problems of inner-city education. In the short term, the physical structure needs repair. In the long term, so do the programs employed to teach those who, in all likelihood, have not been as well grounded in the basics and often have little motivation to catch up.

In the short term, for residents of the inner city to become employed, employment opportunities must exist. Here is where the deal makers, to their credit, have provided good advice and worked to create relatively isolated, but usually successful, results. On the whole, however, successes have been few and far enough apart to point out as individual achievements and not panaceas to the ills of distressed neighborhoods nationwide, although many of them are called "models." The problem with a model is that it assumes a specific set of parameters as a prerequisite, and few cities have the same specific opportunities for and obstacles to growth.

But there are two common denominators: Long-term economic growth will depend both on expanding the tax base and on providing *long-term* employment opportunities for the inner city. It is the second phase of the economic revitalization program; and it is, by far, the more difficult challenge.

Traditional Jobs

Numerous efforts can and have been undertaken to help distressed neighborhoods make their communities attractive to business and industry. Atlanta, Georgia, which has most recently boosted its economy by hosting the 1996 Summer Olympics, will use its newly received U.S. Department of Housing and Urban Development (HUD)-designated status as an Empowerment Zone to attempt long-term renovation of parts of its city. Such designation allows Atlanta to offer businesses who move into the designated zone a property expense allowance of up to $20,000 under Internal Revenue Code Sec. 179. Employers will be entitled to a 20 percent credit on the first $15,000 of wages paid to certain zone employees. Six cities received such a designation.

The Los Angeles Community Redevelopment Agency (CRA) seeks to help the local economy by cobbling together parcels of land, either through purchase or right of domain, to create areas large enough for use by commercial or industrial developers. This makes enough contiguous real estate available for large development in an area of dense population. The CRA can also float the bonds for the development effort. These and other efforts in distressed neighborhoods throughout the United States attempt to set the stage for the influx of jobs into the inner city.

But the real problem lies in finding the jobs themselves. Traditionally, manufacturing has been one of the few industries that pays excellent wages to blue-collar workers. And today there remains a perceived need to draw heavy industry into an area of urban blight because, apart from high-tech jobs (many of which require advanced degrees), manufacturing is one of the few employers of large numbers of people. Unfortunately, many of these types of industries no longer exist in the United States, or, like the mini-mills, operate on so-much-smaller margins that wages cannot match those of the old-time steelworker. Employers in most industries today that are willing to relocate their facilities are looking for cheap, nonunion labor in parts of the country where large parcels of land can be found at a low cost and where state wage and environmental statutes provide few obstacles to their bottom-line results. Despite the much-touted end to the recession, it is still a buyer's market.

Community leaders are beginning to realize that alternatives to heavy industry must be found as the United States moves from an industrial- to a services-based economy, which implies a shift in the basis of today's urban plans. Experts recommend that distressed neighborhoods look to light industry such as food processing, packaging, and storage; apparel manufacturing; printing and publishing; computer component manufacturing; and medical and chemical research labs operating in niche markets.

Michael Porter, a professor at Harvard Business School and an advisor to companies and governments, espouses the idea of developing entrepreneurial businesses based on the local ethnic makeup of the community. In an article entitled "The Rise of the Urban Entrepreneur" (Porter 1995), he cites the progress of Americas' Food Basket, a Cuban-owned grocery store based in Boston's inner city. Porter notes that

> *[The business] has developed a product mix that satisfied local demand better than mainstream supermarkets do. And unlike nearby mom-and-pop stores, Americas' Food Basket has developed a partnership with a leading national wholesaler, which helps it make its selection, prices, and services better than those of its smaller competitors. (p. 106)*

In a similar vein, he mentions Handy Andy Supermarkets of San Antonio, Texas. The firm focuses on the Latino market and has 23 stores in Texas.

Geographically limited and distinct areas that are falling into disrepair but have not yet succumbed totally to urban blight, or which are shedding their image as blighted areas, are prime candidates for development of multi-entertainment centers. The idea here is to lure couples to the now decidedly upscale refurbished area to have a leisurely dinner; take in a show, play, or concert; and finish the night out with a drink or two, dropping somewhere in the neighborhood of $100 or more during the evening.

Through innovative use of public and private funds, Pasadena, California is doing just that, rejuvenating an area of historic structures, and bringing in restaurants and theaters and a community playhouse to what is known as the Old Pasadena and the Playhouse districts. (This is a more expensive effort than it might seem; significant seismic upgrading accompanies the renovation.) Unfortunately, boutiques and theaters and restaurants and bars employ people who need little advanced education, but wages tend to be low. Additionally, crime—or its perception—can undermine redevelopment results in some areas, especially where the areas are designed to draw people after dark. However, Pasadena is overcoming these latter problems through creative development of streetscapes and alleyways and stepped-up security. In addition, the first two-story Target store in Southern California will operate as an anchor store for the area, and will help provide the desired draw of people during other hours.

HUD Secretary Cisneros believes that inner cities, often economic deserts by themselves, must look to develop industries and associated business clusters based on opportunities derived from the surrounding thriving community (Cisneros 1996). Cisneros describes several cities that fit under his theory of regional cluster development. One of the oldest is Research Triangle in the Raleigh-Durham area of North Carolina.

The initial Research Triangle committee was established in 1955 as part of a strategy to induce companies and organizations engaged in research and development to relocate to the newly developed Research Triangle Park and surrounding area. The decision was based on the fact that the community, which was falling into disrepair after the downturn in the tobacco, textiles, and furniture markets, was surrounded by three major state universities with special strengths: chemistry, electronics, and pharmaceuticals.

By the early 1980s, the development supported 20,000 employees with annual salaries of almost a half-billion dollars.

Other successes have come from reviewing opportunities *within* the community. Miami saw a decrease in its popularity as a tourist destination for northern-tier Americans at the same time that the city experienced an influx of immigrants from Cuba and other parts of Latin America. Today, however, Miami is remolding itself as an international trade center. Trade connections have reportedly leveraged other local industries, as well.

Boston has survived the industrial era and the more recent bust of big-time high-tech production around Route 128. Today, the city is characterized by smaller firms such as software producers and similar companies within niche markets. The city has successfully renovated its run-down Marketplace to meet the needs of the downtown area as well as much of its historic waterfront, improving its tourism trade.

Cleveland, Ohio discovered that the city still supported considerable manufacturing, although the industry giants were gone, and that a large share of the region's growing service sector existed primarily to support it. The city has worked to encourage the retention of production activities within the region and has promoted attendant local businesses most likely to survive as the market changes.

Telecommuting and the Virtual Office

Traditional economic revitalization programs have focused on bringing business and industry to the inner city to stimulate economic growth. But telecommuting—working from home through the use of a networked computer—may offer a viable employment alternative. While virtual offices will not provide the same opportunities for the community to increase its corporate tax base, they offer opportunities to companies who would not otherwise venture into the inner city.

Telecommuting offers an alternative to owning or leasing real estate in areas beset with crime and violence.

C. Austin Fitts, who worked on Wall Street and, for a time, was head of the Federal Housing Administration under President Bush, believes that many jobs in virtual offices can be developed for inner-city residents. She contends that companies that would never consider moving their direct operations into an area of urban blight may find it profitable, nonetheless, to have an arm's-length relationship with inner-city employees. In an article by Neil R. Peirce, Fitts is quoted as describing other ways telecommuting can be used in inner-city businesses (Peirce 1995).

> *If I'm Safeway . . . a half-million-dollar store in the South Bronx [may seem] risky and maybe dangerous for my employees. But if I can fly in on-line, have my grocery orders taken by a co-op of residents who've organized their own micro-enterprise, then I have just one delivery to make and can build up a presence slowly and risk-free in that neighborhood.*

Computer aptitude becomes more essential every day to employability in the service economy. Fortunately, aptitude is not linked to formal education, and much of the practical training in commercial software applications does not require that the trainee have a college degree. And because the proliferation of computers has taken place outside the realm of academia, access to computer training and usage is not the select privilege of the formally educated.

In 1995, HUD Secretary Cisneros proposed that public housing facilities be turned into lifelong learning centers.* On the surface, the idea sounded vague and far-fetched, meriting consideration only because funding was made available to support it. However, its purpose makes sense: to change the image of public housing and to provide safe havens for learning. Integral to this new learning paradigm is computer usage.

To take the paradigm further, consider that computers that can be used to provide individualized instruction in the community can also be used to telecommute from it, making it a viable alternative to bringing businesses into the inner city while at the same time providing on-the-job training. It would not entirely eliminate the risks associated with the more traditional entrée of a business into an area of urban blight, but it would help to minimize them. And inner-city workers would gain technical skills in an area where the wages can be good and the potential for growth is considerable. If money is going to be provided to redevelop public housing and create havens of learning, largely through the technology of interactive computing, perhaps public housing is a good place to introduce the virtual office. Theoretically, computers will already be in place, the building will already be cabled, computer support networks will already be set up, and security will already be high.

International Export and the Inner-City Entrepreneur

In the past, small entrepreneurial enterprises have been brought into or reprised in the inner city primarily for the purpose of servicing the

---

*Editor's note: See Chapter 10 for a more detailed discussion of the Campus of Learners concept.

local community. Additionally, Small Business, Woman, Minority, and Veteran Business Enterprises qualifying under federal statutes have sprung up as contracts for repair of the infrastructure have been let within or near the community. Individual businesses then bloomed to serve the new local economy. Often certain types of chain stores could be brought into the community, and, where the money could be found, franchises could be imported. Today the federal Small Business Administration (SBA) offers low-interest loans and, thanks to the Community Redevelopment Bank and recent changes in banking regulations that seek to prohibit discrimination against minority businesses, other loans may be available to the local businessperson.

To date, most small or smaller businesses have looked inward. Support has been based on community need and community potential. However, in the last four years, considerable effort has been made at the national level to assist small and medium-sized firms in competing overseas. Under the auspices of Vice President Al Gore's "Reinventing Government" and with the late Commerce Secretary Ron Brown's lead, 16 government agencies have been working to streamline the export process. Results include the harmonizing of SBA and Ex-Im Bank's working capital programs, increased advocacy overseas for U.S. goods and services, and streamlined processes in the area of export commerce. Through the federal Trade Promotion Coordinating Committee, a national export strategy is evolving with a focus on helping the nation's smaller firms sell their products and services outside the United States.

This means that, in the course of looking for suitable small and medium-sized business opportunities to support the inner city, firms that would provide no direct products or assistance to the local community but with reasonable export potential might also be considered in the economic development effort. Companies looking to minimize overhead costs and create new markets may be good candidates for urban revitalization programs should it be proved that they offer potential as exporters. Homegrown export operations could be developed as well.

However, while this innovative idea has been widely circulated, it should be remembered that opportunities to sell products overseas will be limited by one free market given: A local enterprise in the nation that is importing the product may soon discover that it can manufacture the same item more cheaply (due to much smaller shipping costs if nothing else), thus taking over the market. Along much of the Pacific Rim, where intellectual property laws vary greatly from that of the western world, even patented products are copied and sold on a daily basis.

Additionally, the European Union has enacted statutes that discourage outsiders, and the Asian countries, taking their lead from Japan, have stringent protectionist laws. The United States has entered into a somewhat similar relationship with Mexico and Canada through the North American Free Trade Agreement (NAFTA) and hopes to extend that web of "regional community" to the southern tip of South America. But until that market blossoms, successful export of generic products overseas will be difficult at best.

Small entrepreneurs looking to make substantive sales outside the United States must develop or manufacture products for which there is not only a market niche, but which cannot be easily reproduced, say, precision tools for a particular industry. Alternatively, the entrepreneur can look to the services industry. Here, too, it must be remembered that many of the world's professionals have been tutored in American or European educational systems; often they can perform those same services just as well and at a lower cost. Niche markets are hard to develop and maintain.

Oftentimes, when American companies go outside U.S. borders, they "piggyback" onto other U.S. firms. For example, one of the nation's largest engineering and construction companies contracted with the U.S. Army Corps of Engineers (USACOE) to renovate buildings in six former Soviet republics for use as American embassies. Thanks to the fiasco of the Moscow embassy a few years ago—in which microphones were found implanted in the concrete along with the rebar—USACOE decreed that all items the company brought into the former Soviet bloc countries had to come from the United States. This included everything from wire cable to doorknobs. Not only did all procured items have to come from the United States, but a percentage had to be purchased from qualified Small Disadvantaged or Minority Business Enterprises. A small entrepreneur might do well to tap into government contracts not only here at home, but overseas.

The Need for an Attendant Social Support Structure

While the major hurdle to economic redevelopment lies in creating jobs in areas of urban blight, others, just as formidable, are often overlooked. In the inner city these larger obstacles tend to be child care, health care, housing, and education. These are the basics that a person must have or have access to in order to function as a valuable employee in the workplace.

Child Care

Many inner-city households are headed by young, single parents. Perhaps the most immediate problem, then, is that of good, affordable child care, available well past 6:00 P.M. From all indications, its lack is one of the most compelling forces keeping single parents on welfare. Meanwhile, the advantages of offering such day care programs in the inner city are enormous. Children can be brought up in a nurturing atmosphere, be made ready to enter kindergarten, and spend long periods of time in a secure environment. Although day care may not be considered a good alternative to parental child rearing, it is essential to the economic vitality in a community of single-parent households.

In the earlier example of Indianapolis, the story didn't end with training the women in construction. Rather, it ended when those same women were themselves given a parcel of land that they also developed and sold. The profit was then used to purchase another piece of land and build a much-needed day care center. That is an innovative quality approach to funding a much-needed facility, and it can be replicated nearly everywhere.

Corazón, a nonprofit organization headquartered in Southern California, is dedicated to helping Mexico's poor. To that end, they build a number of structures in blighted neighborhoods—houses, schools, and day care centers. During the day, the centers provide a combination of free time and structured programs designed to teach the children basic skills. In the evenings, the centers hold classes in basic life skills such as parenting, prenatal care, healthy cooking, and so on. On a routine basis, but seldom more than once a month, one adult member of each family with a child in one of these day care facilities (often a grandparent; poor families in Mexico are often headed by extended-family members, but seldom the traditional breadwinner) is required to volunteer at the facility for a day. There, surrounded by professional caregivers, the family member sees good caregiving skills in action. Such programs might be successfully replicated in public housing, where occupants who are unemployed could assist professional caregivers.

Health Care

The need for free, quality health care for their children keeps single parents on welfare rolls, too. Despite that, the infant mortality rate in the inner city surpasses that of some Third World countries (Turner 1993). Altogether, children's health care, teenage pregnancy, drugs, alcohol, and HIV are the most pressing health issues in distressed neighborhoods today. In these geographic areas, where the risk of illness and violence is greater (or perceived as greater), free-market health care insurers, which are themselves compelled to maintain healthy profits, find their profit-taking significantly reduced in high-crime areas. For this reason, they are reluctant to provide health insurance to inner-city residents. That, and the fact that the poor often simply cannot afford health care, places extraordinary financial stress on the health care systems that do exist in the distressed neighborhood. Government-funded clinics are overcrowded and understaffed and often operate under government rules that restrict their ability to give complete medical advice. (For example, government-supported Planned Parenthood clinics cannot discuss the option of abortion except in particular circumstances.)

Like most citizens, inner-city residents need access to affordable health care. This, however, runs counter to the incentives that distressed neighborhoods need to offer businesses to motivate them to move into the community. Experts generally agree that burdens (primarily in the form of taxes and disability insurance) and benefits (primarily health care and pension plans) cost the average employer an additional 37 percent more than the cost of salaries and overhead expenses. As a result, businesses often seek a large pool of people that they can employ part-time.

Attempts have been made to provide government-sponsored health insurance through Medicaid, and many agree that, eventually, some form of national health insurance will be required to keep health care costs in check. Today, perhaps, an answer to the problem lies in the experience of the international financial arena. Over the past five years, multilateral lending institutions have sought to limit exposure to high-risk loans (usually to unstable or former Communist countries) by syndicating them. They form tiers of lenders, each willing to risk a little, but none willing to risk large amounts of capital against significant lack of collateral.

Just as banks in the United States have, by law, been required to make what they consider to be higher-risk loans to minorities and women, insurance companies may find themselves required by law to provide health coverage to a larger portion of the population, including claimants in high-risk locales. It would behoove them to develop a syndicated system of support to these areas before the government steps in and takes legislative action.

Housing

Housing is another prerequisite to work, if for no other reason than that employers are reluctant to hire people who do not have permanent addresses. Additionally, owning a home provides an impetus for local citizens to remain in their neighborhoods; it gives them pride and a sense of belonging. In the past, public housing has been the federal government's answer to the problem, an attempt to take an unproductive piece of land and build high-rise apartment complexes. Today, more effort is made to create pockets of attached housing within middle-class communities in the hopes that the strength of the neighborhood itself will eliminate many of the problems associated with older-style public housing. However, most efforts face an uphill battle from the community.

Other efforts have been made to help lower-income persons achieve home ownership status. By the end of the 1980s, the beginnings of a national nonprofit housing development sector had emerged. According to Mitchell Sviridoff in his article "The Seeds of Urban Revival," national-level intermediaries to the Community Development Corporations include Local Initiatives Support Corporations, the Enterprise Foundation, the Neighborhood Reinvestment Corporation, and the Housing Assistance Council, to name just a few. He also noted that financing can be found through low-income-housing tax credits, community development block grants, HUD subsidies, and Federal Housing Assistance programs. However, Sviridoff refers to these support mechanisms as "patchwork" in nature (Sviridoff 1994).

The city of San Antonio, Texas has found an innovative way to "patch together" its housing resources. The city has used funds from its community development block grant to redevelop housing within its inner city. In 1974, an organization called Communities Organized for Public Service (COPS) started the Select Housing Target Areas program, whose purpose was to refurbish, rather than tear down, low-income housing. Working with city officials and the San Antonio Development Agency (SADA), the program reportedly rehabilitated more than 2600 older homes and built 900 new ones.

In 1988, COPS, a sister organization called Metro Alliance, and SADA created the Home Ownership Incentive Program (HIP). The group realized that many lower-income working families could afford monthly house payments, but not a down payment and closing costs. HIP helps families who qualify for FHA-insured loans to receive 30-year, zero-interest second mortgages for use as down payments. In these ways, San Antonio has found innovative quality solutions to the problems of providing suitable housing for its poorer citizens.

Training

It may appear that the most important incentive of all—schooling—has been overlooked. But for many undereducated Americans, formal schooling is drudgery. Just ask a vocational education student in any middle-class school anywhere in America how many days are left in the school year, and the student can probably answer you in days, minutes, and hours. Schooling implies hard work, extra hours, and the specter of failure. For many, anything other than the most basic training would not be an incentive to work.

Apprenticeship or certificate programs, however, can be well founded, particularly if they are geared to match the jobs that are brought into the inner city or if they can be used to help capture the interest of a business or industry. There are many programs underway in distressed communities across the nation. They address everything from basic hygiene in the workplace to financial management systems for the entrepreneur.

At the Tulsa Technology Center in Tulsa, Oklahoma, a program called Craftsmanship 2000 combines academic study and on-the-job training. Eleventh-grade students who can meet the admission standards begin a four-year program that, supporters say, leave the students "versed in the industry's most advanced computerized machining and lathing operations—and have an academic foundation for understanding how they work" (Stinson 1994). At the center, technology is integrated with all aspects of the curricula. Everything from the most fundamental software in the students' reading and math center to modeling programs for computer-aided manufacturing exists on a network, allowing for less actual commuting and more telecommuting among the center's four main campuses and three satellite training locations.

The effort, sponsored by local businesses, pays student stipends, worker's compensation insurance, and a bonus. Students, in effect, become employees of the program. They emerge, four years later, with an associate's degree, 25 credits of which can be applied to a four-year degree, and the potential to go to work for area businesses, including American Airlines (with a major maintenance facility in Tulsa) and TD Williamson, a worldwide manufacturer of pipelines headquartered in Tulsa.

A Holistic Quality Approach

There's a saying in the quality industry: Quality is remembered long after the costs of the project are forgotten. Certainly a community should not squander its funding to execute a few programs with all the bells and whistles at the expense of all others. Rather, quality in this sense refers to the level of effort required to produce a program with a reasonable chance of success. An architect must develop an "equation," measuring form against function against cost in the process of master planning a single structure or a multiuse facility, keeping in mind a particular architectural style that will meet his or her clients' needs and some of their wants. So must an urban revitalization program develop form, function, and cost within an overriding theme of quality.

If the theme is one of quality, then the policies and procedures of program development and use must be measured in terms of the quality of the results. It becomes the bellwether against which to measure cost and schedule. (At times, it is the fulcrum that keeps cost and schedule in balance.) Developing quality standards and measurements against which to judge revitalization projects and programs strengthens the foundation of a well-run revitalization effort, be it in terms of economic base building, crime prevention, education, or another issue.

To provide good overall management of all such programs is to achieve total quality. It is the framework upon which to implement revitalization efforts. It is a way to do business: the cultural ideology against which to judge activities and results. For economic revitalization to become a reality, total quality must cover all related revitalization programs and include the following:

- Identifying and correlating needs; breaking them down into manageable parts.
- Developing one-year, five-year, 10-year, and "generation" urban strategic quality plans that wean the community from subsidies and propel it toward self-sufficiency.*
- Managing projects and programs with an emphasis on doing the job right the first time. Often that means hiring qualified people to do the work (not the cheapest, but the best qualified within the budget of the plan), providing qualified management oversight of planned infrastructure projects, and ensuring that social programs contain some "meat."
- Determining measurable quality goals. Verify upfront the expenditures that can be tracked against baselines. Determine the viability of schedules. Develop reasonable but far-reaching standards for acceptable performance in each program and project, and get these quality goals into the contract language. Track goals routinely, failing forward where necessary.
- Looking for incremental change as well as quantum leap improvement. Total quality including the use of both "soft" and "hard" quality. It means recognizing that soft quality is often difficult to measure, but worth pursuing—just don't let it be an excuse for not measuring quality at all.
- Empowering people with a knack for getting things done, and giving them direct lines of communication to the top.

---

*Editor's note: See the Appendix for a brief overview of a representative four-year plan.

- Avoiding in-fighting. Debate may be healthy, but no revitalization effort will succeed if there is not a united front among the program's leaders.
- Making sure that those in authority lead with conviction. Programs of magnitude commonly move forward on the sheer will of a select few.
- Operating in alignment with contractors, consultants, and other program management personnel. Develop an attitude of partnering from the beginning. Make them all a part of the revitalization process so they will be committed to the effort. They will give better service at less cost and like doing it.
- Remaining focused but flexible. Much changes in five- and 10-year spans of time. Determine needs annually. Trash programs that don't work. Be ever on the lookout for quality innovations that can be incorporated with the revitalization process.
- Developing fallback positions, particularly within the first five years of development during which the process is most vulnerable. A change in the political winds may spell the end to critically needed funding and support. Be prepared.

Marian Wright Edelman, head of the Children's Defense Fund, also touts the need for a holistic urban revitalization program, although (as would be expected) for her economic revitalization is just part and parcel of a program to rescue the family—and thus the children. But her words are prophetic (Edelman 1987).

> *The first step in bringing about change is caring. But caring is not enough. The second step is trying to see a problem whole and then breaking it into manageable pieces for action. One must proceed step by systematic step to mold and assemble the pieces until the whole is positively affected. (p. 103)*

One final note should be taken from the experience of the group that helps the poor in Mexico. Despite having worked in the border communities for more than 20 years, Corazón still suffers periodic setbacks. Day care equipment gets stolen, volunteers' cars are broken into, and families stage destitution far worse than their actual situations in attempts to get more help from the group. Structures that go up one day burn to the ground the next. New programs flop. Occasionally, funding dries up.

However, because the organization has been doing this work for so long, its leaders know when to ignore such problems and when to deal with them. They recognize that poverty drives people to crime, but so does greed; that unfortunate events happen; that at times they will fail. They recognize that there will always be problems. They recognize that they can change some people's lives, but not all. But they do not let themselves be ambushed by those who would point fingers and claim that their programs don't work at all. They have the quality procedures in place to make things happen and the documentation to prove that it has. Theirs is a lesson in successful, holistic, systemic management. It is a lesson in total quality.

Part III
Quality Techniques

Chapter 12

Planning the Quality Program for Customer Focus and Effective Implementation

John P. Jackson

> *Why build these cities glorious*
> *If man unbuilded goes?*
> *In vain we build the world unless*
> *The builder also grows.*
>
> —Edwin Markham, *Man-Making*

In recent years, city managers have been deluged with information concerning the need for using quality management in their urban development plans. They have been confronted with ISO 9000, total quality management (TQM), process reengineering, and so forth. In many cases they are not sure what they are trying to solve but believe that a quality program is a must for their organizations to be strong in the future. Meanwhile, they are confronted with reports that many segments of public and private industry are having difficulties implementing quality programs consistent with the recently generated ISO 9000 and QS-9000 quality standards; the ISO 9000 series has been sweeping the industry and now has been used by more than 3000 companies and several government entities with mixed results.

Against this backdrop of confusion, let us look at "a nation reconstructed." A nation reconstructed really represents each U.S. city addressing the important challenge of effectively using taxpayers' money by instilling quality in the reconstruction effort—a formidable task. Although I will focus largely on quality assurance (QA) principles related to the construction and operation of major buildings, a parallel can be drawn to those same important quality concepts as they relate to all facets of rebuilding the social structure of the city, including education, health care, welfare programs, and all of the other aspects of the sociological reconstruction of the nation. However, my purpose here is to illustrate some of the key principles of quality assurance as they relate to the constructed project. Let us begin, then, with the development of our understanding of these important quality assurance concepts.

Key Elements of QA Implementation on City ("Owner") Mega-Projects

The typical U.S. city has an elected mayor who oversees all facets of the city government, which is usually directed day in and day out by a salaried city general manager. The general manager, in concert with the mayor and the taxpayers (through their duly elected representatives on a city council), determines the city's top priorities in terms of the overall reconstruction program. In many cases, these priorities take the form of major construction efforts to be accomplished by the city. It is not uncommon to have major construction related to subway systems, large new library complexes, new county courthouses, or improved water purification systems.

The most important thing to note here is that the key to successful project execution by the city ("owner') is that owners must recognize that they are solely responsible for the effective use of taxpayers' money in the overall construction effort. The city's success or failure as an owner has the greatest impact on overall cost overruns. An owner with appropriate quality controls will have a major impact on cost savings and the effective implementation of urban development or revitalization programs.

Typically, the general manager will have an assistant general manager or chief engineer, who is the person with primary responsibility for the city's construction program. The key to implementing proper oversight over major architects/engineers involved in a multimillion- or multibillion-dollar project lies in the chief engineer having a strong technical management team coupled with an equally strong QA program. The typical city organization should have a good multidisciplined engineering team, a strong procurement and contracts administration organization, a seasoned construction field organization, and a senior QA management team. The QA manager must be well versed in construction QA methodology gained from years of experience in using cost-effective QA programs.

In order to properly discuss the organizational principles involved in a city's effective oversight of construction in the revitalization effort, let us use terminology as follows.

- We will define the top person in charge of all design and construction activities for the city as the general manager of construction (GMC).
- We will define the person reporting to the GMC who is responsible for all engineering as the engineering manager.
- The person responsible for all construction we will identify as the construction manager.
- The person responsible for all procurement and contracts management we will call the materials manager.
- The person responsible for the implementation of an effective QA program we will call the QA manager.

An Appropriate, Well-Qualified Team

Let us now discuss the important responsibilities and accountabilities of each of these people and their organizations that make up the overall city design/construction management team. As indicated

Major urban projects require significant quality systems.

above, the head person or GMC is the individual held totally accountable for the successful revitalization effort. When it comes to the disbursement of funds that can approach billions of dollars, the GMC is the person who will have the most significant influence on the success or failure of the design and construction program. The city manager is certainly accountable to the city council for overall management of city functions within a budget, but when it comes to the technical complexities of managing a major rebuilding program, the city manager must rely heavily on the prudent management capability of the GMC.

The success or failure of big-ticket urban renewal programs can have a major impact on the city budget. It must be understood that the fact that the GMC hires a nationally known architect/engineering management firm to implement an effective construction program does not relieve him or her of the inherent responsibility for all of these activities. Recognizing this awesome accountability, it is most important that the GMC have a management team reporting to him or her that controls all facets of the construction process and has the authority and accountability to effectively implement that control.

The GMC's engineering manager (EM) must be accountable for an appropriate degree of review and quality checking of all engineering activities that take place on all city revitalization efforts. The EM must perform a sufficient technical review of all design activities to ensure that the architect/engineer is properly using an effective design control system. This usually requires an engineering management team of top-flight engineers representing anywhere from five to 100 personnel. They must perform a general review of design specifications, key design drawings, and key construction contracts to ensure that these design documents are technically sound in all design disciplines, including mechanical, electrical, civil, environmental, instrumentation and control, and so on.

The materials manager (MM), likewise, is accountable for all of the cost disbursements and must coordinate closely with the engineering manager to ensure that all technical requirements are met. Additionally, the MM coordinates with the construction manager to ensure that all construction management requirements are being fully implemented in the procurement and contract documents. And last but not least, he or she must assure that all QA management requirements contractually binding all architects, engineers, equipment suppliers, and construction contractors are being fully implemented.

The construction manager (CM) has the responsibility to ensure that the entire construction team fully implements all facets of the design. From a QA perspective, he or she must also ensure that any deviations from the design are being properly reported and dispositioned by discipline engineers, construction engineers, and QA engineers. The CM is responsible for the entire construction effort. He or she must insist on a well-trained workforce, a rigorous and effective safety program, and effective labor management.

In all probability, the concept of having a QA manager as a part of a city management team is a new concept for most U.S. city "owners." To be effective, the QA manager must be independent of the engineering, procurement, and construction management activities. This is an essential element of organizational alignment to ensure that the QA organization has sufficient authority to carry out its important independent oversight role. The QA manager must be experienced and sufficiently qualified to clearly understand the objectives of a QA program as set forth in documents such as the ISO 9000 series standards. This experience and knowledge can come only through exposure to quality assurance implementation on project activities over a period of years. The QA manager must report to the GMC because he or she must have immediate and timely access to effect corrective action on problems that occur anywhere on the revitalization project.

Cities, of course, do not have the staff of hundreds of people necessary to perform the multiplicity of management activities associated with the engineering/construction and other activities of a major project. Consequently, they find themselves required to hire a major architectural/engineering or construction management firm who will assign a senior project manager to monitor the complete execution of all facets of the project. The key to effectively controlling the work of the architect/engineer is the existence at the city level of the previously mentioned top-level organization. The days are past when a city, through a single general manager, can hire an architect/engineer and set forth a multimillion- or multibillion-dollar project for the architect/engineer to complete without having a controlling oversight role. The GMC's team must sign off on key design documents, key procurement and contract documents, and key revitalization management documents, and have a strong QA involvement in the overall construction effort.

In the last decade, we saw major city construction efforts such as the Denver, Colorado airport, the Los Angeles, California rail system, and the Boston, Massachusetts harbor modifications wrought

Planning the Quality Program for Customer Focus and Effective Implementation 205

An effective quality system should be the first step toward bringing an area of urban blight out of decay.

with significant quality problems as a result of ineffective oversight by the municipality/owner. By the year 2000, cities will need to have matured in their organizational approach to minimize the potential for such major construction catastrophes to happen again. The effective city QA manager must have a team of quality engineers representing all disciplines that will be actively involved with the EM, MM, and CM as a part of the overall city management team reviewing the quality of the construction effort.

Many will notice that we have used the phrase *quality assurance* versus *quality control* in this discussion of quality. I have purposely avoided making a distinction between these two concepts. The construction industry has used the phrase *inspection and quality control* for years. If one area has contributed negatively in getting urban redevelopment quality assurance programs off the ground, it is the concept of quality assurance activity versus quality control activity.

Let me elaborate. I have seen many major architects/engineers labor under the misconception that they have had quality control systems for years in engineering, in purchasing, and in construction; they just didn't document it. I would like to dismiss that concept as utter nonsense. What they had was what every good company has: each organizational element attempting to do a quality job. Certainly an inspection group did represent an aspect of QA, but it was just one aspect, not a QA program.

The point to be made here is that QA, which was often previously referred to as quality control, is a formal program that integrates the overall management disciplines of engineering, procurement, and construction management into an effective management system.

A QA Manual

Cities have been performing little control over the revitalization process for years and, for the most part, have never had what could be called a formal QA program. Cities of the future should have a QA manual that specifically states how major project efforts are controlled. It must clearly delineate the responsibilities of the engineering management, procurement and contracts personnel, the construction management, and the QA organizations. It must delineate their specific roles in controlling the entire project process.

This QA manual must be authoritative; the procedures set forth therein must be mandatory. To accomplish this, the procedures must be signed by the key city program managers and made mandatory requirements for urban rebuild programs. It is the road map for how the city will control all future projects. All future contracts related to construction that are assigned to architects/ engineers, construction managers (CMs), and/or construction contractors will require that they recognize that the city's program has interfacing requirements with their specific quality requirements. They must understand that acceptance of formalized QA oversight by the city is a given. Consultants and contractors must have effective QA programs; this will be mandatory to do work with the city.

It is important to recognize that the quality assurance manual refers to a formal program and includes procedures to control such management issues as the following:

- QA manual update
- A description of the city's organization for quality assurance and defined responsibilities
- Design control
- Purchase order review and procurement control
- A means for handling program nonconformances
- A means for documenting inspection so that the document becomes objective evidence of quality
- A method of planning for inspection so that important revitalization elements are not missed
- A means for calibrating, measuring, and testing equipment on a construction site
- A system of controlling special processes such as welding and nondestructive testing
- A quality audit program
- A formal system of corrective action or preventive action

Let us look at the key elements of the QA program and how these management factors are implemented.

Key Project Engineering Issues
Owner Design Control

Owner (or city) design control is critical to the project's success. Design control as defined in ISO 9000 is one of the most important aspects of an effective QA program. It represents all those activities associated with a thorough design review of the drawings and specifications defining the project. The engineering management team must be thoroughly integrated with all design coordination activities on every major project underway in the city.

Before discussing design review, let's first define *design quality*. The whole quality assurance system is based on the definition of quality: a measure of how closely we adhere to the customer's expectations as defined in design documents, drawings, specifications, and contract language. With this definition in mind, it is important, then, to recognize that we must start with a good foundation: the design. It is impossible to build quality into a poor design. Let us go through the normal chain of events in developing the design of a major city project. Design sequence is accomplished in the following manner.

• The architect/engineer originates the design concept; this is considered a baseline design that is thoroughly coordinated with the city.

• The engineering management organization defines the owner's requirements for the project to be built.

• The specifications and calculations of the originating design engineer are checked by his or her group supervisor.

• The design is then turned over to others involved in the architectural/engineering or design firm who look at such important areas as quality engineering, environmental requirements, construction management requirements, the effect on the community, and so forth.

• Upon completion of these reviews, the specification or design is published in a draft form and then submitted to the city engineers, who perform additional independent review of the design and transmit their comments back to the architect/engineer. This results in a multilevel design review by the city engineers, the architect/engineer, and all of the various management disciplines within the architectural/engineering firm that cover quality engineering, environmental engineering, and materials engineering to ensure the effectiveness of the design.

In summary, the city, as the owner, must perform sufficient design reviews to ensure that the city is getting top performance from its architect/engineer in the implementation of an effective design, prior to the start of construction.

Design Release

Design release is the mechanism to ensure that work is completed according to approved designs. Once a design is approved by the city, it is released for procurement or construction. A sign of such a release should be obvious on the designs to ensure that work gets done following a design that is mature and has been fully reviewed and approved by the owner and the design system. One of the major contributors to construction errors is work done to preliminary design information. It can be extremely costly and dangerous and often results in major project problems. Good QA dictates that a design release is indicated in a highly visible fashion—with a stamp on documents, drawings, and specifications that says "Released for Construction" and/or "Released for Procurement," as appropriate. Only then does the owner have reassurance that all work done in the field and all materials procured are being handled according to designs that have been through this mature design review process. Once designs are released, the project moves to the configuration management phase.

Configuration Management

Configuration management is an important part of any effective QA program. In this computer age there is no reason that we cannot effectively manage the configuration of our revitalization projects. It is essential that all aspects of project management—whether scheduling, QA, purchasing, or construction management—be accomplished to a well-defined configuration management system. By *configuration management,* I mean the broad management discipline that takes into account design change management to ensure that the product ultimately built is in full compliance with the final released design. Successful configuration management produces a mechanism whereby each member of the project organization can determine at any given time the current design as defined by release of the documents, drawings, specifications, and changes.

All revitalization project participants must have a common, systematic vehicle, computerized or not, that communicates the current design at any point in time. The system must take into account that design changes can number in the thousands on a revitalization project. With an excellent design agency, as many as 20 to 50 design changes a day may be generated. The important thing is that the project/construction manager, field engineers, and inspectors must know what approved design changes apply to the job. Management assessments of troubled urban redevelopment projects have indicated that the lack of design control is probably the primary contributor to construction failures and to degradation of construction scheduling efforts.

The design firm must thoroughly understand that its main objective during the project is to produce a quality design and to provide that design to the field on a timely basis so as to minimize the impact on schedule. Further, the design firm must fully recognize that all of its designers, as a matter of priority on a daily basis, must give top attention to changes and conformance reports being generated by field personnel at the construction site. Accommodation to field-generated design requests in a streamlined manner is a major contributor to a successful quality project. In a well-run design control system, 90 percent of all field-initiated changes will have a one-day turnaround. Such a goal usually is achievable when proper thought and management attention are given to the design change process.

Key Revitalization Project Procurement Issues

The city's MM must understand that his or her primary responsibility is to deliver quality products to the construction site on a timely basis. Included in this responsibility are several important concepts that require close coordination with the engineering and quality assurance organizations.

Procurement Requirements

First, and most important, is to clearly establish all of the product requirements in the procurement specification or, in the case of contract work, to ensure that revitalization contracts delineate all of the requirements imposed on the contractor. One of the major problems in this area is the lack of specificity in the QA requirements to be imposed at the design stage on both suppliers and contractors. Such a problem in a procurement specification or a contract specification usually can be minimized with a thorough quality engineering review by senior quality engineers to make sure that the appropriate QA provisions are detailed in these design documents. If requirements are properly stated, the potential supplier or contractor knows precisely what his or her cost will be to produce the product or provide the contracted services with all appropriate QA requirements.

Only with such provisions appropriately specified in contract documents can appropriate quality assurance evaluations of the supplier or contractor be made. Only then can the MM ensure that a supplier or contractor is qualified. Millions of dollars have been paid to repair bad welds as part of the seismic modifications of various bridges in Southern California. Major modifications were required when poor welding was not detected because nondestructive testing was performed by an unqualified contractor. These are the types of things that must be held fully attributable and accountable to the owner's lack of control in employing an effective procurement and revitalization QA program.

Pre-Award Surveys

One of the city's quality roles is to ensure that pre-award surveys are completed. A multitude of problems have been brought about in the construction industry by awarding contracts to the lowest bidder, particularly when that bidder lacks the complete qualifications to manufacture, inspect, and test products or services in accordance with the specifications. It is imperative that the MM have organizational interfaces with the rest of the city's management team so that he or she has total knowledge of the requirements imposed on the suppliers and contractors and their day-to-day performance record in meeting those requirements.

Design Changes During the Procurement Process

There should be no informal communications with suppliers or contractors that result in design changes without appropriate documentation. The MM must be fully aware of his or her responsibility to keep the design requirements and QA requirements imposed on suppliers and contractors well defined and documented throughout the contract documents. All design changes and nonconformance report approvals must be well documented and communicated systematically to suppliers and subcontractors. The system should involve formal purchase order revisions to the supplier and contractor that emanate from a formal communication channel that will, at any time, provide complete factual data on design configuration changes and commitments. In short, the city's procurement system must be designed to ensure that the city as the owner defines the acceptance of any product or service in a controlled quality process.

Key Construction Management Issues

Let us look at the role of the city construction management organization. Its purpose is to provide a close, coordinated overview of the architect/engineer's or construction manager/general contractor's field engineering organization and participate in the review of key construction documents prior to release. Such a review permits the construction group to oversee the field's approach to constructability, lift sizes, piping piece configurations, field weld locations, sequencing of work, and so forth. As an adjunct to this design review by construction engineering, it is important that the owner's construction management organization ensures that appropriate time is allowed within the schedule to permit construction engineering to perform construction planning activities.

The owner's CM should assure that the architect/engineer prepares work packages, performs material take-offs for each work package, and thoroughly coordinates with quality engineering the inspections that will be performed consistent with the sequencing of the work. Such a review will permit adequate processing of last-minute field design changes prior to the assignment of work to the craft superintendents.

A program must be in place to ensure that construction engineering checks inventories and make allowances for missing equipment or materials that will require stub-outs, block-outs, and so on. All provisions for special hold points imposed by state or federal inspectors or the design agency must be clearly coordinated and provided for by construction engineers and quality engineers as a part of the work package planning review. The owner's construction management organization must establish control mechanisms for ensuring that all construction management activities are carried out on a quality basis at the job site.

Key Quality Assurance Issues

The city's QA organization should provide top-level quality engineers in each discipline—mechanical, electrical, civil and so forth—

who are totally accountable for all activities related to that discipline. The owner's organization should provide lead quality engineers who are fully accountable for their discipline, the subcontractors' QA programs, and all quality engineering review of designs related to that discipline. They should also be accountable for all quality engineering planning input to be provided to construction. In this organizational arrangement the quality engineer must be fully accountable for what gets inspected, including the degree or frequency of inspection, and must provide all clarifications to inspectors on matters of interpretation.

Nonconformances

Control of nonconforming work is an important element of the QA program. The nonconforming control system is one of the most important procedures for achieving a quality facility from start to finish. Routinely, deficiencies resulting from human error or design anomalies result in procurement or project deficiencies. Regardless of whether these nonconformances are large or small, it is important that the design engineers be knowledgeable of the occurrence and that they participate in the ultimate disposition of each nonconformance.

To accomplish this review, the project may have a material review board that has the responsibility for dispositioning the hundreds or perhaps thousands of nonconformances that will occur at the supplier's plant, at the job site, or during the final start-up of the facility. The board is usually comprised of representatives from the city's engineering, procurement and contracts, construction, and QA groups and their counterparts within the lead contracted firms. They must disposition all items as "accept," "reject," "repair," or "rework." Such a system permits the owner to monitor the nonconformance control system, which provides assurance that all defects occurring during the procurement and rebuilding effort are formally reviewed for their technical impacts on the project.

In summary, then, we see that the owner's QA oversight and control is best accomplished with experienced, seasoned, multidisciplined quality engineers in a key role related to the oversight of all major urban renewal projects.

QA Records

ISO 9000 clearly points out the need to maintain important QA records that provide objective evidence that the project is being completed in accordance with the design requirements. Although this is a broad, generalized statement, ISO 9000 has significant requirements related to records management, and an owner has a vested interest in ensuring that, upon project completion, the city is left with those important records providing evidence that requirements have been met. In today's world of increased regulation, prime consideration should be given to such issues that have significant records requirements, such as environmental assessments related to site characterization, concrete sampling and testing, structural steel placement, bolting, welding, mechanical equipment installation, electrical cable runs, and all necessary activities related to start-up testing and final project acceptance.

Considerable thought must be given prior to commencing any project as to the documents to be retained and the overall records management program. Further, all requirements related to project acceptance should be thoroughly discussed and defined in design specifications prior to commencing work. The records management plan should be defined early in the project and changed as necessary to ensure that the final records program meets all regulatory needs to ensure acceptance of the completed facility.

The Human Element

The human element of a QA program is very important. I have just described a QA program that many owners may be implementing on a project for the first time. It is one thing to introduce a QA program concept to a management team in the form of a manual but it is quite another to get all persons involved to really accept the concepts in the short term and fully execute them. This is the human element in QA that can be a difficult challenge to overcome. To illustrate this point, let's review the impact of a new QA program on the key managers involved: the EM, MM, and CM.

The design firm determines customer needs, develops the baseline design criteria and system descriptions, and ultimately, issues the approved job working drawings and specifications. On the one hand, field engineers can no longer make any technical decisions without design office–approved change notices. They must abandon the technical authority that they unilaterally assumed for years in the trade. All of the questions related to the design must revert back to the design office, often hundreds of miles away from the work site. The QA program mandates that the home office must be involved in all resolution of design changes and nonconformances, which will number in the thousands on a given job. This, of course, is a new way of life for the CM and his or her field technical team. Much of their previous authority has been removed. Also, at the design office it is a new way of life for the design engineers, who must remain assigned to the same design task, handling the technical issues until job completion. Problems may come back to haunt them for years. They may long to be assigned to a new and challenging assignment.

Let us now look at the material and procurement issues. The MM's team members were accustomed to looking at bids and picking the low bidder based on the fact that he or she had performed successfully in the past. Now they are saddled with an additional requirement: the same suppliers that they have dealt with for years must be prequalified to ensure that they have effective QA programs in place. This is a new way of life for procurement managers. Their work is now being hampered by QA requirements. They do not like the idea that purchase orders and contract documents must be approved by a QA professional to ensure that provisions are included for source inspector access, contractual language is adequate, a QA manual is provided for, owner approval is mandated, and myriad other important QA requirements have been met.

In summary, we see how QA can have a negative impact on key line managers—the EM, MM, and CM. There is a natural reluctance to embrace the QA program, since they can probably point to the good old days when facilities of all types were constructed successfully (even though there may have been significant cost and schedule overruns). There will be significant confrontations between the QA management team and their counterparts in engineering, procurement, and construction. The key point here is that these confrontations are healthy; a patient GMC will rationally support these new QA concepts with key managers. Without this singular top management support, the QA manager will be beating his or her head against the wall and the program will fail.

The first and most important task the QA manager faces is the need to rationally explain the QA program to the city manager and GMC. This should involve a full explanation of the entire program as defined in documentation such as ISO 9000 and should include discussion of its effective implementation and, most importantly, how it affects the business-as-usual approach to engineering, procurement, contracting, and construction. The city manager and GMC must be completely convinced of the value of this dramatic change. Without such support, an effective QA program will be significantly hindered.

The Value of a Formal QA Program
Litigation Avoidance
A well-run QA program can be a major contributor to litigation avoidance on completion of a project. If records exist that clearly show all design changes, all nonconformance reports, and all audit findings related to management systems as they were continuously

audited throughout the project, these records will help clarify many issues that can be the subject of litigation. If such records are in place, they represent a well-documented record of all these activities. Many potential disputes can be avoided by simply looking at the historical facts related to the project and arriving at settlements without going to court.

Scheduling Cost Improvement

Some of the nation's top development programs that have come within schedule and cost parameters can be attributed to effective use of a QA program promoted by strong project management that adopted the sophisticated techniques represented in programs such as ISO 9000. The integration of good design, good procurement management, good inspection, and good project controls will result in an improved revitalization program effort with cost overrun and schedule delays risks minimized.

Improved Safety

A good QA audit program ensures compliance with all procedures; for years many audit programs included observations of safety violations. Many corporations now are integrating safety and quality into a single organization. The latest Occupational Safety and Health Administration (OSHA) requirements discuss the importance of QA programs. OSHA is moving toward programs to ensure that companies formalize safety audits, similar to formalized quality audits. The end result will be that the audit process will effectively address both safety and quality. The two disciplines, both safety and QA, do go hand-in-hand in terms of oversight methods to ensure compliance with requirements.

An Overall Total Quality Effort

An effective owner-driven total quality effort ensures a win-win outcome for all stakeholders. The time has come for all of those involved with revitalizing our cities to realize that a quality assurance revolution is taking place. Sophisticated project managers representing the owner, the designer or architect/engineer, and the construction manager/general contractor recognize that all engineering and construction must be done in a formalized, controlled manner. They recognize that the concepts of QA as briefly addressed here are essential to bringing about a top-notch deliverable product. The industry has come to realize that activities such as design engineering, material management, purchasing, construction management, and training are all integral parts of the project quality program and significantly impact the overall quality of the revitalization effort. Sophisticated city managers who are responsible for overall urban programs now recognize that shortcuts in systems or approval requirements are no longer acceptable for the sake of schedule expediency. They have come to realize that, in the final analysis, the potential for completing a well-built project within cost and schedule requirements is best served through strict adherence to these quality systems.

History has taught us that, on many problem projects, the city starts with pride in its architect/engineer or construction manager/general contractor until the project gets in trouble. When problems become visible to the public at large, the city quickly adopts the position that the consultant or contractor was the key problem and created the project failures. The key to the success of any project is when the city has prime responsibility for the project such that any key problems of the architect/engineer or construction manager/general contractor are the *city's* problems.

Cities as owners must recognize that good consultants and contractors deserve to make a fair profit for good performance. Too often, owners lose sight of this fact and fail to provide proper executive support in defense of a decision to award contractors fair profits for such performance. Additionally, an owner who has genuine control over the project is totally knowledgeable of all of the technical ramifications involved in the design and construction of the facility and is then qualified to take over ownership and operation of the facility upon its completion.

I have attempted to address a few key elements of an overall total quality program related to an urban revitalization effort. There are many other factors that impact a program of urban development or revitalization (such as the project planning and controls function, adequate staff training, and a strong safety program), all of which are essential to the effective management of associated projects. I have tried to focus on the significant issues related to using QA on these types of imposing programs. For the big-ticket revitalization projects that will characterize a nation reconstructed, an old adage takes on even greater significance: "Quality is remembered long after price is forgotten."

Chapter 13

Deming and Juran and a Quality Strategy That Incorporates Their Philosophies

Eugene Danylyshyn

> *Quality is never an accident; it is always the result of an intelligent effort.*
>
> —John Ruskin, English scholar and critic

We do not have to go to the oldest cities in the United States or to the oldest buildings in the oldest neighborhoods in blighted areas, to find shoddy construction, shoddy products, and shoddy social/educational attitudes toward quality. "Cutting corners," "planned obsolescence," and "getting by" are in danger of becoming acceptable excuses for poor quality in areas where the demand for attention to the bottom line effectively supersedes the value of good management and fine work. In the inner city, where the cohesiveness of any revitalization effort is often fraught with problems of time and money, there is a real risk that short-term, short-lasting results will override the longer-lasting tenets of quality. The fear is that we will rebuild the physical and social structure of our cities only to see them crumble in our lifetimes thanks to our own ineptitude, negligence, lack of forethought, and desire to be done with this complex issue in the span of a few years.

A great deal of lip service has been given to the concept of quality. In terms of urban revitalization, it implies a form of management that embodies the best of hard and soft quality philosophies; the idea that quality can be defined in terms of systems and quantitatively measured results coupled with the understanding that those quality results are more than the sum of those systems and statistics. It encompasses not only the need to use the best and most appropriate methods to achieve desired results, but to motivate people to put those methods to use. J. M. Juran and W. Edwards Deming, leaders in the field of quality, spoke to these points.

Quality Management in the Inner City

As part of rebuilding the infrastructure of a blighted area, a special effort must be made to ensure that quality practices are employed during all phases of the program as time and budget constraints vie for attention. A system must be devised to allow for the repair of salvageable buildings and social programs and the construction of new structures.

A "planned community" must be put in place. It must encompass and blend with the systems already there to meet the needs of the community. Too often the high demand to meet particular goals (such as building new housing) and the dearth of city inspectors and auditors allows too many project and program administrators, working under contracts that fail to allow enough time for quality work, to produce substandard results.

Although there are sterling exceptions, many firms in this "rebuilding" industry cut corners as a means to remain competitive. Lower-quality or inappropriate materials are used because they are cheaper or perhaps more readily available. Concrete is poured in the hot sun and cures too fast, causing structural cracks. Nails are inadvertently driven through air conditioning hoses improperly installed behind drywalls, and the unit fails to cool. In the worst cases, seismic, wind, or other codes are not met, and a few years later the structure collapses during a natural disaster.

In today's world, where time is money, insurance policies have been substituted for quality workmanship. Consultants and contractors routinely purchase them to cover expenses incurred for repairs needed after the structures have been completed and the owners have taken possession. Granted, these policies are costly, but the cost is figured into the profit margins as a price of doing business. Builders that file bankruptcy leave the insurance companies to assume responsibility for monetary losses. Sometimes these same builders relocate and continue to do business under a new name. Meanwhile, the conscientious, dependable, reliable builders pay higher rates for their insurance coverage. This is then passed on to consumers. According to some experts, as much as half the cost of a structure is a result of various types of insurance the builder must pay to ensure its own survival.

Social programs often fare no better. Standards of success—measurable results—are lowered to make the program look more successful. Funds are spent on boondoggles. Policies are ignored and procedures forgotten. Accounting is sloppy. Waiting lists are long. And "empowerment" means just too much work carried out by too few people—people who make too little money, for the most part. Programs rely too heavily on volunteers, nonrecurring subsidies, and community support. Social programs deal with social challenges, and the end product is never a sure thing. Human success cannot be legislated; it can only be fostered. Good will has lost its place in our society today.

In an urban revitalization program, quality means more than good work; it includes proper management and oversight of what will be, in fact, a series of projects all being undertaken at once. This is where the marriage of J. M. Juran's and W. Edwards Deming's quality philosophies can play such a vital role. Together, these philosophies can create the synergy of a total quality program that offers not only quantifiable quality control but addresses the intangible issues of quality management.

J. M. Juran (left) and W. Edwards Deming (right) transformed Japan using quality principles and techniques. We can transform urban communities using the same practices.

J. M. Juran

J. M. Juran first published his *Quality Control Handbook* in 1951. Now in its fourth edition, it has since grown to more than 1500 pages (Juran and Gryna 1988). In comparison to Deming's early, detailed statistical quality control approach, Juran emphasized planning, organization, and systems to achieve quality in products and services. A quality management plan designed by Juran would emphasize quality control through evaluation, analysis, verification, survey, inspection, testing, measuring, and controlling processes and results, as well as through developing a well-qualified, appropriate quality management team. He believes in matricing project activities with quality (control) activities. He believes in overall quality management and in quality control throughout each phase of a project. In terms of a rebuild program in an area of urban blight, his quality management techniques would include those detailed as follows.

Project Quality Management. Develop and schedule quality activities against project tasks. Evaluate the costs of instituting quality efforts against the costs of possible defects. Control, standardize, and communicate instructions and procedures, documentation and records, and training, indoctrination, and certification. Manage nonconformances and corrective action. Define required quality evaluations.

Quality of Design. Check project/program documents for accuracy and completeness. Control and verify project/program design quality through reviews and tests. Address field-identified concerns (constructability or programmability). Evaluate the qualifications of the people who will undertake the work.

Quality of Procurement. There are three phases to this: precontract, contract, and postcontract activities. These may include pre-award surveys and approved vendor list development, specification and contract review for quality issues, prebid conferences, shop inspections (where physical infrastructure is involved), and inspection of materials received.

Quality of Construction/Implementation. Quality in this phase of a project includes controlling selected critical processes and monitoring overall efforts to produce quality results during the work process.

Quality of Operation. Quality control during the life of the facility or program involves much the same activities as those previously outlined. Ensure that equipment, materials, and/or resources are managed properly and that audit, inspection, and test schedules are adhered to. Review methods of operation to help ensure optimal use of the funding/budget for the facility or program. In addition, educational activities should be monitored for quality and relevance.

W. Edwards Deming

Initially, W. Edwards Deming held to a philosophy of statistical measurement to ensure quality. His efforts were directed toward time efficiency programs that could, in fact, be measured. However, eventually he realized that improving processes caused only so much improvement and that statistical analysis could not be applied to every situation. In fact, once quotas for efficiency were set, he found that employees tended to work to meet the quotas rather than focusing on producing quality goods or providing quality services within a reasonable time frame.

As a result, Deming developed the concept of what is now generally known in the industry as "soft" quality (as opposed to procedures, systems, and measurements, known as "hard" quality). Receiving little support in the United States for this paradigm shift toward quality management, Deming implemented this program in Japan. The results are obvious; Japan has moved from producing cheap, unreliable products to taking a leadership role in developing products of considerable quality and reliability at competitive costs. Today America scrambles to catch up.

If urban revitalization efforts are to succeed, they must incorporate Deming's soft quality concepts as well. These are spelled out in some detail as follows.

Create Constancy of Purpose for Improvement of Product and Service. Do not veer from a course of total quality. In terms of urban revitalization, do not propose a "band-aid" fix, but work with an eye toward solid and lasting improvement of the whole. Organizations involved in a program of urban upgrade must have consistent goals and purposes in both good times and bad. Obviously, an investment in ideas, programs, and technologies will not always have an immediate payoff in the short term, so an emphasis on long-term, reliable results must be sought. There must be quality in terms of the construction of buildings and infrastructure, the design of neighborhood areas, and the social opportunities made available for improvement of the total quality of life. Making this happen implies the use of best techniques, new innovations, and sound management.

Adopt a New Philosophy. Believe that total quality management will, in the long run, save money and positively effect change in the community. Believe in empowering people. Believe in root cause analysis.* Identify the problem, the cause, and what needs to be done. Develop remedial action tasks and long-term correction goals. Operate with the enthusiasm of a child and the wisdom of Methuselah. Believe in a program of management that rests on the concepts of quality.

Cease Dependence on Mass Inspection. One cannot completely eliminate inspections in production, execution, and revitalization. But don't "overinspect." Use measuring devices such as statistical control judiciously. Don't shy away from quantitative measurements, but make sure that interim results are not confused with end results. Recognize the importance of critical milestones in urban revitalization programs and measure their progress, not the progress of each and every task that affects the result. This would bog down the system. Use inspection or audit/survey techniques to get feedback on what has already occurred and evaluate the data against the process of continuous improvement and total quality management. Make them proactive tools for future tasks, rather than reactive tools for tasks that have been completed.

End the Practice of Awarding Business on the Price Tag Alone. Never confuse short-term low cost with that of long-term low cost. Work smarter; work with those who affect the bottom line upfront and honestly. In the long run it will save in the rework that results from procuring shoddy materials and services.

Improve Constantly and Forever the System of Production and Service. Improving on what has been learned will lead to increased productivity. Recognize that there is more to successful business than profit—that beyond profits are systems. Good systems will

---

*Editor's note: See Chapter 7 for more information on root cause analysis.

result in long-term profits in as little as three to five years in many instances of urban revitalization.

Institute Training. Training is a key tenet in sustaining quality performance. New technology requires new expertise; new ideas need dissemination, and they are seldom learned thoroughly through osmosis. Revere training in the community as part of the new attitude and show that reverence in the way that training programs are initiated. Training in the inner-city arena is the key to productivity improvement and sustained social, educational, and economic growth.

Institute Leadership. A couple of old adages are appropriate here: "You can't lead a horse to water;" "You'll draw more flies with honey than with vinegar." One leads well through good instruction, by providing a proper example, and by encouraging others (coaching them) to do their best. Leaders need to understand the job, the people, and the systems. Leaders need to build trust and offer help. Leaders need to do more than manage the work; they must be prime motivators toward whatever goals have been set. For that reason, it is important that they set quality goals. Most importantly, leaders must train others to take their places if the revitalization effort, which will take years, is to continue its momentum.

Drive Out Fear. Using negative motivation instills fear in most people. This type of motivation can be very counterproductive. Reinforcing positive action usually brings out the best in people. For example, if an employee or citizen makes an honest mistake and is allowed to "fail forward," improved services and products will be the result. If, instead, the employee has been taught to fear failure, he or she will not be open to new ideas and techniques and will likely attempt to hide all evidence of failure.

Break Down Barriers Between Staff Areas. Reach for consensus. Effective accomplishment of revitalization tasks requires performance by individuals working as a group or team. Competition or politics will drag the redevelopment program off course. On the other hand, innovative ideas, often conceived in group brainstorming activities, can shorten that course dramatically.

Eliminate Slogans, Exhortations, and Targets for the Workforce. These are all cheerleading exercises that belong in competitive sports. Do not mistake this for the kind of positive motivation that is created through employee recognition, training, and teamwork processes that enhance workflow and improve the working environment.

Eliminate Numerical Quotas. Developing too many numerical quotas in an urban revitalization program risks the loss of the total quality concept. Physical and social structures may be poorly designed or installed/implemented if the emphasis is on meeting quotas and not on quality. Work instead toward a goal of "doing the job right the first time." There can be little pride in sloppy work and less in poor workmanship, especially when that workmanship is a result of a need to make a quota at all costs.

Remove Barriers to Pride of Workmanship. Beware of providing the kind of incentives that lead to sacrificing quality for quantity. People like to be recognized for performing well. Their chests swell proudly from knowing that they have properly assembled a roof on somebody's house or that their programs are working. People have a right to be proud of their craft skills and should be able to enjoy considerable self-worth from doing their jobs well.

Institute a Vigorous Program of Education and Retraining. Everybody involved in urban revitalization needs to continuously update their knowledge and skills through educational programs or other training sessions. This will give them better tools with which to improve themselves as well as the products and services they provide. Education and retraining are often the most efficient ways to introduce workers to new techniques that can be applied to their jobs.

Take Action to Accomplish the Transformation. Recognize that quality management is underutilized in the United States today and that the nation underuses its vast natural and human resources. America has great potential and can become greater through the leadership and empowerment of its workforce at every level of urban development. The result will be a cultural transformation that allows today's distressed neighborhoods to rejoin the ranks of the surrounding areas. That, in turn, will provide the means for achieving the objective of being world-class cities that others will use as a benchmark.

A Total Quality Management Plan for Urban Development

This is a brief overview of a total quality strategy for use in an urban revitalization program. It is designed to be cohesive but flexible; it is meant to guide and not to limit. It provides the framework upon which to develop a specific quality program for use on a particular revitalization program. It is divided into 10 categories.

1. Organization and responsibilities
2. Training
3. Communication
4. Alignment
5. Total quality measurement
6. Total community involvement
7. Positive reinforcement
8. Citizen review process
9. Total quality status update
10. Total quality plan update

These categories are described in more detail as follows. Additionally, Figure 13.1 shows the primary roles and relationships among the major players in an urban revitalization program and briefly outlines their responsibilities during the first 100 days of program implementation.

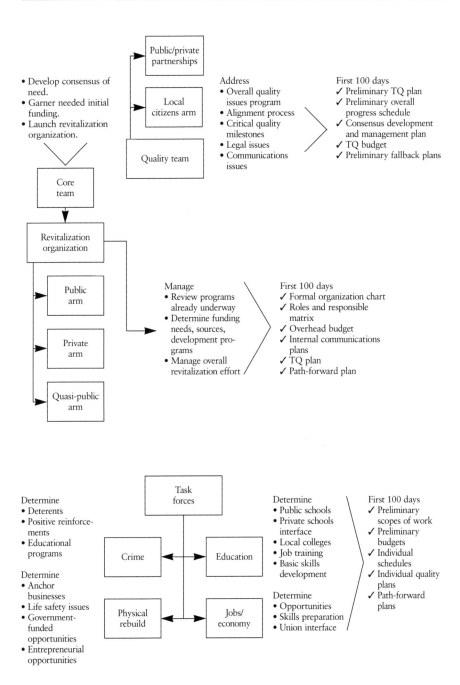

Figure 13.1. Urban revitalization program: Organization, roles, and initial responsibilities.

Organization and Responsibilities

City team members are responsible for the application of total quality (TQ) concepts in their daily work. Personnel are expected to review and suggest ways to improve their own processes. They should observe and identify opportunities for improvements in related areas and may be called upon to participate in process improvement teams.

The *city manager* is responsible for focusing the implementation process on the achievement of city goals and for providing the resources for implementation.

The *TQ steering committee* is composed of a mix of city management and department personnel. Members are responsible for providing leadership and guidance to the TQ effort by developing the strategy for all aspects of TQ implementation. They solicit and evaluate improvement opportunities, select those key processes that support the city's goals and help meet citizen requirements, charter teams, select team members, provide coaching and resources, authorize training, evaluate and support implementation of team recommendations, and provide recognition. It is their responsibility to foster the TQ culture in the city by creating an environment that supports innovation, teams, and trust, and by performing their tasks in a manner consistent with the principles of TQ.

The *TQ coordinator* is the focal point for TQ and work process improvement training, facilitating the city's TQ steering committee and guiding work process improvement teams. The coordinator facilitates the alignment process and provides coordination among city departments. The responsibilities of the TQ coordinator include management of a suggestion box program and communication of TQ information throughout the city via appropriate media.

The *quality assurance manager* is an external advisor to the city manager, the TQ coordinator, the steering committee, and work process improvement teams on the measurement of city quality performance.

The *department managers* are responsible for communicating this plan to their groups and fostering active participation in the TQ process.

Work process improvement teams are multidepartmental teams, including citizen representation (wherever appropriate), that focus their attention on key improvement opportunities. It is the team members' responsibility to learn and apply relevant structure to their task. They must be trained in basic work process improvement steps and other tools, as required. Periodic feedback to the steering committee on progress is also a team responsibility. Recommendations are made to the steering committee for review and implementation.

Training

To maximize the benefits of TQ, all city team members should participate in some form of TQ training. Of primary importance are the leadership skills necessary to facilitate the TQ process and the implementation skills required to apply TQ principles and tools. In particular, every work process improvement team members should receive just-in-time training on the TQ processes and tools that are relevant to their specific tasks. All other city personnel should receive orientation in TQ principles and exposure to the basic concepts and tools. This orientation will help them apply the concepts and disciplined approach to their daily work.

Communication

Communication is an integral part of the TQ process. It is critical to the success of the overall implementation plan to keep the city team informed of progress on strategic processes. Various communication methods can be used, including the discussion of TQ topics at meetings, periodic all-hands meetings, lunchtime forums, TQ bulletin board announcements, recognition coffeebreaks, and face-to-face communication among those contributing suggestions and the steering committee contact person.

Alignment

The city must conduct one or more alignment sessions with its citizens. The focus of the alignment sessions should be agreement on the following items.

- Purpose/vision
- Goals and measurements
- Clarified roles and responsibilities
- Corrective action plan
- Reinforcement plan

Out of these alignment sessions should come a formal city total quality plan, including a budget and schedule.

TQ Measurement

The TQ Steering Committee and/or the individual work process improvement teams must have the responsibility and authority for developing a specific set of measures for each area. Goals measurement should answer the following questions.

- Have goals been set?
- How will each goal be measured/quantified?
- Who is responsible for tracking the measurement?
- Who is responsible for updating the measurements?
- Who is responsible for displaying the measurements?
- Who will administer positive reinforcement (rewards and recognition) when a goal is attained?
- At what frequency (for example, daily, weekly, or monthly) will positive reinforcement be applied?
- What level/types of awards will be given?

Total Involvement

The involvement of every city team member in the process of continuous improvement should be facilitated through implementation of several programs. These may include the following:

- Work process improvement teams
- Quick action teams
- Problem-solving teams
- Value awareness (suggestion system)

Rewarding employees at all levels is a vital component of a successful TQ culture. Rewards are both extrinsic (recognition or awards) and intrinsic (responsibility for outcomes or the opportunity to give input). Recognition and awards are tailored to reinforce appropriate behaviors. It should be noted that the opportunity to give input and seeing one's ideas put into practice are powerful motivators. Participating on teams to improve processes and having more control or the say-so in how the work gets done reduces frustration and provides valuable intrinsic rewards. External recognition might include the following:

- Participant recognition at city team meetings
- Certificates of recognition
- Reception/coffee with the city mayor
- Letter of appreciation from the city mayor

Citizen Review Process

Reviews must be held with the local citizens to keep them apprised of the progress of social and structural programs. The frequency, timing, and responsibility for this review should be established after the goals measurements have been determined.

TQ Status Update

The city manager must receive periodic updates of the activity and progress of TQ activities. Specific subject matter will vary but should include the city's level of TQ activity, such as process improvement team progression, suggestion systems, and any special activities planned or conducted.

TQ Plan Update

The material in this plan will need updating as the city changes. Every effort must be made to ensure consensus about these changes, to get them in writing, and to communicate them to all TQ personnel and to those with whom they interface, as appropriate.

Chapter 14

Getting Started and Getting Results

Roger D. Hart

> *Discontent is the first step in the progress of a man or nation.*
>
> —Oscar Wilde, *A Woman of No Importance*

With the best vision and plan and using the right techniques, there is still one important component missing. It is that of ensuring that urban revitalization gets real and quantifiable results. To be able to measure results, and to be reasonably sure that those results represent a total quality (TQ) effort, measures must be developed early in the program. In a program of urban reform, cost control is one of the critical measures of success. Failure to control costs leads to cutting back or cutting corners, both of which adversely affect quality. Alternatively, failure to control costs leads to cost overruns. Depending on the nature of the city's contracts, reimbursable or lump sum (and the size of the city's legal staff), either the city, the contractor, or consultant is sure to lose. For these reasons and others, I have focused on quality costs as a critical measurable factor in the urban revitalization process.

Getting Started

The primary reason for instituting TQ is to ensure that all the tasks of large, diverse, and unwieldy urban programs operate in lockstep—that the interrelated activities are well coordinated and the work is orchestrated for optimum results. While much of this chapter focuses on the means to set up a program to measure costs using quality techniques, it is important to remember that other activities are equally important for cost control. Some of the more critical efforts that affect the outcome of any urban revitalization program include the following.

- *Prepare a budget and forecast.* This is a priority for the first 100 days of program mobilization. It should include the award of any state or federal grants.
- *Prepare collaborative agreements.* Formalize public/private partnering on behalf of the urban community. This task will

There is no single logical progression in getting started, but there is real work to be done.

result in the formation of a formal urban revitalization entity and will include all necessary supporting documentation. The purpose of this entity is to act as an industrial resource for the citizens of the urban community.

- *Develop a TQ program.* This task will include the development and training of all quality-effecting personnel involved in this revitalization effort.*
- *Provide assessments/benchmarks from other organizations.* This should include, but not necessarily be limited to, other cities, similar organizations, and world-class benchmarks. This should also include identifying problems and opportunities and reporting them in a timely manner.
- *Provide appropriate support in Washington, D.C.* This should include efforts agreed to by a city manager to assist the process at the federal level and maintaining the support of congressional or other government representatives.
- *Develop master planning tasks.* These tasks should include holding alignment sessions, providing a mission and vision, and developing a framework for a master plan design for the overall urban revitalization program.
- *Let master plan contracts.* This includes necessary master planner experts in appropriate construction, social services, and education fields to ensure completion of the master plan.
- *Prepare phased scopes of work.* Provide a transition plan for full use of economic, social, and infrastructure revitalization plans within the overall revitalization program.
- *Keep a virtual database.* Have a videotaped work product that is available for viewing by officials in Washington, D.C., state officials, and the citizens of the urban community.

---

*Editor's note: See Chapter 13 for details on developing a TQ strategy.

- *Final packaging.* As part of the public/private partnership concept, help the urban community obtain the necessary funding to complete a comprehensive revitalization plan.

As one gets into the specifics of the latter phases, thousands of interrelated tasks occur from within community interest groups, schools, colleges, and public housing, and to the urban infrastructure, that will impinge on each other and affect the overall plan of the revitalization process. It is important that these be identified and tracked.*

Quality Techniques

Fifty years ago, ensuring quality meant inspecting finished products and judging productivity based on time and motion studies and quota reports. Today, ensuring quality is the means by which we encourage a certain level of excellence through *direct quality participation* in the processes that affect that excellence. Because of its complexity and multiple-project nature, urban revitalization programs are prime candidates for the infusion of quality techniques. They can be employed at all operational levels to positively impact schedule, budget, and the degree of excellence required to consider every part, and the program as a whole, successful.

No single quality model can be developed to meet the needs of all urban renewal programs, because the programs themselves are so diverse. However, a number of quality-effecting principles and techniques have been commonly employed as distressed neighborhoods have turned themselves around. Urban planners and municipal governments can help to make quality an integral part of their efforts by incorporating and/or customizing, as appropriate, the quality activities listed as follows. Once an attitude of quality is embodied in the program and its integral parts, it is anticipated

---

*Editor's note: For a brief overview of a representative phased urban revitalization program, see the Appendix.

that those involved in the revitalization process will add others to fit their needs.

Quality at the Individual Project or Program Level

Table 14.1 lists quality-effecting techniques for both physical rebuild projects and social programs, as the two go hand-in-hand in any revitalization process. Although corollaries cannot be matched across the board, many of the techniques that have been employed in more traditional construction projects are equally applicable to the development, implementation, and maintenance of far-flung, highly diverse social programs such as those associated with education, welfare, crime prevention, and health care. Not only do these various social programs often overlap (such as the need to care for children who come to school hungry), but they often interface with physical urban development or redevelopment (children need to go to clean, safe, up-to-date schools).

Quality, embedded in both physical and social revitalization activities, will help to minimize friction and strengthen the bonds between the two as the inevitable tradeoffs are negotiated. Ask the question, How can we achieve excellence in this project/program with the time and resources available?, rather than wondering if we can better please the individual client or society on the whole by saving a few bucks. This does not imply that using alternative materials, techniques, and approaches is not permissible in a quality setting. Instead, it implies that substandard materials, shoddy techniques, and superficial approaches to solving problems are not acceptable to those who embrace quality as the keystone in their revitalization programs.

Quality at the Overall Program Level

If quality is the key to managing individual projects and programs, it is the framework upon which the entire program—the integration of all of these projects and programs—should be instituted.

Table 14.1. Quality-effecting activities.

Physical Rebuild	Social Program
Leadership	**Leadership**
Minimize project politics by choosing apolitical leaders, directors, or managers.	Same.
Ensure that quality personnel are experts in their field.	Same.
Expect quality results; accept nothing less.	Same.
Data and analysis	**Data and analysis**
Check engineering calculations at critical junctures.	Check the pulse of the program at critical junctures.
Collect objective data; perform analysis based on a strategic quality plan.	Evaluate statistical data on the community based on the linkage to a strategic quality plan.
Strategic quality planning	**Strategic quality planning**
Develop a formal quality policy and institute procedures.	Same.
Ensure that critical activities are scheduled; monitor tasks that affect those activities.	Ensure that critical aspects of the program receive appropriate attention.
Where practical, put quality activities on the schedule.	Same.
Develop formal protocols for dealing with schedule slippages.	Same.
Human resource management and development	**Human resource management and development**
Develop an attitude toward quality by placing emphasis and recognition/reward on pride of workmanship.	Same.
Work to create an atmosphere of partnership; work tenaciously to avoid adversarial relationships.	Same.

Table 14.1. *continued.*

Provide open and appropriate lines of communication.	Same.
Educate those not knowledgeable of practices but who will influence the project.	Educate the community as to the nature and goals of the program.
Give quality team members real authority to act.	Same.
Train workers to become better able to complete their work.	Same.
Managing process quality	**Managing process quality**
Work with experts who have done the job before (and well).	Same.
Conduct independent assessments, audits, and tests.	Same.
Provide written policies and procedures on work processes; monitor adherence.	Same.
Document all work processes in a formal manner.	Same—but beware letting the paperwork overtake the program.
Perform constructability reviews; invite construction leads to take part.	Perform periodic reality checks—social programs tend to get bogged down in theory or minutiae.
Review bid packages before they go out to ensure optimal construction staffing and scheduling.	Review funding requests before sending them to ensure the optimal spread of possible resources.
Prequalify vendors and contractors; do the homework up front.	Same.
Insist that company inspectors have unlimited access (within the bounds of safety and taking into consideration the nuisance factor) to vendor shop floors.	Employ "management by walking around," especially if the program operates at more than one site.
Approach local labor from a partnership point of view.	Not applicable—labor climate is seldom a concern in social programs.

Table 14.1. *continued.*

Monitor safety practices—they will be an indication of pride of workmanship.	Monitor morale—it will be a good indicator of program success.
Write airtight contracts that spell out the scope of work and schedule in detail, as well as the payment guidelines.	Employ some sort of structured social contract with program recipients to ensure that they understand program goals and rewards as well as the consequences of their actions.
Review construction planning tasks against such things as critical activities, crew densities, and material and equipment availability.	Review tasks against budget, resources, and an accountability index.
Ensure that contractors have formal, practical quality programs in place that complement the overall project's quality program.	Ensure that partnerships with other social programs enhance program goals.
Review engineering done in the field before it's implemented.	Critique pilot programs before proceeding to full-scale efforts.
Ensure that change orders are negotiated by personnel who understand the design or construction process (as appropriate); document negotiations.	Ensure that needed changes are not instituted superficially; document everything.
Communicate change orders quickly and efficiently; document the same.	Communicate program changes quickly and efficiently; document the same.
Quality results	**Quality results**
Establish a baseline budget; ensure that changes are reflected in it as the project progresses.	Establish a baseline budget; monitor adherence to it.
Ensure that the budget is reasonable—you get what you pay for.	Ensure that the budget is workable—nonprofit does not necessarily mean things cost any less.
Trend measurable quality results for adverse effects.	Survey community to establish and evaluate quality trends measured over time.

Table 14.1. *continued.*

Customer focus and satisfaction	Customer focus and satisfaction
Focus on the customer and the customer's customer.	Focus on program recipients.
Develop systems to measure internal and external client satisfaction.	Develop systems to measure participant and citizen satisfaction as well as to effectively address inter- and intradepartmental needs.

The complexity of the urban revitalization program can make or break the bank, the local political powerhouse, and the will of the citizens to strive toward excellence. Again, if decisions are made based on quality (rather than politics or budget), then discussions can focus on the degree of excellence required to sustain any particular project within the overall program and to sustain the program itself. If formal (even better, quantifiable) agreement can be reached on these issues, and if the leadership is in place, either through the city or a hired program manager, then the process of revitalization can move forward. While many of the quality activities listed in Table 14.1 are applicable to the overall management of the renewal effort, there are a few quality issues that are particularly crucial to the success of revitalization. They include the following:

- Overcome political partisanship through the use of cross-functional teams and quality champions. Develop horizontal teams crossing over multiple organizations for important, broad-based issues (such as reducing drug trafficking). Develop vertically integrated teams to solve critical specific issues (such as the need for a distance learning center).*

---

*Editor's note: See Chapter 7 for details of these methods.

- Ensure that communications are open and that people are informed. Develop a public relations program to report positive progress; beat the media in reporting setbacks. It will allow you to tell the story in your own way and will give you an aura of respect you would not otherwise have.
- Strive for community consensus. This is difficult because it involves the democratic process, which works slowly. Ensure that the city council, or whoever represents the citizens, is in a position to operate for the good of the entire community and not just the good of selected constituents.
- Ensure that someone uses a formal methodology to maintain all records. The system must be kept up-to-date by someone who cares.
- Work to ensure that the vision is not lost over time and with personnel changes.
- Design a flowchart to identify project and program interfaces. Develop a list of critical interface activities.
- Assign a small task force to research and evaluate new ideas and technologies for use in the revitalization program.
- Determine the significant few program activities that are critical to the overall success of the revitalization effort. Concentrate on applying quality techniques to these, as it will be impossible, at this level of detail, to apply them to the whole.

Theory of Obtaining Measurable Results

As stated previously, if the reconstruction of our cities is to make significant progress using quality techniques, those cities must have in place a distinct method to practically measure the effect of applying those techniques. Traditional quality measurement tools can provide an effective means of improving performance on many urban projects. This chapter attempts to demonstrate the methodology of improving performance on this type of program. The methodology includes the following stages.

- Identifying practical opportunities
- Analyzing quality costs for the opportunity
- Defining responsibility
- Remeasuring the process to set new goals
- Continuing improvement of the significant few

Urban development projects and programs require a unique application of quality measurement tools because they include efforts to both rebuild the community and to mend its social fabric. Nevertheless, a standard industrial process of quality measurement will work for both types of revitalization efforts. This process includes the identification of workflow items from project or program conception, design or model criteria definition, design output or model development, procurement, project construction/installation/erection or program implementation, facility start-up or pilot program start, and operation, including maintenance. Quality performance improvement methods need to address this type of industrial process.

Certainly, there are various ways of preventing or minimizing quality concerns or problems other than a formal TQ program. Many communities across the nation have attempted to provide numerous methodologies, most of them based primarily on a "wealth of experience." It is known, for example, that it is more effective to provide vendor surveillance at a city supplier's facility than to wait until the material or component arrives at the revitalization project site. It is known that, generally speaking, it is more effective to provide for city inspection in-process than to wait until the facility has been completed. It is known that social programs that start small and expand carefully generally work better than programs that attempt to address too many needs at once. Because of this general knowledge, some people question whether there is any real need to develop a formal TQ program at all.

The question as to how extensive the TQ efforts should be can become quite difficult to answer. In most cities undergoing development or renovation today, it is answered by experience, trial and error, and intuition based on education and experience and collective intelligence. But in order to systematically address the question in terms of the use of early quality tools, one has to understand the functional relationships among urban workflow activities.

In the hopes of finding any functional interrelationships among the vast assortment of potential concerns and solutions surrounding even the simplest project, one has to compare items to a common base or a common unit of measure. As mentioned, it is recommended that costs in dollars be used as the unit of measure in urban revitalization programs. This focus on the base unit is the most appropriate, given the present state of quality measurements. With this in mind, quality cost analysis is the method described here to effectively address these functional relationships.

Quality Cost Analysis and Its Use

Quality cost analysis is a method whereby one can systematically analyze a quality attribute in order to determine the most effective application of prevention and appraisal techniques. There are many detailed texts on quality cost analysis and the cost of quality. I have not attempted here to explain the theory of quality cost analysis, but to explain its application to urban projects. In the market today, many excellent texts on the subject are available (Juran and Gryna 1988).

In theory, a quality cost analysis is based on the improvement of a particular quality attribute in one independent, isolated case. However, the urban revitalization process contains workflow items that are interdependent and influence other workflow items for the same project. The objective here is to present a method whereby this may be accomplished. Again, in order to accomplish this, one must understand the fundamentals.

As in so many other processes, there is a complex interactive set of probability density functions and a method to measure the interaction in only one set in isolation (quality cost analysis or cost of quality). But as mentioned, even the simplest of urban projects are complex tasks that cannot afford to be put on hold while significant statistical data are assessed. It is necessary to have a way of studying multiple interactions and to make corrections quickly and effectively.

The technique known as *design of experiments* (Hicks 1982) is used to study multiple interactions. A two-by-two or three-by-three experiment is easy to perform, but as the experiment events are increased it becomes increasingly more difficult to execute and is exponential in nature. However, it has been generally agreed in urban redevelopment that there are usually a significant few quality concerns versus the trivial many; in other words, perhaps 20 percent of the items important to quality have an 80 percent effect on quality. If it is assumed that a handful of quality items executed early on in an urban project are really important, one can indeed set up a designed experiment using, for example, a five-by-five matrix.

The Practical Process

This section provides a practical approach to the process of using costs and the costs-of-quality method to measure the results of urban revitalization efforts. This process is as follows:

- At the very early stages of an urban revitalization project, define each work order and task breakdown clearly and distinctly. There may be as many as 200 or more of these tasks from the beginning stages of the project to completion.

- Before one proceeds, one must have an objective third party provide a clear cost estimate of each of the 200 or so tasks carefully and without bias.

- The next step is to carefully select an accounting system that is able to honestly account for the prevention, detection, and failure costs segregated to each task. This step is usually the hardest, because most accounting systems tend to "bury" these quality costs.

- At this point, use the concept of Pareto analysis to clearly identify the significant few tasks that will make or break the revitalization program. In the case of 200 tasks, there may only be 8 to 10 tasks that, if quality efforts were concentrated, would prevent 80 percent of the potential problems.
- After selecting the significant few tasks, concentrate quality improvement techniques there (for example, audits, training, rewards/recognition, process control, and partnering).
- At this point, work the project, collect all costs including quality costs, and watch the results. They will likely be staggering. Do not be surprised if there is an immediate 25 percent to 30 percent improvement.
- After the project is completed and costs have been collected and accounted to each individual task, the results should show an astounding correlation of significantly reduced costs with each of the significant few tasks.

Figure 14.1 provides a sample matrix to use when developing a quality cost analysis.

Employing Unique Measurable Results

Earlier in this chapter, I mentioned quality cost analysis. Here I more carefully investigate its use in the urban revitalization process. In order to perform a quality cost analysis, one must develop and implement methods to identify and quantify quality-related costs. What are quality-related costs? Do these include inspection, checking and calculations, costs for quality planning the urban project, or accounting for the quality costs? The answer is clearly "All of the above."

There are many direct and indirect quality costs. To fully understand the effect of any one quality action, all actions must be considered. Since the quality function has traditionally required reporting performance in rejection and nonconformance reports, and since this information is often difficult to interpret in terms of

Workflow item or task	Independent estimate	Total final costs	Prevention quality costs	Appraisal quality costs	Failure quality costs
Strategic plan					
Organization/ management					
Community needs					
Funding costs					
Mobilization					
Permits/fees					
Environmental/ clearing					
Design conception					
Detailed design					
Contracts/ procurement					
Construction					
Start-up					
Education and training					
Special needs					
Programs prototypes and adjustments					
Six-month operation					
One-year operation					
Operation and maintenance					
Communication to the community					
Totals					

Figure 14.1. Sample quality cost analysis form.

cost, opportunities for savings or real quality improvement are often overlooked. Successful project TQ management requires the use of sound financial quality planning and control. When quality failures are presented in financial terms, increased management attention and interest is generated. Unfortunately, it is normally too late for the completed urban project.

1. Failure costs, however caused, reduce profits; and quality control activities, as well as the appraisal of quality standards, cost money to operate.
2. Quality-related costs can be classified as prevention costs, appraisal costs, internal failure costs, and external failure costs. Investment in prevention and appraisal will substantially reduce internal and external failure costs and assist in maintaining client (in this case, the community) satisfaction.

These two factors are particularly relevant to urban revitalization programs. When expenditures are increased on prevention costs, the costs of failure fall. However, there is a point at which the total costs are at their lowest (optimally balanced). Conditions such as satisfaction, prestige, and safety can often make it more desirable to carry increased prevention costs.

Quality costs that are appropriate to an urban project should be identified and monitored. The classification of quality cost data should be relevant and consistent with the other accounting practices of the project so that direct comparisons can be made. Quality costs (direct and indirect) should be separately recorded within the accounting system such that they can be easily classified into the following categories.

- Prevention quality costs—quality planning, quality engineering, and training and education
- Appraisal quality costs—checking, inspection, and assessment
- Internal failure costs—failure to serve the public, repair of schools, or rework of city government

- External failure costs—electorate dissatisfaction, loss of regional market opportunity, or high facility repair and maintenance

By knowing where quality costs have been incurred, action can be taken to control and reduce them. This should be accomplished by focusing on using preventive quality techniques, applying effective appraisal techniques, and implementing programs to preclude the repetition of both internal and external failures. The financial report presented to the public should be an accurate, separate statement of the costs of failure and costs of operating quality measures. For control purposes, quality costs should be allocated to the accountable area, and appropriate account codes within the cost centers should be used. This known allocation of all quality costs is important to the analysis and prevention of failures. This should include both direct and indirect quality costs.

To have sufficient impact, the report can be presented in a style similar to other management cost accounts and supported by financial ratios and trend analyses related to the business of the company within the urban community. This should enable management to better understand the relevance of TQ and to allocate effective financial resources to it.

Quality costs may be collated and reported based on the quality data collected. If one is approaching the subject of quality cost analysis for the first time, the first step to consider is a pilot study. Choosing the project for this pilot study can be perplexing. Generally speaking, the following criteria should be employed when making this decision.

- Most importantly, the project for the pilot study should be one with a quick beginning and short time duration, as one needs to measure the results after project completion. Focusing on pieces of the project or project phases is not sufficient. To look at the whole or big picture, one must use a holistic approach to quality cost analysis.

- The project should contain particular work breakdown items that are relevant ways to make an impact on one's organization. This should be a strategic decision based on what is, indeed, important to one's business in the urban community.

- The project should contain particular work breakdown items that are easily quantified and measured. Some particular quality parameters in urban development projects are complex and sometimes hard to quantify. Try to avoid this obstacle in a pilot study. Remember that this can sometimes be difficult; however, all quality parameters can be quantified. (Be honest, pragmatic, and realistic.)

This first step in quality cost data collection for the pilot study is to determine the scope of work to be carried out. Initially, the work scope of the first quality cost data collection activity will be dictated by the work breakdown structure. Preliminary figures must be established from a small area or single project line to gain public approval and commitment to the TQ costing system. A list of categories and elements for operating quality costs must be included as the basis for development to meet the public's specification requirements.

During the pilot study, it is important that each possible quality cost source be covered by a fairly explicit and definitive element or work breakdown item. In many cases it does not always make sense to track all work breakdown item quality costs. Any good city manager can review the list of work breakdown items and know that many of them will have little, if any, impact on the quality of the urban development project. Therefore, the work breakdown items should be arranged in terms of importance to quality; the significant few that it appears would have a significant impact on quality should be selected. Using Pareto analysis to sort out the significant few versus the trivial many can help with this decision. When experience is gained with this quality cost system, it will be apparent where these definitive elements can be combined or eliminated.

When the list of quality cost elements has been identified, the collection of cost data can begin. The costs directly and indirectly attributable to the quality function must then be accumulated. These initial quality costs should be concerned primarily with prevention and appraisal. Next, the internal costs of budgeted failures should be identified and recorded. Then the internal quality cost of unbudgeted failures should be completed. In many cases, one may have to wait until this first pilot study project is complete to understand the true magnitude of the quality costs. In this manner, an efficient collection system can be established before a full-scale quality cost program is established.

After all costs have been collected, they should be tabulated to present a breakdown of quality costs by element. The report format will depend on the nature of the project and the level of management to which the information is presented.

Effect on Urban Change

Many decades have passed since World War II and the institution of modern quality concepts. Quality can seem quite elusive in the concept of urban change. How can quality be used to bring positive urban change and create project value? The answer lies in organizing quality into a logical flow pattern in two respects: the flow pattern of traditional urban projects, and the flow pattern of the quality discipline itself. When we effectively blend these two together, we create a step-by-step building block of the community and the quality discipline. We provide quality in urban change by

- Creating quality ideas
- Providing innovative quality policy
- Measuring quality in relation to cost and schedule criteria
- Exceeding public expectations
- Defining our work

- Establishing a traditional quality system that induces the traditional quality assurance elements of design control, document control, corrective action, assessments, or audits (which incidentally, are well defined in the ISO 9000 series standards)
- Motivating using TQ techniques
- Focusing satisfaction through partnerships
- Measuring the effects of quality programs

Part IV
Epilogue

Chapter 15

A Vision of the Cities That Can Be in 2010

Roger D. Hart

> *Go to the people*
> *Learn from them*
> *Love them*
> *Start with what they know*
> *Build on what they have.*
> *But of the best leaders*
> *When their task is accomplished*
> *Their work is done*
> *The people will remark*
> *"We have done it ourselves."*
>
> —Ancient Chinese poem

Where We Are and Where We Can Be

As clearly shown in Part I of this book, the United States faces serious challenges in the area of urban revitalization. The vicious cycle and concentration of poverty, social despair, and fiscal distress plagues too much of urban America today. It weakens our social,

Urban blight represents the worst this nation has to offer its citizens.

political, and economic health and undermines the ability of metropolitan regions to compete in a global community (Cisneros 1996). Solving the problems of urban decay has become mired in the reality of the enormity of the challenge. Public schools provide educational opportunities too disparate from one district to another. Federal, state, and local government structures are so fragmented by petty jealousies and vicious in-fighting that it is difficult to believe they will ever accomplish anything. Businesses strive for huge profits hiding behind a mask of global competitiveness while workers struggle to survive. At the most fundamental level, Adam Smith's tenet that man is basically good finds a tenuous foothold in today's society, and we mourn a past that discriminated against women, minorities, and children and saddled men with huge responsibilities and unrelenting expectations as the guardians of the larger whole, because, we thought, naiveté and acceptance bred contentment. The real problem today lies in waging war against the selfishness and stupidity of humankind that, thanks to untold technological advances, has spread beyond the boundaries of the geopolitical and sociocultural isolation of earlier decades.

Part II of this book sought to provide some of the knowledge and vision needed to promote urban revitalization. It is an admittedly eclectic response to the problems of urban decay with its focus on the importance of a democratic foundation, leadership support, and specific, grassroots safety, education, financial, and economic solutions. But it provides knowledge of what others have done or believe it is possible to do and, by giving specifics, shares insight into the tools used to effect change. The most important tool, evident throughout all of these chapters, is that of total quality (TQ) as embodied in quality champions, quality strategies, and a holistic approach to solution planning and execution. It is described as the framework on which to build a program to meet these disparate challenges, the glue that holds this program together, and the ideal, managed in real-life and real-time organizations and activities and really measured, toward which to strive in planning an urban revitalization program.

Part III dealt with specific quality techniques designed to serve the revitalization effort. It includes a detailed overview of specific means to ensure quality on urban projects and programs, emphasizing the responsibility of the city in designing and managing urban renewal and emphasizing the importance of a TQ management team on the city's payroll. In another chapter we attempt to provide, in outline form, a strategy for introducing quality into a program of urban revitalization based on the philosophies of J. M. Juran and W. Edwards Deming. And finally, after frequently touting the need throughout the book to provide well-documented quantitative and qualitative measures of program or process progress, we provide specifics on how to measure quality. The material in this section is geared to the physical rebuild of the nation, but much of it could be adapted easily to the development and implementation of quality social programs in the inner city.

Fortunately, we as a nation and we as individual citizens are aware of the problems of urban revitalization, some of us on a more conscious level than others. And the taint of sloth, indifference, and greed is not so great as to have indelibly stained the rich fabric of our culture. Our governments desire to operate reasonably and responsively. Our most prized institutions struggle toward excellence. And, most notably, the typical people on the street bind themselves to others to improve the lot of their neighbors. In fact, in the area of urban reform, we have seen greater success at the grassroots level than at the national level—perhaps because the challenges are more manageable there; perhaps because leadership is less threatened and so much less weary there; perhaps because we can appreciate the need to maintain our own backyards; perhaps because we can feel the plight of one neighbor while, thanks to the numbing effect of today's mass media, we can muster little empathy for the masses. Whatever the reason, *We the People* still believe that together we can plan our own destiny. We may not have all of the components quite right, but we believe that we can effect change.

Sir Isaac Newton said, "No great discovery was made without a bold guess." This book is our attempt to make that bold guess as it affects urban revitalization.

Key Forces, Major Themes, Objectives, and Strategies

We have touched on many of the forces, themes, objectives, and strategies related to urban revitalization, all of which have had and continue to have a significant effect on the well-being of our nation's cities. As Martin Luther King Jr. said, "We are caught in an inescapable network of mutuality, tied in a single garment of destiny." The result is a web of seemingly unstoppable "givens" that directly impact any TQ program of urban reform. These include trends in growth of the global population, the evolution of mores and values, the explosion of technology, and the changes our citizens will face in their everyday lives in the next millennium. Additionally, key forces will shape our nation and the future of our cities. These include the acceleration of change, the focus on the customer, the metamorphosis of our systems of education, the role of government and business, and our perception of the meaning of life itself. These trends and forces are outlined in the Figures 15.1 and 15.2.

Globalization
- U.S. population increasing more slowly; however, with a significant increase in diversity.
- World population continuing to explode, particularly in Third World countries.
- Urbanization continuing and increasing in the areas of intelligent-based processes and products. Referred to by some as a *third wave*.
- Asian countries continue to play a significant role in the world economy, politics, and business structures.

Values
- Information crime may become critical as information plays an increasingly vital role in both business and personal lives (cyberspace criminals).
- Global terrorism growth rate is expected to top 15 percent per year for the next 15 years.
- Manual workload will continue to decline; however, computer technology continues to expect more out of humans.
- Many generational issues will explode in areas such as the ability to use information technology.
- Social responsibility can create vision and high levels of commitment.
- Increasing disparity will be seen between the "haves" and the "have nots" on an economic scale.

We the People Will Also Change
- Many changes will occur in terms of demographics, workforce, religious/sexual/cultural diversity, declining relative wages, knowledgeable workers, telecommuting, microbusinesses, and virtual organization.

Technology
- Growth and use of the World Wide Web (part of the Internet) will continue at a rapid pace.
- Growth of security technology will explode.
- Practical development of technologies such as artificial intelligence or expert systems will continue at a rapid pace.

Figure 15.1. Key factors affecting our nation's cities and their revitalization efforts.

> **Acceleration of Change**
> - Technological automation, the ability to customize down to a lot size of one, and raw processing power will increase exponentially.
>
> **People Focused on the Customer**
> - With the ability to provide smarter markets, focusing on the person (or in the case of business, the customer) will play a key role.
>
> **In Search of Meaning**
> - With accelerated change and global uniqueness, humans will feel the need to search for meaning and wisdom in all our actions and roles in life.
>
> **Education**
> - On-line and long-distance learning will play important roles.
> - Higher education will be reorganized to play a more responsive role and to better respond to changing conditions.
>
> **Government and Business**
> - Government and business will reflect society and be smaller and more responsive to citizen needs.
> - Many factors such as electronic money, the environment, taxation, and the media will play a dominant role.
> - Global relationships will play a significant role, as well.

Figure 15.2. Trends shaping our nation's cities and their revitalization efforts.

A Look at the Future: Possible Scenarios

Every generation has faced an uncertain future. Our vision of 2010 is cloudy at best, with our crystal ball prophesying many different forms and permutations. Based on the forces at work in the world today, we can predict both optimistic and pessimistic results. ASQC's recently published Futures Project report outlines a few scenarios (ASQC 1996).

- Scenario 1: Global reality—By the year 2010, technology has created a prosperous economy around the world, including in the United States.

- Scenario 2: Hard times—In the year 2010, drug-plagued urban cities, functional illiteracy, and large, unemployed segments of the population confront affluent minorities behind gated communities in desperate and hopeless anger.
- Scenario 3: Dynamic tension—During the year 2010, technology is a "double-edged sword." Tension around the globe continues. The world's population of very poor decreases; however, the separation between the "have" and "have nots" widens dramatically. Few people can afford luxury products.
- Scenario 4: Quality dominates—By the year 2010, we as human beings have evolved into a higher order. Issues affecting our government, economy, urban cities, information technology, education, culture and quality have been addressed and attendant problems have been resolved.

A scene from the Waterworld theme park: Will our future be as depicted in the movies "Blade Runner" and "Waterworld"?

What will be the logical scenario in our "quest of the cities?" I tend to be optimistic, if cautiously so. Jonathan Swift once wrote, "There is nothing permanent except change." I believe that the crossroads of change are fast approaching. There are choices we have to make today in order to have Scenarios 1 and 4, and prevent Scenarios 2 and 3. Will our future be as in the movie "Blade Runner," or will we see the positive evolution of man? I believe that we will see one extreme or the other. Which do you believe it will be?

I Have a Dream: The Physical Future

I *do* have a dream.

I dream that I am driving in my automobile (which no longer uses polluting gasoline) that powers itself along networks of freeways that are designed to ease the flow at every critical point. An on-board navigational system provides additional safety assurance. I am driving with my family. The children are in the back seat "video talking" to their friends in the community we will soon visit. That community is no longer a city, but truly a "greenbelt" village community. It has safe playgrounds and campus-style schools with a diverse population. There are many nationalities and cultures of people working together in this community. There are many underground buildings, ensuring energy efficiency and allowing more public green space on the surface. The community's integrated urban design was developed to reduce crime, travel, and pollution.

I make a left-hand turn on an architecturally pleasing roadway past a power station that provides electricity from waste and gas from a landfill in the old quarries. The plant also uses information technology to reduce energy use and renewable energy from an appropriately sited reservoir. There are wildlife runways, housing schemes designed to deter street crime, and specially designed barrages to improve flood prevention. A mile or so down the street is the local social housing association designed to support the community's people in need. Everyone in the community assists and aids those in this housing complex. The population in this social housing has been decreasing because few are in need anymore. (See Figure 15.3.)

Quality social programs have at last been developed and implemented that provide appropriate safety nets without encouraging dependence on the welfare state. Much of this is attributable to the paradigm shifts in education and economic reform that have improved the lot of employers and employees, a result of embedding quality techniques into these programs. While competition is still seen as healthy, the concept of winning at all costs has been largely replaced with responsible free-market reform.

People have once again found the value of respecting others as well as themself, a philanthropic quirk that took root at the turn of the century. Ethics, civic duty, and inalienable rights have made a comeback. Humankind has learned that social well-being is directly linked to economic well-being and that, in a global community, this means that certain minimum standards must be maintained, even if at the cost of gross profits. Everyone, it is recognized, is *not* equal, but the inequalities are not so great as to cause the kind of general miasma that gripped so many in the previous millennium. All is not fair or sane or safe, but there is reason for hope.

My automobile passes over a rapid transit system that is integrated with other public transportation, has concrete sleepers to reduce energy use per mile, and whose tunnels leave the landscape undisturbed. I travel over a bypass specially designed to relieve traffic congestion in this key intersection. There is a bike path colored by special aggregates to identify it. Next to the bike path is a steep embankment that is unobtrusively reinforced with "Geotextile grass."

Most single-family homes now have insulating blocks to reduce energy and noise transmission and use reconstituted stone; plumbing fittings are designed to reduce water consumption, and all home utilities are run by a central home processing unit.

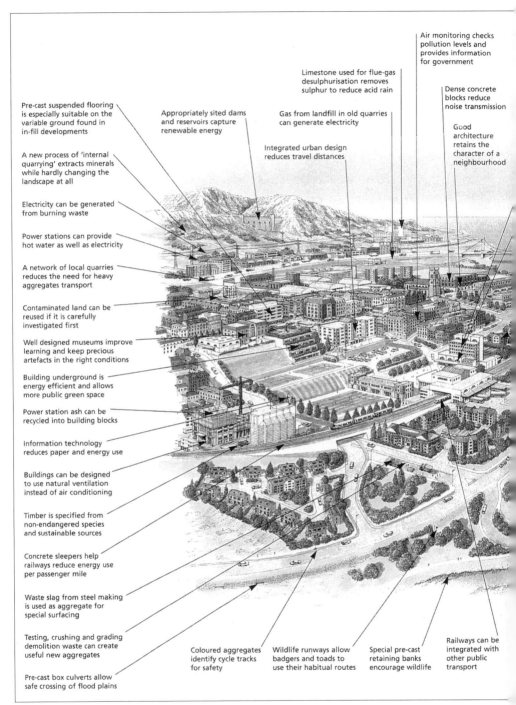

Source: "TARMAC in the Environment," reproduced by courtesy of TARMAC Professional Services Ltd.

Figure 15.3. What will our cities look like in the next century?

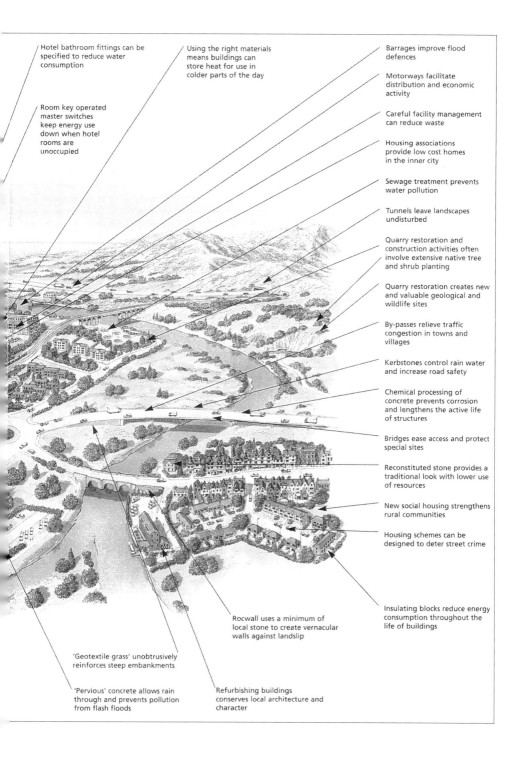

I park in my friends' driveway and we go into their home, where their children are watching multimedia vision (MV). A special is on tonight. It's the 2010 Academy Awards for Peace. This has become the most popular special show of the year on MV.

We the People's Future

"Future shock [is] the shattering stress and disorientation that we induce in individuals by subjecting them to too much change in too short a time," according to Alvin Toffler (1971, 104). The difficulties faced in the coming decade will tax our ability as humans to cope with massive change. That ability will be based on our understanding of where we are going. The authors of this book believe that the information provided here will help convince people that there are means and methods to cope with what the future will bring.

There is little disagreement that neighborhoods should be defined by more than geographic proximity or geopolitical boundaries, or

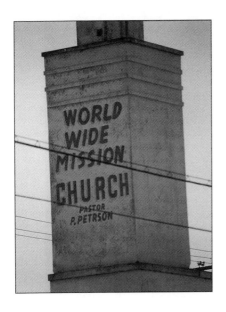

Can we return to the livable city?

even by traditional material wealth. The youth of today need strong values and sound role models, both human and organizational. This should start with a basic tolerance of each other and a firm commitment to the structure of the family. Human beings have to be morally, spiritually, and fundamentally happy and responsible as world citizens. It all begins with hope.

I believe that the concept of total quality described in this book allows one to proceed along this path. Revitalizing cities have to start with this firm foundation and end with the revival of the human spirit.

The Future Is in Your Hands

Isaiah 61:4 says, "And they shall build the old wastes, they shall raise up the former desolations, and they shall repair the waste cities the desolations of many generations." As bleak as some realities are, the Yankee belt, eastern corridor, eastern foundry, western foundry, midsouth, southern Appalachia, Florida, the Great Plains, western, mountain, north Pacific and Hispanic America all have pockets or wombs of modernization and models to restore the national economy to health. In summary, I would like to offer the key points the contributing authors made.

- Change priorities to get at the root cause of problems in lieu of using current "band-aid" methods.
- Continue the long American tradition and reputation of being, for the most part, an optimistic people.
- Work together toward the challenges of tomorrow.
- Do not waste the human capital of our urban communities.
- Provide the true equality and excellence of education that allows family support structures to work, and create a community as a village.
- Create vision to solve the many issues involved in urban revitalization.

- Create test beds of quality solutions.
- Rethink government roles through democratic and total quality techniques.
- Changing the pattern of urban decline will change the pattern of crime; deal with the underlying quality problems in order to fight crime.

"May our guardian angel, sweet companion, not abandon us . . . neither by day nor night." Faith abounds in the inner city.

- Solve municipal problems by pragmatically solving financial woes.
- Use technology and other methods to bring industry to the urban community.
- Use traditional quality management techniques to holistically execute urban revitalization programs.
- For success, depend on clear and measurable results.
- *We the People* have to understand ourselves and work together.
- Work for our future and our children's future.

> *"A great democracy must be progressive or it will soon cease to be a great democracy."*
>
> —Theodore Roosevelt

Appendix

An Example of a Holistic Total Quality Approach

Within the framework of this book, we have described many different aspects of a total quality solution to the critical revitalization of America's cities. Because of the comprehensiveness of this subject, its encompassing nature, and its many facets, it was sometimes difficult to keep our discussions from seeming too generic. We tended to describe the scope of work in broad quality terms (although not always) or to chop up the subject of urban revitalization into discussions of particular challenges. What was lacking—what we could not do in the format of the chapters—was to provide a time frame against which to develop and carry out the ideas. The reason, as we stated, was that the needs of each urban center are so diverse that those kinds of specifics are impossible. How long it takes one community to repair its schools and another to institute an innovative, quality education program depends on any number of interrelated variables too numerous to mention within the structure of this book. This difficulty is compounded by the fact that, in urban revitalization programs, we are dealing with people development and not necessarily with just physical infrastructure issues. Nevertheless, we believe that it is important to give the reader an appreciation of the symmetry of using an effective quality system in the urban revitalization process.

The following is an attempt to describe an integrated and holistic approach to urban revitalization using an effective total quality system by describing the way East St. Louis, Illinois, has proposed to further address its challenges. In the course of developing its proposal for designation as an Enterprise Community (EC) or Empowerment Zone, a new U.S. Department of Housing and Urban Development (HUD) initiative, city leaders proposed leveraging its achievements and natural resources through a unique approach to public/private partnerships, education, and total quality. Basically, they proposed to bring on board a private (nongovernmental) firm of experts in program management, placing them in an organization where they would operate in a not-for-profit* partnership with the city. They would not be just subcontractors. East St. Louis proposes to provide incentives for the new organization to operate in the best interests of the city. That is, if the organization helps the city increase its tax base faster than scheduled, it will reap cash benefits. It is a truly innovative idea in the public sector on such a large and comprehensive scale—a definite shift from the attitude of choosing the lowest bidder and operating in an adversarial relationship.

The mission of the public/private partnership will be to coordinate an integrated, commercially viable revitalization program for the city. It will implement policy determined by a board of directors made up of both partners as well as the community. The organization will give/receive direction to/from a project management office. It will likely have the following subentities.

- Development corporation
- Architectural/engineering and construction corporation

---

*Technically, a nonprofit organization makes no profit. These kinds of organizations are described as "public charities" with 501(c)(3) tax designations. Not-for-profit organizations, on the other hand, operate for the public good, but plow some of their funding back into their organizations for such purposes as leadership development. These are referred to as 501(c)(4) organizations.

- Education and training institution
- Operations and maintenance corporation
- Social and community foundation institution

Additionally, East St. Louis has proposed to institute HUD Secretary Henry Cisneros' "Campus of Learners," extending the campus well beyond the boundaries of public housing (as originally envisioned by HUD) by making it part of the campus (public housing is in close physical proximity to the campus). The thought is to improve the housing *and* the school. The catalyst of the effort will be the formation of a Quality Institute at this college. Programs at the Quality Institute will be focused on the specific needs of the community in terms of urban rebuilding and address both the physical rebuilding of the community and the redevelopment of the social fabric of the city.

The city has proposed to leverage its human capital assets in part by training large numbers of its citizens to do high-quality remediation work. Under its EC designation, leaders are trying to arrange with the federal government to receive contracts awarded sole source for nearby federal remediation projects. While they are still in process of meeting this goal, they have put in motion the idea of negotiating contracts from that standpoint. They are prepared to offer eager workers with experience in local remediation gained as part of the city's life safety remediation program. (This is described in greater detail later in this Appendix.)

Leaders in East St. Louis believe that this form of "public assistance" (much better than a handout), combined with the programs they already have in place, will move the community forward by providing jobs that are exportable (see Figure A.1). They believe that remediation efforts in other nearby communities—and across the nation—will continue long after this particular project is completed. They see a long-term future for their citizens in this arena.

Though it has not been formally placed in the revitalization schedule, East St. Louis is also actively pursuing the development of riverfront land between the Casino Queen and the downtown area.

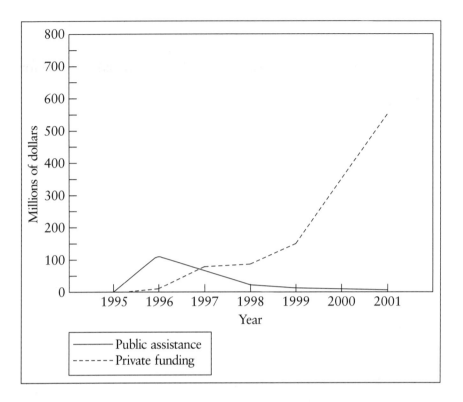

Figure A.1. Cities may be able to create an economic base through participation in a major federal infrastructure or remediation program. The key lies in being qualified to get a significant chunk of the work.

Although this has been under discussion for several years, a formal urban plan is expected to get underway by the end of 1996. The vision includes a hotel with an auditorium, a factory outlet mall, space for commercial recreation (probably an entertainment center with a musical orientation), a golf course, restaurants, and rental apartments. Recommendations include the improvement of the MetroLink East Riverfront light-rail line station and the extension of the National Expansion Memorial Park from the Missouri shore (where the Gateway Arch stands) to the Illinois side of the river. It is anticipated that this development will enhance the tourist trade garnered by the current riverboat casino and further improve the employment and revenue resources available to East St. Louis.

What follows is a brief discussion of East St. Louis's timeline for the next four years. Because the actual schedule lists by line item hundreds of tasks (see Figure A.2), we have chosen to condense them into a short overview by phase (see Figure A.3). For more detail, the reader will have to contact city officials. Keep in mind that East St. Louis's leaders believe this schedule can be met because they intend to put in place a formal total quality program that addresses the many issues of the innovative marriage of education and opportunity. All of the quality techniques, practices, and concepts discussed in this book will be evaluated and, where appropriate, incorporated into this program to best ensure its success. It will happen because the city and the program management firm will operate in concert, a team in which each member stands to profit by working toward mutually acceptable goals in a formally spelled-out program that they both agree is attainable, if aggressive, using the quality tools at hand.

The East St. Louis example may be too simple for application to another complex program or project. On the other hand, it may be too complicated for some more straightforward and smaller-scale revitalization efforts. It is recognized that many interactions and effects during a revitalization process can cause significant changes in philosophy and direction. Therefore, the description provided here and Figures A.2 and A.3 represent a snapshot of a living document.

Schedule Summary

In the first phase (the first 100 days), the city and a private consortium address physical emergencies and set in motion a community revitalization–based training program. The formation of a public/private corporation at the city government level occurs during the first phase. The second phase (first 12 months) extends infrastructure social revitalization activities through an aggressive integration

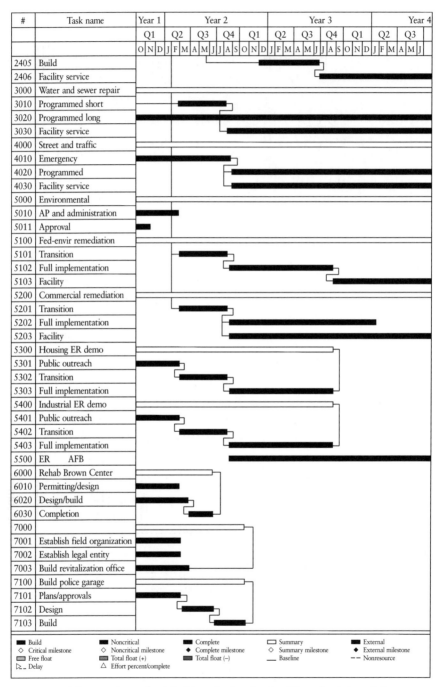

Figure A.2. This city has scheduled hundreds of tasks. The schedule, while aggressive, allows for quality interface at every level. This figure shows a portion of the detail schedule.

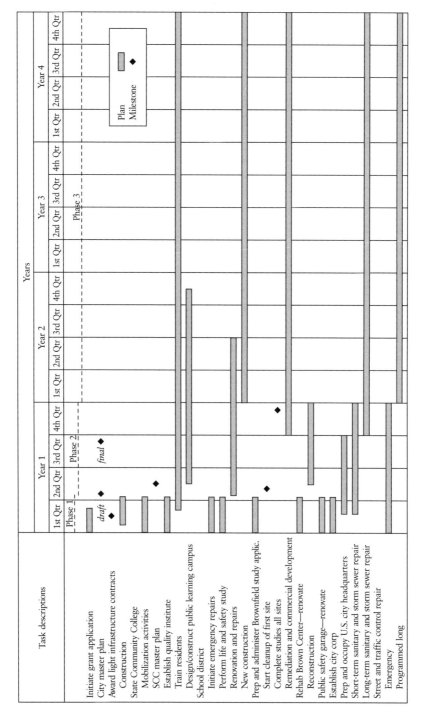

Figure A.3. First page of the roll-up summary schedule.

of a local community college,* public housing, and the surrounding communities at large. During this phase, a private consortium temporarily helps the public/private partnership establish a learning campus in the city. The consortium phases out as the partnership takes the reins. The third phase envisions the partnership managing the entire program. Late in that phase, that relationship, too, phases out as the city turns from salvaging itself to promoting its own growth and regeneration. This phase builds on training and opportunities created in the earlier phases.

Phase 1 (100 Days/Mobilization)

The purpose of this phase is to address the majority of emergency and life safety issues and provide the master plan process for establishing public housing campuses, transforming the community into a lifelong learning campus, and establishing the public/private partnership that can be used as a role model for other communities. Much of the Phase 1 effort is directly conducted by the private consortium.

Emergency Grant Application and Administration. The city prepares applications for HUD Block Grants, Educational Grants, Public Works Grants, Infrastructure Planning Grants, Title Grants, and FMHA Planning Grants. This role will be later filled by the public/private corporation.

Master Planning. A range of planning efforts are underway. The key is to develop a comprehensive plan that reflects the community's vision and focuses on commercial and private sector growth. Existing data are assembled and protocols are developed from which an integration of these activities will occur.

Emergency Light Infrastructure, Including Sewers. The city lets emergency contracts to local firms as part of its capital improvement program. These contracts primarily pertain to emergency sewer

---

*It does not have to be a community college, but this is the vehicle of choice for East St. Louis.

repairs related to washed-out mains, collapsed road beds, and combined sanitary and storm sewers.

Schools. The private consortium develops a Quality Institute at the local college. This institute will become the link between the college educational activities in the revitalization program and the management activities of the public/private corporation. Among the key education-focused projects, the Quality Institute addresses the conceptual designs of the Campus of Learners.

The local K–12 school district requires significant emergency repairs for most of its facilities. During this phase, some of the more severe repairs related to roofs, heating plants, hazardous materials, and bathroom facilities are undertaken on an emergency basis. In addition, a complete and comprehensive life and safety inspection and study is performed.

Environmental Remediation Activities. This project includes the preparation and associated administration of a Brownfield study application.

Formal Establishment of the Public/Private Partnership. A major effort is made to prepare for a large-scale revitalization beyond the 100-day effort. A public/private partnership is put in place and fully staffed within 45 days of contract approval. The partnership is expected to employ local personnel. An expected goal is to draw 65 percent of these people from within the community. Once fully operational, it will provide permanent infrastructure revitalization program management, development of city-owned properties, environmental cleanup, facilities services, training of the local employment base, and a community foundation.

Phase 2 (101–365 Days/Transition)

This is a transition phase that sparks the beginning of an expertise within the community and shifts the responsibility from external expertise to emerging local firms and people. Some visible projects are completed, such as emergency physical repairs to the schools.

Design and construction work on the Campus of Learners is executed in this phase. The upgrade of vital water and sewer systems is finalized. In addition, the quality partnering will focus on training resources to complete the physical restoration of the entire economic complex. Significant amounts of work will be performed by local contractors under the direction of the program management office. Contaminated sites are identified throughout the community. Since the remediation efforts required by the nearby clean-up can be undertaken after a 40-hour safety training course, citizens are gaining needed experience through local community remediation programs. Arrangements are made with the federal government for performing nearby remedial work.*

Phase 3 (Year Two to Year Four/Full Revitalization Implementation)

This is a full-scale effort of two to four years depending on the extent of the revitalization effort required within the community. Many more people are employed and new businesses are opening. The partnership is reevaluated and a new contract drawn up with the program management office, depending on need. A majority of the work is being executed by local firms. Most importantly, most members of the community are directly employed.

Vision of the Future for the City

East St. Louis sees itself as a revitalized, environmentally sound city with a new technology base and increased employment and population. By the year 2010, it wants to be a center of excellence for urban revitalization, with a highly skilled workforce and a strong economic base. The skyline will be indicative of the degree of economic wealth and demonstrate that the community has become the successful city it once was. Its citizens will enjoy a high standard of living. Once again the nation will speak proudly of East St. Louis.

---

*This works for other federal programs as well, largely in the infrastructure arena.

Author Biographies

Roger D. Hart, MS, CQE, CRE, LCS, author of the ASQC Quality Press book *Quality Handbook for the Architectural, Engineering, and Construction Community,* is the director of quality services for Fluor Daniel, Inc., the largest publicly held A/E&C firm in the United States. Hart is also an immediate past vice president of ASQC and founded its Design and Construction Division. With a masters degree in math and physics, his expertise lies in developing dynamic organizations of experts in technical systems to directly impact international development and industrial communities. Hart has worked closely with the city of East St. Louis (Illinois), the U.S. Army Corps of Engineers, and the U.S. Department of Housing and Urban Development to develop new and innovative techniques in support of quality urban reform in the areas of Empowerment Zones, Campus of Learners, and other Hope VI initiatives. A well-known quality expert, he has served on the boards of ASQC and the U.S. Koalaty Kid Alliance, and board of examiners for the Malcolm Baldrige National Quality Award; is a senior judge for the U.S. Secretary of the Air Force Unit Quality Award; Chairman, Non-Government Panel 10 Laboratory Infrastructure, Civil Engineering, Battle

Space Environment, and Environmental Quality; and a judge for the *USA Today* Quality Cup. Hart has held numerous other posts and received many honors in the quality field. Over the last 20 years, Hart has authored numerous technical papers and publications, and has lectured for courses at the State University of New York, Massachusetts Institute of Technology, and the University of Massachusetts.

Sheryl L. Cooley is a professional writer and researcher. Her work includes nearly 15 years in the engineering and construction industry, where she has functioned as a technical writer and trainer. Cooley's background in this arena includes research in the global competitiveness of American contractors overseas, development of appropriate marketing tools and materials for the A/E&C industry, design of global communications programs for A/E&C companies, and collateral support for national advertising programs. A published author in her own right, Cooley provided editorial assistance to Hart for his book, *Quality Handbook for the Architectural, Engineering, and Construction Community*. More recently, she worked with him and, through him, with East St. Louis as it tendered its bid for Empowerment Zone/Enterprise Community designation to the U.S. Department of Housing and Urban Development. A former journalism instructor, Cooley has taught high school in the United States and abroad.

William H. Brown has served in a variety of capacities in state government, including special assistant to the governor of Illinois for Employment and Training, director of the Governors' Office of Planning, and special associate for community and economic development for the State Financial Advisory Authority. On the municipal level, he has functioned as director of business for the City of East St. Louis, Illinois and director of purchasing for the City of Alton, Illinois. Brown holds a masters degree in public administration and a masters of science degree in public policy from Southern Illinois University at Edwardsville. He received a bachelor's degree in public affairs from Wayne State University in Detroit. Brown also served in the U.S. Army for four years.

Gordon D. Bush was elected mayor of East St. Louis, Illinois, in 1991 and again in 1995. Born and raised in East St. Louis, he has served the city as a city planner, city commissioner, and treasurer. He was also elected and served on the St. Clair County Board of Review from 1982–1991. Bush is a member of the National Conference of Mayors, vice president of the National Conference of Black Mayors, and president of the Illinois Conference of Black Mayors. He is founder of the East St. Louis Youth Commission; board member emeritus, East St. Louis Boys Club, a board member Boy Scouts of America Okaw Valley Council; a board member of the East West Gateway Coordinating Council; and a board member of the Greater United Way of St. Louis. Bush holds bachelor's and masters degrees in urban planning from Southern Illinois University at Edwardsville. He received a doctorate of human letters from Wiley College and the Distinguished Alumnae Award from Southern Illinois University at Edwardsville in 1996. Additionally, Bush was a featured speaker at the Million Man March in Washington, D.C., in 1996.

Wilbur L. Campbell, Ed.D., is president of Workforce Writers Planners and Trainers, an educational consulting company. He was the assistant to the president, office of curricular and instructional services and served as director, vocational and technical programs at State Community College in East St. Louis, Illinois, directing the reform of vocational programs serving the area. Campbell was a tenured associate professor in the School of Business, Management Information Systems Department at Southern Illinois University at Edwardsville. He taught at Northern Illinois University and Niles Township High School in Skokie, Illinois. He was a student in the Upward Bound program for inner-city youth at Northern Illinois University (NIU) and earned a bachelor's degree in accounting and masters and doctorate degrees in education at

NIU. He has served as consultant to Clark Oil, East St. Louis School District 189, the ESL Regional Vocational System, and Southern Illinois University at Edwardsville East St. Louis Center. He has served on the boards of many professional organizations, including the Illinois Vocational Association, the Illinois Business Education Association, and the Illinois Association for the Advancement of Black Americans in Vocational Education.

Eugene Danylyshyn, P.E., is director of quality assurance for Fluor Daniel, Inc., one of the nation's engineering and construction giants with projects worldwide. Danylyshyn's background includes managing financial and technical control of quality engineering projects such as equipment, process, and product validations; in-process and final product specifications; quality control test and operating procedures; statistical quality history and costs; final product and facility audit; quality training; and compliance from R&D through production. He has implemented technical operations for consulting services and assessment of quality systems for numerous major public and private firms, including the Chicago Transit Authority, Vitek, Inc., and the city of East St. Louis. He provided key support to the successful assessment of Fluor Daniel's Irvine office to ISO 9001. With a B.S. degree in mechanical engineering and an M.B.A., Danylyshyn is chair-elect of the ASQC Design and Construction Division; a certified reliability engineer and certified quality engineer (ASQC); and a committee member for both the International Organization for Standardization and the American National Standards Institute, among other professional affiliations.

John P. Jackson, P.E., is the founder of Management Analysis Company, a management consulting firm specializing in hands-on management support to clients undertaking multibillion-dollar construction projects. He directs the Construction Quality Assurance Division of this company in diverse global management consulting assignments. A former director of quality for Kaiser Engineers, he has authored more than 30 papers on quality assurance worldwide and has been honored as a Fellow of ASQC for his contributions to quality in the commercial nuclear industry. He is a past chair of the Design and Construction Division of ASQC and a certified ISO 9000 quality systems lead auditor.

Ishaq Shafiq is chief of staff for the mayor of East St. Louis, Illinois after serving as East St. Louis's city manager. His prior experience includes 20 years as the CEO and president of Nationwide Guaranty Corporation, a mortgage banking firm. He has served on the executive committee of the Million Man Local Committee, the Economic Development Committee at the National African-American Leadership Conference (1995), chairman of the Economic Development Task Force for the Illinois Black Legislative Caucus, and has served on the board of directors for several corporations. He was a guest of President Bill Clinton at the White House in 1996. Shafiq has written several articles on economic development in African-American communities. He holds a bachelor's degree in political science and a masters degree in urban planning from the University of Illinois at Champaign-Urbana.

**Dick Swett,** a former member of Congress representing the state of New Hampshire, is running for election to a seat in the Senate. With a B.A. from Yale University and an honorary doctorate degree in laws from Franklin Pierce College, Swett is currently president of Dick Swett Associates, Inc., an architecture and energy consulting firm serving companies nationwide. He background includes hands-on management of large projects for several development companies, with particular emphasis on residential and mixed-use projects and international telecommunications programs. Swett has used his considerable knowledge and experience in the AE&C industry to promote legislation designed to improve today's urban and rural communities. Such bills include the Transportation for Livable Communities Act, where he authored legislation to ensure that community needs are considered as transportation programs are adopted. The bill was strongly supported by the American Institute of Architects; key provisions of the legislation were included in the Intermodal Surface Transportation Efficiency Act. He also coauthored the Congressional Accountability Act, legislation requiring that Congress abide by the same laws it passes for the remainder of the country. Swett is a member of the American Institute of Architects.

Bibliography

Preface

Cisneros, Henry G. 1993. *Interwoven destinies: Cities and the nation.* New York: W.W. Norton & Co.

Chapter 2

Edelman, Marian Wright. 1987. *Families in peril: An agenda for social change.* Cambridge, Mass.: Harvard University Press.

Chapter 4

Voice of the people. 1996. *Chicago Tribune,* 30 April.

City of East St. Louis. 1995. *East St. Louis 20/20: A strategic vision/The East St. Louis enterprise community, a national test bed learning campus 1995.* East St. Louis, Ill.: City of East St. Louis.

Kozol, Jonathan. 1991. *Savage inequalities: Children in America's schools.* New York: Crown Publishing.

North Central Association of Colleges and Schools. 1990. *Comprehensive evaluation for the commission on institutions of higher education: State Community College.* North Central Association of Colleges and Schools.

State Community College. 1992. *Policies and procedures manual*. East St. Louis, Ill.: State Community College.

Chapter 5

Edelman, Marian Wright. 1987. *Families in peril: An agenda for social change*. Cambridge, Mass.: Harvard University Press.

Ormell, Catherina. 1995. The decline and rise of the family. *Focus Magazine* 10, no. 3 (January): 34–37.

Rodham Clinton, Hillary. 1996. *It takes a village: And other lessons children teach us*. New York: Simon & Schuster.

Weston, Bonnie. 1996. The case for welfare reform. *The Orange County Register*, 17 March, Accent section 1, 4.

A whole village for the children. 1994. *The Washington Post*, 9 April, G4.

Chapter 6

Furdell, Phyllis. 1995. Joint effort by cities, community organizations will bring success. *Nation's Cities Weekly*, 19 June, 9.

Porter, Michael E. 1995. The rise of the urban entrepreneur. *Inc.*, 16 May, 104–115.

Rubin, Marilyn Marks. 1994. Can re-orchestration of historical themes reinvent government? A case study of the Empowerment Zones and Enterprise Communities Act of 1993. *Public Administration Review* 54, no. 2 (March-April): 161–169.

Williams, Michael R. 1985. *Neighborhood organizations: Seeds of a new urban life*. Westport, Conn.: Greenwood Press.

Chapter 7

ASQC. 1996. *Quality, the future, and you: An ASQC consideration of the year 2010*. ASQC Futures Project. Milwaukee: ASQC.

Hart, Roger D. 1994. *Quality handbook for the architectural, engineering, and construction community*. Milwaukee: ASQC Quality Press.

Juran, J. M. 1995. *A history of managing for quality: The evolution, trends, and future direction of managing for quality*. Milwaukee: ASQC Quality Press.

Kessler, Sheila. 1995. *Total quality service: A simplified approach to using the Baldrige Award criteria.* Milwaukee: ASQC Quality Press.

Peasle, Amos J. 1970. *Constitutions of nations, Volume IX: The Americas.* The Hague: Martinus Nijhoff.

Russell, J. P., and Terry Regel. 1996. *After the quality audit: Closing the loop on the audit process.* Miwaukee: ASQC Quality Press.

Toffler, Alvin, and Heidi Toffler. 1995. *Third wave information society?* Atlanta, Ga.: Turner Publications.

Toffler, Alvin. 1980. *Third wave.* New York: Bantam Books.

Chapter 8

Bluestone, Barry, and Bennett Harrison. 1982. *The industrialization of America: Plant closings, community abandonment, and the dismantling of basic industry.* New York: Basic Books.

Franke, C. A. 1906. *Pictorial East St. Louis: Views of its business, manufacturing and home life.* East St. Louis, Ill.: East St. Louis Publishing.

Morton Hoffman and Co. 1973. *Preliminary findings on the East St. Louis riverfront.* East St. Louis, Ill.: Morton Hoffman and Co.

Hunt, V. Daniel. 1993. *Quality management for government.* Milwaukee: ASQC Quality Press.

Illinois Department of Revenue. 1969–1974. Business reports. Springfiled, Ill.: Illinois Department of Revenue.

Judd, Dennis, and Robert E. Mendleson. 1972. *The politics of urban planning: The East St. Louis experience.* Urbana, Ill.: University of Illinois Press.

M.M. Beal and Co. 1990. *City of East St. Louis Phase I: Diagnostic report.* East St. Louis Ill.: M.M. Beal and Co.

Rudwick, Elliot. 1982. *Race riot at East St. Louis.* Urbana, Ill.: University of Illinois Press.

Shafiq, Ishaq. 1992. *Economic development in East St. Louis: The Carl Officer administration, 1979–1991.* Urbana, Ill.: University of Illinois.

Stanback, Thomas, and Thierry Noyelle. 1982. *Cities in transition.* Totowa, N.J.: Allan Held-Osmun.

U.S. Bureau of the Census. 1990.

U.S. Bureau of the Census. 1972. *Census of manufacturers.* M-70 (As) report no. 6.1 to 6.9. Washington, D.C.: U.S. Bureau of the Census.

U.S. Bureau of the Census. 1967. *Census of manufacturers, geographic area series.* MC-67. Washington, D.C.: U.S. Bureau of the Census.

Wilson, William J. 1980. *The declining significance of race.* Chicago: University of Chicago Press.

Chapter 9

Thomas, Clarence. 1994. The rights revolution and America's urban poor: Victims or beneficiaries? *Vital Speeches* 60, no. 17:514–517.

Chapter 10

East St. Louis Public School District 189. 1996. *Blueprint for School District 189 Plan.* East St. Louis, Ill.: East St. Louis School District 189.

NCREL. 1995. *Learning through technology: Study group framework and profile tool.* North Central Regional Educational Laboratory.

HUD. 1996. *Campus of learners: Bringing education and computer technology to public housing communities.* Washington, D.C.: U.S. Government Printing Office.

Illinois Department of Education. 1996. *Education to careers in Illinois: Marketing notebook.* Springfield, Ill.: Illinois Department of Education.

Chapter 11

Cisneros, Henry G. 1996. *Urban entrepreneurialism and national economic growth.* Fourth in a series. Washington, D.C.: U.S. Government Printing Office.

Edelman, Marian Wright. 1987. *Families in peril: An agenda for social change*. Cambridge, Mass.: Harvard University Press.

Mann, Eric. 1993. The poverty of corporatism: Los Angeles—A year after (part 1). *The Nation*, 29 March, 406–410.

Peirce, Neil R. 1995. 1995. Why computers make sense in low income housing. *Nation's Cities Weekly*, 14 August, 5.

Peterson, Paul E. 1993. The changing fiscal place of big cities in the federal system. In *Interwoven destinies: Cities and the nation*, edited by Henry G. Cisneros. New York: W.W. Norton & Co.

Porter, Michael. 1995. The rise of the urban entrepreneur. *Inc.*, 16 May, 104–115.

Sclar, Elliott, and Walter Hook. 1993. The importance of cities to the national economy. In *Interwoven destinies: Cities and the nation*, edited by Henry G. Cisneros. New York: W.W. Norton & Co.

Stinson, Joseph. 1994. Beyond shop talk: Reinventing high school. *Electronic Learning* 13 (February): 18–24.

Sviridoff, Michael. 1994. The seeds of urban revival. *The Public Interest* (winter): 82–103.

Chapter 13

Juran, J. M., and Frank M. Gryna. 1988. *Juran's quality control handbook*. 4th ed. New York: McGraw-Hill.

Chapter 14

Hicks, Charles R. 1982. *Fundamental concepts in the design of experiments*. Orlando, Fla.: Holt, Rinehart & Winston.

Juran, J. M., and Frank M. Gryna. 1988. *Juran's quality control handbook*. 4th ed. New York: McGraw-Hill.

Chapter 15

ASQC. 1996. *Quality, the future, and you: An ASQC consideration of the year 2010*. ASQC Futures Project. Milwaukee: ASQC.

Cisneros, Henry G. 1996. *Urban entrepreneurialism and national economic growth*. Fourth in a series. Washington, D.C.: U.S. Government Printing Office.

Toffler, Alvin. 1971. *Future shock*. New York: Bantam Books.

Index

14 points, of Deming, 226–30

A

Accounting systems, 249
Adolescents, sexual activity of, 58–59
A/E&C. *See* Architecture/engineering and construction community
AFDC (Aid to Families with Dependent Children), 14, 55, 63, 66
African-Americans, population of, 114–15, 117
AIA (American Institute of Architects), 16, 17, 25
AIDS, 58
Aid to Families with Dependent Children (AFDC), 14, 55, 63, 66
Alignment, in total quality management, 234
Alton, IL, 143
American Institute of Architects (AIA), 16, 17, 75
Amos, Kent, 65
Appraisal costs, 252
Architectural, Engineering and Construction Division, ASQC, 74

Architecture/engineering and construction (A/E&C) community, xxi, 36. *See also* Construction projects
partnerships and, 74–75
quality control and, 88
rework in, 89
ASQC, 74–75, 264
Assessment, of programs, 90. *See also* Measurable results; Measurement tools
Atlanta, GA
African-American population of, 114
Empowerment Zone for, 180

B

Balance of power, in government, 96
Baltimore, MD
African-American population of, 114
economic revitalization in, 173
Bank loans, 72
Bankruptcies. *See also* Finances
of builders, 223
of cities, 113–14
Bay St. Louis, MS, financial problems of, 114
Benchmarking, 107, 239

297

Birmingham, AL, African-American population of, 114
Bonds. *See* Debt, restructuring of
Bookstores, college, 155, 158
Boston, MA
  entrepreneurship in, 181
  quality problems in, 204
  school-to-work programs in, 161
Bridgeport, CT, financial problems of, 114
Brownfield sites, 27, 178, 283
Budgets. *See* Costs; Finances; Quality cost analysis
Buildings. *See also* Construction projects
  in East St. Louis, 119, 282–83
  minimization of decay in, 8
  quality issues and, 79–82
  for schools, 4, 49, 52, 86–87, 282
Bureaucracies, 13, 17, 18, 131
Businesses. *See also* Partnerships
  crime fighting and, 143–45
  in East St. Louis, 117–19, 136, 143–44
  emigration of, 115
  key role of, 264
Businesses, revitalization of, 8, 38, 80–81, 85–86, 273
  elements for, 108–10
  ethnic needs and, 181
  exporters and, 185–88
  telecommuting and, 183–85
  traditional jobs and, 180–83

C
Campus of Learners program, 166–69, 277, 283, 284
Capital. *See* Human capital
Casinos, 143–44, 173
CETA (Comprehensive Employment Training Act), 122, 126, 129
Change. *See also* Economic revitalization; Urban revitalization
  in design, 210–11, 212
  in employment skills, 34
  as a key factor, 263, 264
  quality and, 255–56
  responsibility for, 270–73
  revolutionary, 95–96
Chelsea, MA, financial problems of, 114
Chicago, IL
  diversity in, 5, 35
  school-to-work programs in, 160–61

Child care, 188–89
Children. *See also* Adolescents; Education
  neglect of, 63–64
  in poverty, 33
  religious institutions and, 64–65
  role models for, 61–62
Churches. *See* Religious institutions
Cisneros, Henry, 86, 87, 182, 185
Citizen review process, 235
Citizens. *See also* Empowerment; Human capital; Human factors
  diversity of, 36
  as valuable assets, 38
Cleveland, OH, financial problems of, 114
Clinton, Hillary Rodham, 65
Collaborative agreements, 238–39. *See also* Partnerships
Colleges. *See also* Campus of Learners; Quality Institute
  alternative, 86
  community, 49–52, 153–58, 163, 169, 281
Commitment, long-term, 90
Common good, 3
Communication, 233, 246
Communities, and families, 57, 63–65, 271
Communities Organized for Public Service (COPS), 191–92
Community colleges. *See* Colleges
Community Development program, 72, 122, 123, 191. *See also* Enterprise Community
Community Oriented Policing (COPs), 143
Community pride, 9
Community Reinvestment Act, 72
Community revitalization. *See* Urban revitalization
Competitiveness, business, 11–12, 88
Comprehensive Employment Training Act (CETA), 122, 126, 129
Computer age, 77, 183–85. *See also* Technology
Configuration management, 209–11
Consensus management, 18, 131–32
Constancy of purpose, 226, 234
Constitutional Conventions, 99, 102. *See also* U.S. Constitution

Construction community. *See*
    Architecture/engineering and construction community
Construction managers, 203, 205, 213, 216, 217
Construction projects
    economic revitalization and, 177–79
    engineering issues in, 208–11
    general managers of, 201–05, 217
    procurement issues in, 211–12
    quality assurance and, 200–220
    quality management and, 225
    social programs vs., 152–53
    teamwork in, 201–06
Continuous improvement, 227–28
Contracts, 239
Coordinators, of total quality, 232
COPS (Communities Organized for Public Service), 191–92
COPs (Community Oriented Policing), 143
Costs. *See also* Quality cost analysis
    control of, 237, 238–40, 250–55
    of education, 40, 41, 46, 48, 51, 61, 84
    of empowerment, 223
    of environmental remediation, 81
    of food, 55
    management of, 202, 218
    of programs, social vs. construction, 152
    quality and, xxi, 87–89
    of services, 3–4
    short- vs. long-term, 227
    of transportation, 21–23
Craft training, 85, 192–93
Creditors, 126, 128, 129
Crime, 8, 31, 62, 273
    drugs and, 135–40, 146–49
    programs to fight, 139–49
    as a revitalization issue, 83–84
    U.S. Constitution and, 97, 98, 99
Cross-functional teams, 103–07, 108
Cultural diversity, 35–36
Culture of desperation, 30–32, 35, 36, 37
Customer focus
    American attributes and, 101–02
    as a key factor, 264

D
DARE program, 147
Data collection, inadequacies of, 33

Debt, restructuring of, 125–29, 145–46
Decision making, web of, 131
Deming, W. Edwards, 100, 222, 223, 261
    14 points of, 226–30
    on soft quality, 226–30
    on statistical methods, 225–26
Democracy, and total quality, 93–111
Demonstration Cities and Metropolitan Development Act, 71–72
Denver, CO
    Campus of Learners in, 168
    quality problems in, 204
Design change management, 210–11, 212
Design control, 208–09
Design of experiments, 249
Design quality, 208, 225
Design release, 209
Despair, psychology of, 78–79
Desperate cultures, 30–32, 35, 36, 37
Detroit, MI, African-American population of, 114
Distressed Cities Act, 29, 141, 143
Diversity, 5, 28, 29
    cultural, 35–36
    in revitalization, xix, 259–61, 275
Documents. *See* Quality records
DOD. *See* U.S. Department of Defense
Drug abuse, 62, 84
    as a business, 135
    crime and, 135–40, 146–49

E
East St. Louis, IL, xiv
    anti-crime program in, 139–49
    background information on, 116–23
    drug crime in, 135–36, 139–40, 146–49
    education in, 39, 41, 48–52, 146–47, 153–58, 169, 277, 283
    financial problems of, 114, 117–23, 141
    financial solutions for, 123–31, 133, 141–46, 148–49, 173
    holistic approach in, 276–84
    police force improvements in, 142–43, 148
Economic revitalization, 171–77. *See also* Finances; Urban revitalization
    child care and, 188–89
    construction projects and, 177–78

Economic revitalization—*continued*
   employment, and, 177–88
   employment, telecommuting, and, 183–85
   employment, training, and, 192–93
   exporters and, 185–88
   health care and, 189–90
   holistic quality approach to, 193–96
   housing and, 190–92
   long-term approach to, 179–88
   short-term approach to, 176–79
   social support for, 188–93
Economy. *See also* Costs; Finances; Poverty
   national, 11–13
   urban, 27–35
Educate America Act, 162
Education
   after-school programs for, 65
   alternate environments for, 86, 87
   Campus of Learners for, 166–69, 277, 283, 284
   case study of, 48–52, 153–58
   costs of, 40, 41, 46, 48, 51, 61, 84
   craft training in, 85, 192–93
   drug crime and, 138, 139, 146–47
   employment and, 40, 41, 42–43, 61, 185
   family lifestyle and, 61
   human capital and, 34–35, 37
   improvements in, 9, 10, 42–43, 53, 109, 154–70
   inequalities in, 39, 46, 48
   as a key factor, 40–41, 264, 271
   lack of measurement tools in, 44
   lack of quality focus on, 52–53
   lack of technology in, 44–45
   need for, 228, 229
   organizational control in, 45–46
   partnerships in, 42–43, 157–58, 160–62, 165, 281–83
   problems in, 8, 42–53, 61, 151–53
   public housing and, 166–69
   Quality Institute for, 277, 283
   as a revitalization issue, 84–85
   of slaves, 34
   standards for, 155–56, 159, 162
   strategic planning in, 155–57
   technology and, 44–45, 163–65
   total quality and, 42, 51, 52–53, 102–03
   vocational, 109

Effectiveness
   in education, 44
   pof quality, 87–88
Elections, 97, 98
Employment, 9, 38, 144, 277
   construction projects and, 177–79
   education required for, 40, 41, 42–43, 61, 185
   income and, 85–86
   long-term projects and, 179–88
   school-to-work programs for, 158, 160–62
   short-term projects and, 176–79
   telecommuting and, 183–85
   traditional, 180–83
Empowerment, 9, 89
   American attributes and, 100–01
   belief in, 227, 230
   cost of, 223
   of cross-functional teams, 106–07
   in economic revitalization, 194
   in education, 52, 157
   human capital and, 36
   of municipal employees, 130
   for peacekeeping, 84
   for transportation, 24
Empowerment Zones program, 73, 108, 180, 276
Engineering community. *See* Architecture/engineering and construction community
Engineering managers, 203, 205, 216, 217
Enterprise Community (EC), 73, 149, 276, 277
Environment, in the future, 266, 267
Environmental remediation, 38
   cost of, 81
   demonstration program for, 74
   planning for, 283, 284
   solutions to, 82
Excellence, quest for, xxi. *See also* Quality
Experiments, design of, 249
Exporters, 185–88
Export-Import Bank, 186
Extended families, 57
External failure costs, 252, 253

F
Failure costs, 252, 253
Families
   communities and, 57, 63–65, 271

Families—*continued*
  education and, 61
  as a key factor, 62, 271
  single-parent, 55–60
  systematic help for, 67
  traditional, demise of, 56–57, 60–63
  welfare support for, 63, 66
Fear, 228
Federal government. *See* Government, federal
Finances. *See also* Bankruptcies; Costs; Debt; Economic revitalization
  inadequacies of, 113–23, 141
  solutions for, 123–31, 133, 141–46, 148–49, 273
Financial Distress Act, 124
Fire-fighting services, 126, 148
Flowcharts, of critical activities, 246
Food, cost of, 55
Funding. *See* Costs
Future
  government role in, 24–25
  responsibility for, 270–73
  vision for, 264–70, 284
Futures Project, of ASQC, 264

G
Gangs, 59
Gary, IN, African-American population of, 114
General manager of construction (GMC), 201–05, 217
Globalization, 11–12, 185–88, 263
Goals, 105, 226, 234. *See also* Vision
Goals 2000, 162
Government. *See also* Partnerships
  key role of, 264
  rethinking of, 272
  total quality and, 93–111, 272
Government, federal. *See also names of specific agencies, departments, and programs*
  bankruptcy courts of, 114
  budget cutting by, 175
  distrust of, 13–14, 17–18
  education and, 41, 162
  environmental remediation and, 283
  family supports and, 63
  infrastructure projects of, 178–79
  as a partner with localities, 25
  school-to-work programs and, 158
  successes of, 18, 20–24
  support from, 239
Government, local, 17, 25
  case study, East St. Louis, 48–52, 276–84
  education sanctioned by, 39–53
  school-to-work programs and, 158
  transportation programs and, 22–24
  urban planning in, 35–36
Government, state
  budget cutting by, 175
  education and, 40, 41, 49, 51–52, 158
  financial assistance from, 114, 124, 141, 143
  roles of, 108, 109
  school-to-work programs and, 158
  transportation programs and, 22–24
Grant applications, 282
Great Depression, 78
Great Society, 71
Gross domestic product, xxi, 33, 35

H
Hartford, CT, Campus of Learners in, 168
Health care, 189–90
Hierarchy of needs, 79
Highways. *See* Transportation systems
History, of urban revitalization, 71–75
Holistic approach. *See* Total quality, holistic approach to
Home ownership, 50, 191–92
Housing, 72–73, 120, 122
  Campus of Learners program and, 166–69, 277
  economic revitalization and, 190–92
  in the future, 266–67
  holistic revitalization and, 276–82
  value of, 49
Housing and Community Development Act, 73
HUD. *See* U.S. Department of Housing and Urban Development
Human capital, 33–38, 271, 277
Human factors, 106–07, 215. *See also* "We the People"
  for the future, 266–67, 270–73
  key forces and, 262–63
Human resource management, 106, 230

I

Illinois. *See* Chicago; East St. Louis; Metropolitan Community College; State Community College
Illiteracy, 33
Implementation. *See also* Planning
  for quality assurance, 200–07
  for total quality, 237–46, 278–84
Income, lack of, 85–86. *See also* Poverty
Indianapolis, IN, economic revitalization in, 178
Individual rights, 96–97
Industry. *See* Businesses
Inspection, 205, 227. *See also* Quality assurance
Insurance, instead of quality, 223
Integrated deployment, 18. *See also* Total quality, holistic approach to
Intermodal Surface Transportation Act (ISTEA), 18–24
Internal failure costs, 252
Internal Revenue Service, 126, 129, 145
International business, 185–88. *See also* Globalization
Involvement, in total quality management, 235, 240
ISO 9000 standards, 199, 204, 215, 256
Issues, in revitalization, 76–86. *See also* Costs; Finances; Physical property issues; Social issues
ISTEA (Intermodal Surface Transportation Act), 18–24

J

Japan, and total quality, 100
Jobs. *See* Employment; Occupational programs; Unemployment
Judgment funding, 121
Judicial system, 97, 98, 99
Juran, Joseph M., 222, 223, 224–25, 261

K

Kessler, Sheila, 103, 105
Kozol, Jonathan, 48

L

Leadership, 100, 228
Legislation. *See* Government
Lifelong learning, 185. *See also* Campus of Learners program
Life safety issues, 81, 281
Litigation avoidance, 217–18
Local Initiatives Support Corporations, 72
Long-term approaches, xiv, 90, 179–88, 221, 227
Los Angeles, CA
  economic revitalization in, 174–75, 180
  quality problems in, 204

M

Malcolm Baldrige National Quality Award, 33
Malls, shopping, 118
Manufacturing, declines in, 6, 77, 117–19
Marketing, 239–40
Maslow, Abraham, 79
Mass transit, 21–22. *See also* Transportation systems
Master planning, 239, 281, 282
Materials managers, 203, 205, 211, 212, 216, 217
Measurable results, 101, 111, 234, 237, 246–55, 261
Measurement tools, 44
Medicaid, 190
Metropolitan Community College, 157, 163, 169. *See also* State Community College
Mexico, economic revitalization in, 189, 196
Model Cities Program, 72, 122
Monetary system, 97
Moral values, 62, 96, 263, 267, 271

N

NAFTA (North American Free Trade Agreement), 187
NCREL (North Central Regional Educational Laboratory), 163–65
Neglect
  of children, 63–64
  of urban blight, 73
Neighborhood policing, 83–84, 143
Newark, NJ, African-American population of, 114
New Orleans, LA, African-American population of, 114
New York, NY, debt problems of, 113–14
Night life, in revitalized areas, 80
Nonconformances, 214–15

North American Free Trade Agreement (NAFTA), 187
North Central Regional Educational Laboratory (NCREL), 163–65
Norton, Eleanor Holmes, 16, 17
Numerical quotas, 229
Nurturing villages, 65

O

Occupational programs, 158, 160–62, 192–93. *See also* Employment
Omaha, NE, economic revitalization in, 173–74
Omnibus Budget Reconciliation Act of 1993, 73
Operation, quality of, 225
Optimism, 266–67, 270–71
Orange County, CA, financial problems of, 114
Organization, of total quality efforts, 232–33
OSHA. *See* U.S. Occupational Safety and Health Administration
Overinspection, 227
Owners
   design control by, 208–09
   responsibilities of, 200–01, 219–20

P

Parenting, 63–65. *See also* Children; Families
Pareto analysis, 250, 254
Partnerships
   ASQC recommendations for, 74–75
   with churches, 145, 147–48
   cross-functional teams as, 103–07
   in debt restructuring, 127–29
   in education, 42–43, 157–58, 160–62, 165, 281–83
   formalization of, 238–39, 240
   planning for, 277–84
   in playgrounds project, 16
   quality and, 89
   in urban planning, 35
Pasadena, CA, economic revitalization in, 182
Peace, 270
Pessimism, 11–13, 31
Philadelphia, PA, financial problems of, 114

Physical property issues, 79–82. *See also* Buildings
Pilot studies, for cost analysis, 253–54
Planning, xiv, 110, 230–40, 277–84
Playgrounds project, 15–18
Police services
   anti-drug efforts of, 142, 147
   as creditors, 126
   improvement of, 142–43, 148
   neighborhood, 83–84, 143
Political issues, 76, 77, 136–37, 152–53, 245. *See also* Government
Poverty, 6, 31–33, 59, 120
   human capital and, 37
   related to other problems, 138
   as a revitalization issue, 85–86
   root causes and, 31–32
Power relationships, 131, 132
Pregnancy, teenage, 58–59
Prevention costs, 252
Price tag decisions, 227
Pride of workmanship, 229
Prisons, 4
Private sector. *See* Businesses
Problem solving, 94, 103, 105, 106–07, 227, 235
Procurement management, 211–12, 216–17, 225
Productivity, economic, 11, 35
Project engineering, 208–11
Project quality management, 225
Prostitution, 84
Psychology of despair, 78–79
Public housing. *See* Housing
Public relations, 246
Public schools. *See* Education
Public works systems, 115–16, 282–83
Purpose, constancy of, 226, 234

Q

QS-9000 standards, 199
Quality. *See also* Total quality
   as an attitude, xii
   costs and, 87–89
   in education, 154–70. *See also* Education, improvements in
   effectiveness of, 87–88
   in the future, 265, 266–270
   issues of, for revitalization, 76–86
   long-term nature of, 221
   paradigm shifts in, 86–89, 185

Quality—*continued*
  role of, in revitalization, 89–91
  soft, 226–30
  threats to, 221–23
  urban change and, 255–56
  views of, xix–xx
Quality assurance manual, 206–07
Quality assurance (QA). *See also* Total quality
  advantages of, 217–20
  compared to quality control, 205–06
  construction projects and, 200–220
  human impact of, 215–17
  implementation elements of, 200–07
  key issues in, 213–17
  managers of, 232
  project engineering for, 208–11
  project procurement for, 211–12, 216–17
  teamwork and, 201–06
  urban change and, 256
Quality champions, 102–03, 105–06
Quality control
  compared to quality assurance, 205–06
  Juran on, 224–25
Quality cost analysis, 237, 248–55. *See also* Costs
Quality Institute program, 277, 283
Quality management, 221–23
  definition of, 88
  Deming on, 226–30
  Juran on, 224–25
  planning for, 230–36
Quality manual, 207–08
Quality participation, 240
Quality records, 215, 246
Quality techniques, 240–46, 261
Quick action teams, 235
Quotas, numerical, 229

R
Raleigh-Durham, NC, economic development in, 182–83
Rebuilding. *See* Urban revitalization
Rebuild Los Angeles, 174–75
Recognition, of accomplishments, 90, 100–01, 110, 229, 235
Records, quality, 215
Regulations, 77. *See also* Environmental remediation

Religious institutions, 63–65
  partnerships with, 145, 147–48
Research Triangle Park, 182–83
Responsibilities
  for the future, 270–73
  in quality assurance, 200–06, 219–20
  in total quality management, 232–33
Retail firms, 118–19. *See also* Businesses
Reviews, in total quality management, 235
Revitalization. *See* Economic revitalization; Urban revitalization
Revolutionary change, 95–96
Rewards. *See* Recognition
Richmond, VA, African-American population of, 114
Root cause analysis, 94–95, 227, 271
Root causes, and poverty, 31–32

S
Safety, management of, 218
San Antonio, TX
  entrepreneurship in, 181
  housing programs in, 191–92
SCC. *See* State Community College
Schedules
  holistic approach and, 278–84
  quality and, 89, 218
School boards, 42, 45–46
Schools. *See* Education
School-to-work programs, 158, 160–62
Service industry, growth of, 6, 77–78, 86, 181
Severely distressed city, definition of, 29
Sewer systems, 116, 282–83
Sexual activity, of adolescents, 58–59
Short-term approaches, 176–79, 221, 227
Single-parent families, 55–60
Slaves, education of, 34
Slogans, 229
Social issues, 76, 82–86, 137–39. *See also* Crime; Drug abuse; Education; Employment; Families; Health care; Housing; Poverty
Social programs
  construction projects vs., 152–53
  for economic revitalization, 188–93
Soft quality, 226–30
South Bend, IN, Campus of Learners in, 168
South Tucson, AZ, financial problems of, 114

Standards
  educational, 155–56, 159, 162
  ISO 9000, 199, 204, 215, 256
  lowering of, 222–23
  QS-9000, 199
State Community College (SCC), 49–52, 153–58. *See also* Metropolitan Community College
States. *See* Government, state
Statistics, inadequacies of, 33. *See also* Measurable results
Steering committees, 232
Strategic planning. *See also* Planning
  American attributes and, 100
  in education, 155–57
  total quality and, xiv, 110
  U.S. Constitution and, xvii, 96–99
Strategic quality goals, 105
STWOA (School-to-Work Opportunities Act), 158, 160–62
Suggestion systems, 235
Supply-side economics, 37

T
Task analysis, 249–50, 280–81
Tax structure, 8–9, 29, 46
  in East St. Louis, 118, 121, 143, 145–46
  economic revitalization and, 176
Teamwork, 232–33, 235, 261, 271
  barriers to, 228–29
  cross-functional, 103–07, 108
  for debt restructuring, 126, 128–29
  for education, 156
  for overcoming partisanship, 245
  in quality assurance, 201–06
Technology
  changes in, 95–96
  education and, 44–45, 163–65
  in the future, 264, 265, 266–67
  industrial shifts and, 77–78
  as a key factor, 263, 273
  of telecommuting, 183–85
  U.S. Constitution and, 96–98
  use of, 101, 110
Teenagers, sexual activity of, 58–59
Telecommuting, 183–85
Test bed approach, 74, 90, 272
Third wave, of change, 95–96
Total involvement, in quality management, 235

Total quality, 5–10. *See also* Quality assurance; Quality management
  for Constitutional Conventions, 99
  constraints on, 131–32
  cost efficiency and, 116
  democracy and, 93–111
  for economic well-being, 171
  in education, 42, 52–53
  education for, 102–03
  fiscal responsibility and, 130–31
  human capital and, 33–38
  human factors in, 106–07
  as a key, 10, 261, 271
  key factors that affect, 262–64
  long-term approach to, xiv
  measurable results and, 101, 111, 234, 237, 246–55, 261
  planning for, xiv, 110, 237–40, 278–84
  program size of, 246, 247–48
  teamwork in, 103–07, 108
  techniques for, 240–46, 261
  three-pronged approach to, 8–10
Total quality, holistic approach to, xi, xiii, 6, 89, 133, 273
  case study of, 275–84
  for construction projects, 218–20
  economic revitalization and, 193–96
  in education, 51, 53
  families and, 65
  quality cost analysis and, 253
Total quality management, 100, 227. *See also* Quality management
  planning for, 230–36
Trade, international, 185–88
Traditional families, demise of, 56–57, 60–63
Traditional jobs, 180–83
Training. *See also* Education
  need for, 228, 229
  occupational, 192–93
  in total quality management, 233
Transportation systems
  to attract businesses, 115
  demonstration program for, 73–74
  in the future, 266–67
  impact of highways in, 5, 19
  Intermodal Surface Transportation Act (ISTEA), 18–24
Trial by jury, 97, 98
Tulsa, OK, craft training in, 192–93

U

Ueberroth, Peter, 174–75
Underemployment, 32
Unemployment, 6, 32, 118–19. *See also* Employment
Updates, in total quality management, 236
Urban America, diversity of, 28, 29
Urban Family Institute, 65
Urban planning, 35–37
 education and, 41
 quality and, 89–90
Urban renewal
 old model of, 5
 roots of, 71
Urban revitalization, 5–10. *See also* Economic revitalization; Total quality
 American attributes and, 100–02
 cross-functional teams and, 103–07, 108
 diversity of challenges to, xix, 259–61, 275
 education as a key to, 40–41
 history of, 69–75
 implementation of, 237–46, 278–84
 key factors that affect, 262–64
 literature of, xi–xii
 measurable results and, 246–55
 need for, xi, xiv, 259–62
 program elements for, 108–10
 quality cost analysis in, 237, 248–55
 quality elements of, 89–91
 quality issues in, 76–86, 221–23
 total quality plan for, 230–36
 vision of, 71–91
USACERL (U.S. Army Corps of Engineers CERL), 73–75, 82
U.S. Army Corps of Engineers, 187–88
U.S. Army Corps of Engineers CERL, 73–75, 82
US City consortium, 74
U.S. Congress, 72, 97, 98
 distrust of, 14
 role of, 15–16
 successes in, 18, 20–21
U.S. Constitution, xvii, 94–99, 102
U.S. Department of Defense, 73–74
U.S. Department of Housing and Urban Development, 73, 122, 180, 191, 276, 282
U.S. Occupational Safety and Health Administration, 218
U.S. Small Business Administration, 186

V

Value awareness, 235
Values, moral, 62, 96, 263, 267, 271
Virtual database, 239
Virtual offices, 183–85
Vision, xviii, 71–91, 246
 for 2010, 264–70, 284
 creation of, 272
 in democracy, 93–111
 for fighting crime, 135–49
 for improving education, 151–70
 for improving finances, 113–33
Vocational education, 109. *See also* Craft training

W

Wages. *See* Income; Poverty
Washington, DC. *See also* Government, federal
 African-American population of, 114
 diversity in, 35
 family support in, 65
 financial problems of, 114
 playgrounds project in, 15–18
Welfare reform, 66, 267
Welfare system
 AFDC and, 14, 55, 63, 66
 despair and, 78
 family support and, 63, 66
 as welfare state, 6–8, 9
Wellston, MO, financial problems of, 114
"We the People," 94, 100–02, 111, 262, 263. *See also* U.S. Constitution
 in the future, 270–71, 273
Women, employment of, 178
Work. *See* Employment; Occupational programs; Unemployment
Workmanship, 223, 229
Work process improvement teams, 233, 235
World-class cities, 230